GREAT LIVES OBSERVED

Gerald Emanuel Stearn,

EACH VOLUME IN THE SERIES VIEW
ACHIEVEMENT OF A GREAT WORLD FIGURE IN THREE PERSPEC-
TIVES—THROUGH HIS OWN WORDS, THROUGH THE OPINIONS
OF HIS CONTEMPORARIES, AND THROUGH RETROSPECTIVE
JUDGMENTS—THUS COMBINING THE INTIMACY OF AUTOBI-
OGRAPHY, THE IMMEDIACY OF EYEWITNESS OBSERVATION, AND
THE OBJECTIVITY OF MODERN SCHOLARSHIP.

ROBERT S. STAROBIN, *the editor of this volume in the Great
Lives Observed series, is an Associate Professor of History at
the State University of New York at Binghamton. The author
of* Industrial Slavery in the Old South *(New York: Oxford
University Press, 1970), Professor Starobin has contributed the
annual royalties from his study of Denmark Vesey's slave conspiracy to the Southern Conference Education Fund and the
Black Panther Party.*

GREAT LIVES OBSERVED

Denmark Vesey
THE SLAVE CONSPIRACY OF 1822

Edited by
ROBERT S. STAROBIN

Vesey's example must be regarded as
one of the most courageous
ever to threaten the racist foundation of America.
In him the anguish of Negro people
welled up in nearly perfect measure.
He stands today, as he stood yesterday . . .
as an awesome projection of the possibilities
for militant action on the part of a people who have—
for centuries—been made to bow down in fear.

—STERLING STUCKEY

A SPECTRUM BOOK

PRENTICE-HALL, INC., ENGLEWOOD CLIFFS, N.J.

Dedicated to Bobby Seal and in memory of Fred Hampton.

The quotation on the title page is from
Sterling Stuckey, "Remembering Denmark
Vesey—Agitator or Insurrectionist?"
Negro Digest, XV (February, 1966).

Current printing (last number): 10 9 8 7 6 5 4 3 2 1

C–13-198440-3

P–13-198432-2

Library of Congress Catalog Card Number: 71–120796

Printed in the United States of America

PRENTICE-HALL INTERNATIONAL, INC. (*London*)
PRENTICE-HALL OF AUSTRALIA, PTY. LTD. (*Sydney*)
PRENTICE-HALL OF CANADA, LTD. (*Toronto*)
PRENTICE-HALL OF INDIA PRIVATE LIMITED (*New Delhi*)
PRENTICE-HALL OF JAPAN, INC. (*Tokyo*)

Contents

Introduction

When I began to compose this introduction, a white federal judge had just gagged and shackled a black man to prevent him from cross-examining witnesses in the trial of eight radicals accused of conspiring to incite riots at the 1968 Democratic Convention in Chicago. The judge then sentenced the black man to four years in prison for contempt of court. Now as I conclude, Chicago police are alleged to have assassinated two more black organizers while they slept in bed—another demonstration of the depths of racial oppression in the United States.

Against such racism blacks have struggled throughout American history, and the most spectacular forms of black resistance are the conspiracies and rebellions which have surfaced from one generation to another. Major slave unrest occurred in New York in 1712, in South Carolina in 1739 and 1740, in Virginia in 1800 and 1831, and in Louisiana in 1811 and 1812. But one of the most extensive plots of all was uncovered in Charleston, South Carolina, in 1822—the Denmark Vesey Conspiracy. Vesey and his followers planned simply to seize the city of Charleston, kill most of the whites, and, if necessary, escape to the Caribbean or Africa. Whites ruthlessly suppressed the rebels, but they are still revered today for their courage, daring, and determination.

South Carolina society seemed peaceful enough in the spring of 1822, yet beneath the serene surface it seethed with discontent. The 260,000 slaves who worked in the cotton fields and malarial swamps, a majority of the population, had long protested their enslavement. Major rebellions had occurred in 1739 and 1740, 25,000 slaves had escaped to the British lines during the American Revolution, and a conspiracy in Camden, S.C., had been broken up as recently as 1816. Many smaller plots and uprisings had also taken place. Exploitation had increased after the War of 1812, as prices of staples tended to decline and as new lands were opened up in the West. Yet masters had neither entirely dehumanized their slaves nor completely crushed their innate longing for freedom. For obvious reasons, slave dissatisfaction and discontent remained profound enough to inspire thoughts of rebellion.

For such a slave society, where 12,652 bondsmen outnumbered 10,653 whites in Charleston alone, the presence of an active free-black community was both paradoxical and dangerous. Concentrated in Charleston County, the number of freedmen had rapidly increased

1

from 1,161 in 1800 to 3,615 in 1820. Free blacks worked at a variety of occupations that ranged from artisanry to longshoring, from shop-keeping to houseservantry, with the vast bulk earning only very modest livings. A handful had managed to accumulate considerable wealth and to organize fraternal groups, such as the Brown Fellow-ship Society, an elite educational and welfare organization begun in 1790. However, whites despised the free blacks and regarded them as bad examples and potential leaders for those still in bondage.

Beginning in 1815, free blacks and slaves had joined together in an unprecedented act of religious self-determination. When the white Methodist Church canceled certain privileges for blacks within its congregations, the blacks communicated with the newly organized African Methodist Episcopal Church in Philadelphia. They sent two representatives to be ordained as ministers, and finally established their own separate church. Most of the "class leaders," or deacons, resigned from the white-dominated Methodist Church; and almost 5,000 blacks, three-quarters of the black membership, transferred their allegiance to the new African Church.

This blow for independence outraged white officials, and they be-gan to harass the black religious community. In 1817, 469 black Methodists were arrested on charges of disorderly conduct. The fol-lowing year, 140 more were apprehended for violating laws against educating slaves without whites being present. Thirteen of these were either fined or sentenced to imprisonment, banishment, and whipping. In 1820, a group of freedmen petitioned the state legislature for per-mission to conduct separate religious services. Upon the recommenda-tion of the white Charleston assemblymen, the plea was rejected. The next year, the City Marshal again warned the black clergymen that instructing slaves was illegal; yet, despite such threats and intimida-tion, the African Church remained a seedbed of subversion.

To preserve the "domestic tranquillity" of the state, whites moved against the black community again in 1820. An act passed that year forbade any more free blacks from entering the state; if freedmen left the state, they were forbidden to return. Considering the African Methodists' journey to Pennsylvania, the new law was a direct attack on the religious integrity of all blacks. To discourage further entry of free blacks into the state, those not born in South Carolina or residents of less than five years were subject to a stiff, fifty-dollar-a-year tax. Manumission of slaves was also severely proscribed, and licenses were now required of blacks for certain occupations to reduce competition with whites. Altogether, Charleston blacks—both free and slave—found themselves under considerable pressure.

The black population was inspired by other events as well. They undoubtedly had heard of the successful slave revolt in Saint-Do-mingue, since South Carolinians had long traded with the Caribbean islanders and since some Haitian émigrés had settled in the state with their slaves. Blacks also seemed aware of the significance of the debates in Congress during 1819–21 over the admission of Missouri as a slave state. Perhaps they also knew of the Gabriel Conspiracy near Richmond in 1800, and of the plans devised in Washington in 1816–17 to colonize blacks in Africa. Certainly, they were conscious of the suppression of the Camden Revolt in 1816. In short, black Charlestonians had many grievances, sufficient knowledge of the tradition of insurrection, and adequate understanding of antislavery thinking to begin to plan a revolt of their own. Only leadership seemed to be lacking; Denmark Vesey changed that.

Studying the Vesey Conspiracy raises interesting questions about its participants, leadership, and ideology; answering these questions sheds new light on the history of black protest. First, it is clear that rebel recruits came mostly from the slave workers of Charleston and its environs. The conspirators were, according to the *Official Report of the Trials*, "Negroes hired or working out, such as Carters, Draymen, Sawyers, Porters, Labourers, Stevidores, Mechanics, [and] those employed in lumber yards." Others joined from waterfront rice mills, while slaves from rice and cotton plantations surrounding the city were involved.

That recruits came mainly from the urban, industrial slaves of Charleston casts great doubt on the assertion by some historians (like Richard Wade, whose findings are criticized more fully in the Afterword) that urban bondsmen and slave hirelings were more content and less rebellious than rural, plantation bondsmen. Indeed, the evidence suggests that urban slaves were, despite their supposedly greater privileges and higher standard of living, at least as discontented as rural slaves. No wonder whites were mystified and horrified when even their most trusted servants and apparently contented bondsmen were implicated in the plot.

In contrast to the manual-laborer participants stood the rebel leadership, which consisted mainly of skilled slave artisans and religious leaders. Vesey himself was a free black carpenter, and his lieutenants were all slave craftsmen and preachers. Peter Poyas was a "first-rate" ship carpenter, Mingo Harth was a "mechanic," Tom Russell was a blacksmith, and Monday Gell was a harnessmaker who hired out his own labor and kept a workshop in the center of the city. Gullah Jack was a "conjurer" who kept alive African religious traditions, while other leaders were deacons in the black church. Undoubtedly these slaves had through their work gained a greater sense of independence and more education than most common laborers. And artisans and preachers could articulate shared grievances more easily than most workers whose rage at oppression revealed itself mainly through action.

The African background of many of the participants and leaders forms another significant feature of the Vesey Plot. Since the overseas slave trade remained legal until 1808 and there was a great deal of illicit importing thereafter, many South Carolina slaves had been born in Africa or could easily trace their heritage to their former homeland. It is thus probable that many of the participants were either native-born Africans or only first-generation Americans. Moreover, several of the leaders, including Monday Gell, an Ebo, Gullah Jack, an Angolan, and Mingo Harth, a Mandingo, hailed from Africa, while Vesey himself had allegedly been born there. Certainly, these men had not been as acculturated to South Carolina society as those born in the state. The memory of their previous cultural identity and national independence was still strong, and they could appeal to other blacks partly on this basis.

The extent of white involvement forms another interesting aspect of the Vesey Plot, for whites were—as in other revolts—suspected of collaboration with blacks. The authorities never proved that whites actually engaged in the planning of the insurrection; but once rumors about the revolt began to spread, some whites apparently encouraged blacks to rebel. Eventually, four white men were tried for the misdemeanor of "inciting slaves to insurrection," a noncapital offense. Three of these four whites were poor, European immigrants—which suggests the extent of South Carolina's xenophobia—while the fourth man was not a native of the state. However, though the blacks were condemned to death or deportation, the whites received only prison terms and fines, revealing further the racist foundations of southern "justice." Thus, William Allen, a Scottish sailor, was sentenced to twelve months imprisonment, a $1,000 fine, and had to give security for his good behavior for five years after his release. John Igneshias, a Spanish seaman, and Jacob Danders, a German peddler, each received three months in jail, $100 fines, and requirement of security. Andrew Rhodes, a one-time shopkeeper, was sentenced to six months in prison and a $500 fine. The court noted that in Allen's case the punishment might amount to life imprisonment, since he was too poor to pay the fine or the security; the same was probably true for Rhodes. Allen was perhaps the most interesting of the four whites, for when he conspired with the blacks, according to the court, they "objected . . . that he [Allen] being a white man, could not be safely trusted by them." To this charge, Allen replied that "though he had a white face, he was a negro in heart."

The surviving evidence also reveals some surprising information about those blacks who informed against conspiracies. Popular mythology holds that the so-called "house nigger" group usually betrayed revolts; but in this case the informers came from various backgrounds. True, Peter Devany, the fifty-five-year-old slave of John C. Prioleau, and William, slave of J. and D. Paul, seemed to be trusted domestic servants. But William Pencil, another informer, was a skilled, free black tinplate worker, and George, belonging to the Wilson family, was a blacksmith and religious leader in the African Church. It is also true that one rebel leader warned recruits not to reveal plans "to those waiting men who receive presents of old coats, etc., from their masters, or they'll betray us." But other leaders seemed willing to rely on trustworthy house servants to slit their masters' throats or to poison the city's water wells, and even some of Governor Thomas Bennett's personal servants were involved. So incendiary did whites regard these individual acts of sabotage by house servants that references to poisoning wells were deleted from the printed records. In any event, the evidence suggests that a revision of the traditional role assigned to house servants is in order.

The bravery of the conspiracy's leadership contrasts sharply with the treachery of its traitors. All of the leaders, with the exception of Monday Gell and Rolla Bennett, who confessed under coercion, met their death with calm and dignity. Peter Poyas strengthened a fellow prisoner who was being tortured by urging him to "Die like a man." Then, Poyas responded to the court's interrogation with only a "cryptic smile," and from the gallows stated to other blacks: "Do not open your lips; die silent, as you shall see me do!" Vesey defended himself ably in court, challenging witnesses and disputing the charges against him, and faced his execution with complete composure. Before he was captured, Gullah Jack planned to rescue the imprisoned leaders and continue the revolt.

Compared to other insurrections, the Vesey Plot embodied an extraordinarily rich ideology. Beyond a general antiwhite attitude, Vesey combined the Old Testament's harsh morality and the story of the Israelites with African religious customs, knowledge of the Haitian Revolution, and readings of antislavery speeches from the Missouri controversy. "He was in the habit of reading to me all the passages in the newspapers that related to St. Domingo, and apparently every pamphlet he could lay his hands on that had any connection with slavery," testified one rebel as to Vesey's organizational strategy. "He one day brought me a speech which he told me had been delivered in Congress by a Mr. [Rufus] King on the subject of slavery; he told me this Mr. King was the black man's friend, that he, Mr. King, had declared . . . that slavery was a great disgrace to the country." While Gullah Jack provided recruits with African religious symbols to guarantee victory, Monday Gell may have written to the Haitians in order to obtain assistance. It is also possible that Vesey planned, if the need arose, to escape to Haiti or to Africa. A profound consciousness of the African homeland was certainly revealed when Prince Graham, after his conviction, "at his own request was trans-

ported to Africa on board of a vessel which sailed from Charleston."
Indeed, few other slave revolts, except for the one in Haiti, developed
such a high level of political and cultural consciousness.

The hysterical reaction to the conspiracy by virtually all white
Charlestonians indicates the pathological dimensions of the "mind
of the Old South." Officials disagreed over the extent of the plot and
the best means of repressing it, but no one at the time doubted that
the blacks actually intended to rebel. The whole white community
seemed gripped by fear for over two months, and the panic persisted
through the fall legislative session and beyond. Even Governor Bennett
and his brother-in-law, United States Supreme Court Justice William
Johnson, both of whom deplored the panic and criticized the procedures of the authorities, believed that a plot did in fact exist and
became somewhat hysterical themselves. Bennett secretly communicated with Secretary of War John C. Calhoun to request federal re-
inforcements for local garrisons; Calhoun complied by shifting troops
from Savannah and St. Augustine to the Charleston area. Thus, the
military preparations, the numbers of arrests, deportations, and executions, the harsh punishments, and the fears expressed privately by
many whites—all indicate the magnitude of the hysteria.

Most of all, slaveowners feared their "indiscriminate slaughter" and
the rape and "prostitution" of white women. Such fears of sexual
"transgressions" were a prominent theme in both private and public
utterances, just as they had been in earlier crises. A Charleston busi-
nessman, for example, disclosed that "the females were to be reserved
for worse than death," while a newsweekly reported that a slave of Governor Bennett "was to have had his daughter, a beautiful young lady,
as part of his share of the spoils." Even young Anna Johnson (whose
father was urging public calm) believed that "we poor devils were to
have been reserved to fill their Harams—horrible—I have a very
beautiful cousin," she added, repeating the rumor about Bennett's
daughter, "who was set apart for the wife or more properly the 'light
of the Haram' of one of their Chiefts. . . ." Thus one historian's
view that "no conspiracy in fact existed" was not accepted by South
Carolinians in 1822.

Politicians manipulated the hysteria (which they had helped create
and promote) for their own political purposes. By the fall of 1822,
James Hamilton, Jr., the zealous mayor-prosecutor, was elected to
the United States House of Representatives. Robert Y. Hayne, com-
mander of the troops and attorney general, was chosen United States
Senator. And John L. Wilson, owner of a slave informer, became
Governor. By comparison, Bennett left office in disrepute, and had his
report on the conspiracy tabled by a legislature hostile to criticism
of the repression of blacks. Justice Johnson was widely denounced
for his dissenting views, and eventually he was hounded from the

state because of his opposition to states' rights. In general, the policies of the fanatical racists triumphed over those of the liberal politicians in the suppression of the Vesey Plot.

Given the savagery of the white retaliation against the blacks, serious methodological problems arise in assessing the evidence left from the plot, for all of the surviving sources derive either from terrorized blacks or fearful whites. The trial testimony came largely from witnesses who desired to escape death or to direct attention away from themselves. Though two leaders confessed, they did so under extreme duress; the rest of the leadership denied complicity or remained silent. The original court minutes survive, but the whole trial record was edited by the magistrates before publicaion. In sum, the evidence is inherently biased against the conspirators and must therefore be used with skepticism and caution.

The printed and manuscript trial evidence may be criticized on other grounds. Discrepancies appear between the manuscript confessions by Bacchus Hammet and John Enslow and the printed version; contradictions also appear within the printed record itself. However, the manuscript confessions were taken when the slaves were in jail, while the printed version stems from similar, but not necessarily identical, testimony given or read in court. Moreover, the wealth of detail about the rebels' plans, the coincidence of names, and the correspondence of places contained in the printed record—all seem derived more from common knowledge by blacks about the plot than from testimony manufactured by the whites. Also, the rebel leaders had sufficient time to destroy their records and hide their arms, since Peter Poyas and Mingo Harth, after being arrested, were temporarily released, and Vesey and Gullah Jack remained at large for many days.

The means used to extract testimony from the blacks also casts serious doubt on the reliability of the trial evidence. The authorities did not of course hesitate to use various forms of coercion to gain information from the blacks. William Paul, for example, was kept in solitary confinement for nine days until he incriminated other slaves. Other suspects were lodged in separate cells to prevent communication among themselves. Peter Poyas was chained in his cell while another black man was being interrogated nearby. Monday Gell, Charles Drayton, and Harry Haig confessed only after being sentenced to death, but were then promised clemency for cooperation. The court simply delayed their execution so that they had more time to implicate other rebels and testify against them. As a reward, the court commuted their sentences from death to deportation. Little evidence bears on the extent of torture, but even Governor Bennett admitted publicly that "no means which experience or ingenuity could devise were left unessayed, to eviscerate the plot."

The trials took place in a small room in the same building where the prisoners were confined. The public was barred from the court-room and blacks were not allowed within two blocks of the building. Troops guarded the prison and court day and night to prevent blacks from freeing the captives and continuing the conspiracy. The trial procedure was far from equitable: owners and counsel were present, but defendants could not confront those witnesses who gave testimony under a pledge of secrecy. Thus, four out of five witnesses against Rolla Bennett were anonymous, and the fifth was a slaveowner. The court permitted hearsay evidence without objection, and attorneys often did not bother to cross-examine those witnesses who testified openly. There was no jury; only a majority of the magistrates was necessary for conviction. Bennett and Johnson objected that these procedures were so unfair as to endanger valuable slave property, and the court later admitted that it had departed "in many essential features, from the principles of the common law, and some of the settled rules of evidence." However, since blacks were involved, Attorney General Hayne ruled that the procedures were justified. So the trials continued.

It is clear that the purpose of the trials was not only to ferret out and punish slave conspirators but also to terrorize and pacify the rest of the black community. "The terror of example we thought would be sufficiently operative by the number of criminals sentenced to death," explained the magistrates. Governor Bennett conceded that the death sentences were intended "to produce a salutary terror." Altogether, 35 blacks were executed, many in a mass hanging toward the end of July; more than 30 others were deported from the state. Many awaiting deportation were still incarcerated in the workhouse as late as the beginning of 1823; others received public whippings. Those sentenced to death were hung publicly before crowds of spectators, and reportedly "their bodies [were] to be delivered to the surgeons for dissection, if requested." To complete the "terror of example," the black community was prevented from dressing in black or wearing black crepe to mourn its dead.

In order to promote "proper" behavior by blacks in the future, the original informers received substantial rewards from the state legislature in the fall of 1822. The owners of Peter Devany and George Wilson were authorized to emancipate their slaves. The traitors received lifetime annuities and exemption from taxation. The assembly then granted William Pencil, the free black who had counseled Peter to inform, $1,000 outright, while Scott, a free black who had implicated a white man, received a $500 award. Of course the owners of banished slaves also gained compensation for the loss of their human chattel. (For further discussion of the plot, see Afterword.)

Despite white retaliation and repression, Denmark Vesey's slave conspiracy helped politicize the black communities of America. Control of South Carolina's slaves remained a problem for whites down to the Civil War, and the informers were ostracized by Charleston's blacks. Black leaders in the North like Henry H. Garnet, William C. Nell, William Wells Brown, Archibald H. Grimke, and a certain "Colored American" kept alive the spirit of the conspiracy throughout the nineteenth century. Militant whites like Joshua Coffin, Thomas Wentworth Higginson, and John Brown also revered Vesey's deeds. And when the fugitive slave Frederick Douglass recruited troops for the Union Armies during the Civil War, he called upon black Americans to "remember Denmark Vesey."

Chronology of the Conspiracy and the Life of Denmark Vesey

1767 (?) Denmark Vesey born a slave (exact date unknown) either in Africa or the Caribbean.

1781 Transported and sold, along with 390 others from St. Thomas, Virgin Islands, to Cap François, Saint-Domingue, by Captain Joseph Vesey, a Bermuda slave trader.

1781–82 Reacquired by Captain Vesey as his personal servant after being declared "unsound and subject to epileptic fits."

1783 Captain Vesey settles in Charleston, S.C., as a slave broker and ship merchandiser.

1791 Slave revolution begins in Saint-Domingue.

1800 Vesey wins a prize of $1,500 in the East Bay Lottery with which he purchases his freedom from his master for $600 and opens a carpentry shop.

1800 Gabriel Conspiracy broken up near Richmond, Virginia.

1804 Haiti declared an independent republic by its black leaders.

1816 Slave conspiracy uncovered in Camden, S.C., July 4.

1816–17 Morris Brown and other black Methodists of Charleston leave the white Methodist organization and affiliate with the Philadelphia-based African Methodist Episcopal Church. Authorities harass African Church, but Vesey joins its Hempstead branch.

1819–21 U.S. Congress debates whether to admit Missouri as a slave state; Senator Rufus King of New York denounces slavery.

1820 South Carolina legislature imposes restrictions on free black immigration.

1821–1822 In winter, Vesey begins recruiting his lieutenants; then travels outside of Charleston to contact support in plantation districts.

May, 1822 Vesey sets July 14, the darkest night of the month, for commencement of revolt.

May 25 William Paul attempts to recruit Peter Devany Prioleau, who informs Mrs. Prioleau, her son, and William Pencil, a free black who urges Peter to tell his master.

May 30 Peter confides in Colonel J. C. Prioleau and is interrogated by Charleston authorities.

May 30–31 J. and D. Paul's slaves arrested and interrogated; William Paul implicates Peter Poyas and Mingo Harth, who are arrested, questioned, but released; Vesey advances the time of the rebellion to June 16 and begins to destroy all records.

June 8   William Paul makes further confessions, and official investigations continue.

June 14   George Wilson, a slave used as a spy, learns that African Church is one center of the conspiracy and that rebellion will begin at midnight June 16.

June 15—16 Charleston officials organize and deploy military forces; Vesey and other leaders meet, and try in vain to communicate with plantation supporters.

June 17—18 Ten slaves arrested, including Peter Poyas, and Ned, Rolla, and Batteau Bennett; court assembles; Vesey goes into hiding.

June 19—27 Court holds hearings; fifteen more blacks arrested.

June 22   Vesey captured at his wife's house.

June 23   Vesey tried, convicted, and sentenced to death.

July 2   Vesey, Poyas, the three Bennetts, and Jesse Blackwood executed.

July 5   Gullah Jack captured after trying to continue the revolt.

July 9   Gullah Jack, John Horry, Charles Drayton, Monday Gell, and Harry Haig condemned to death.

July 10   Drayton, Haig, and Gell make confessions and are reprieved.

July 12   Gullah Jack executed.

July 13—25 Arrests and trials continue.

July 26   Twenty-two slaves hanged; first court adjourns.

August 1—8 Second court holds trials.

August 9   William Garner executed.

October 7   Four whites convicted of inciting slaves to insurrection.

November— December Legislature meets; reimburses masters and informers; passes further anti-Negro laws.

PART ONE

THE TRIALS OF THE CONSPIRATORS

1

The "Official Report of the Trials of Sundry Negroes, Charged with an Attempt to Raise an Insurrection in the State of South-Carolina"

On October 22, 1822, Lionel H. Kennedy and Thomas Parker, presiding magistrates, published the proceedings of the trials of the Vesey conspirators, along with an appendix containing a report on the trials of four whites indicted "for attempting to excite the slaves to insurrection." The other members of the court attested that "the Report of the Trials contains the Evidence given in each case." Extracted here are the magistrates' introduction, the evidence presented against the most important of the accused, the alleged confessions of the informers and some of the conspirators, the sentences pronounced, a recapitulation of the punishments, and the summary of the trials of the white complicitors.[1] The printed report follows the manuscript version (located in the South Carolina Department of Archives and History) in every detail except for some reorganization of evidence to make the investigation seem more systematic than it actually was, and for the deletion (marked with asterisks) where a slave confessed to poisoning some water wells.

[1] From L. H. Kennedy and T. Parker, *An Official Report of the Trials of Sundry Negroes Charged with an Attempt to Raise an Insurrection in the State of South-Carolina* (Charleston, 1822), pp. iii–viii, 49–51, 61–68, 70–77, 79–83, 85–89, 177–78, 90–99, 103–5, 107, 114–22, 141–47, 179, 180–82, 188, and Appendix, pp. i–v. In all of the following documents the original spelling and punctuation have been retained.

INTRODUCTION

. . . As the public had not an opportunity of witnessing these proceedings, in consequence of the peculiar nature of the investigations, which occupied the attention of the Court; and as a very general desire has been expressed to be informed of the detail of the plot, as far, as it has been developed; the presiding Magistrates of the first Court, in whose possession are all the original documents, at the request and under the sanction of the whole Court, have undertaken the present publication. The whole evidence has been given, in each particular case, in the order of its trial, and wherever any additional, or incidental testimony has been disclosed against any criminal subsequently to his conviction, sentence or execution, it has been duly noticed. The evidence is in most cases preserved, as it was originally taken, without even changing the phraseology, which was generally in the very words used by the witnesses.

Although a different style might have been more agreeable to the ear, it was supposed, that this report would be considered more authentic and satisfactory, if this method were adopted. It will be perceived, in several instances, that hearsay communications have been recorded, and it may be imagined, that they had some influence on the minds of the Court. Such communications were only admitted under the belief, that they might lead to further discoveries, but they had no effect whatever on the decision of the cases; and being preserved, it was thought adviseable, to lay before the public, the whole narrative, as it was given by the witnesses, *and not to suppress any part of it.* . . .

On Tuesday, the 18th of June, the Intendant of Charleston, informed the authors, that there were several colored persons, in confinement, charged with an attempt "to excite an insurrection among the blacks against the whites," and requested them to take the necessary steps to organize a Court for the trial of those criminals. The Intendant, at the same time, suggested the names of five gentlemen, as freeholders, who, possessing in an eminent degree, the confidence of the community, and being highly approved of, were immediately summoned, in the form prescribed by law, to assemble the next day, at 12 o'clock. . . . After the Court had been . . . organized, the Intendant briefly related the circumstances, which led to the detection of the plot, and the preliminary measures adopted, which are detailed in the account published by the authority of the City Council. He at the same time presented to the Court a callender, containing the names of all the criminals, then ascertained, the charges on which they had been committed, and the witnesses against them. Before the Court proceeded to any trial, they were engaged some time, in examining all the testimony they could obtain, in order to ascertain how far, a conspiracy had really been formed: being convinced by these means, of the existence of a plot, they laid down the rules and principles, on which, the trials should be conducted. As the Court had been organized under a statute of a peculiar and local character, and intended for the government of a distinct class of persons in the community; they were bound to conform their proceedings to its provisions, which depart in many essential features, from the principles of the common law, and some of the settled rules of evidence. The Court however, determined to adopt those rules, whenever they were not repugnant to, nor expressly excepted by that statute, nor inconsistent with the local situation and policy of the state; and laid down for their own government the following regulations:—First— That no slave should be tried, except in the presence of his owner, or his counsel, and that notice should be given, in every case, at least one day before the trial. Second—That the testimony of one witness, unsupported by additional evidence, or by circumstances, should lead to no conviction of a *capital* nature. Third—That the witnesses should be confronted with the accused, and with each other, in every case, except where testimony was given under a solemn pledge that the names of the witnesses should not be divulged, as they declared in some instances, that they apprehended being murdered by the blacks, if it was known that they had volunteered their evidence. Fourth— That the prisoners might be represented by counsel, whenever this was requested by the owners of the slaves, or by the prisoners themselves, if free. Fifth—That the statements or defences of the accused should be heard, in every case, and they be permitted themselves to examine any witness they thought proper.

The Court, on mature deliberation, determined that the public generally, or in other words those, who had no particular interest in the slaves accused, should not be present at their trials; but that the owners of all the slaves tried, and their counsel, as well as the owners of those, who were used as witnesses, should be admitted, if they desired it. The Court also extended the same permission to the Intendant and Wardens of Charleston. Among other reasons, which induced this course, were the following; because several witnesses had volunteered their testimony, under a solemn pledge of secrecy, and because the further detection of the plot, would be greatly impeded, if not entirely stopped, by the accused being apprized of the information against them, and being thus enabled to effect their escape before they could be apprehended.

It was also morally certain, that no colored witness would have ventured to incur the resentment of his comrades, by voluntarily disclosing his testimony in a public court. The court was likewise anxious to prevent the public mind from being excited by the exaggerated representations of the testimony which might have been circulated by auditors under the influence of misapprehension or terror.—In the progress of these trials, the propriety of these measures was completely verified, and they were also sanctioned by precedent, on a former occasion, under similar circumstances, at Camden, in this state. . . .

After the execution of the first six criminals [on July 2, 1822], and the conviction and passing sentence on five more, two of the latter made disclosures, which caused the arrest of such considerable numbers, that the court were induced to lay down certain rules of discrimination, in the guilt of the parties, and to adopt two classes of offences. Under the first class were included those who attended the meetings at Denmark Vesey's, at Bulkley's Farm, or at appointed meetings in Monday Gell's shop, for the purpose of obtaining and communicating intelligence of the progress of the conspiracy; all those, who aided and abetted in the contribution of money, arms or ammunition; all those, who persuaded others to join; all those, who were employed as couriers, to communicate intelligence, or convey orders; and generally, those, who, from their acts or declarations, indicated a hearty concurrence in the plot; and all those, who, after the condemnation of the first 6, endeavored to keep up the spirit of insurrection, to promote, or endeavored to promote or excite a party to rescue the prisoners to be executed. Those who were embraced in this class were, upon conviction, to be punished with death. Under the second class were included those, who had merely consented to join in the plot, without taking any active part.—Those, who were included under this class, were to be transported beyond the limits of the United States, not to return therein, under the penalty of death. . . .

Every possible care was taken by the Court throughout the trials, to prevent collusion between the witnesses, or either of them knowing what the others had testified to. Those in prison were confined in different rooms, or when, from their being wanted in Court it was necessary to bring them in the room adjoining that in which the Court was sitting, they were put together in one room, a confidential non-commissioned officer of the City Guard was placed in the room with them to prevent their communicating together. They were brought in and examined separately, none of them knowing against whom they were called, until they entered the Court Room; and the evidence given in the one room could not be heard in the next. Those who were not arrested, as they could not know who were to be the witnesses against a particular individual, or what individual was to be tried, could not well collude together.

THE INFORMER'S CONFESSION

On May 30, 1822, Peter (also called Devany), a personal servant belonging to Colonel J. C. Prioleau, made the following confession before the Corporation of Charleston, Intendant James Hamilton, Jr., and Governor Thomas Bennett. After Peter's disclosures, Peter Poyas and Mingo Harth were arrested, but their behavior was so deceptive that they were released. Soon, however, two other informers appeared; further exposure and the trials followed.

On Saturday afternoon last [May 25] (my master being out of town) I went to market; after finishing my business I strolled down the wharf below the fish market, from which I observed a small vessel in the stream with a singular flag; whilst looking at this object, a black man, (Mr. Paul's William) came up to me and remarking the subject which engaged my attention said, I have often seen a flag with the number 76 on it, but never with 96, before. After some trifling conversation on this point, he remarked with considerable earnestness to me. Do you know that something serious is about to take place? To which I replied no. Well, said he, there is, and many of us are determined to right ourselves! I asked him to explain himself—when he remarked, why, we are determined to shake off our bondage, and for this purpose we stand on a good foundation, many have joined, and if you will go with me, I will show you the man, who has the list of names who will take yours down. I was so much astonished and horror struck at this information, that it was a moment or two before I could collect myself sufficient to tell him I would have nothing to do with this business, that I was satisfied with my condition, that I was grateful to my master for his kindness and wished no change. I left him instantly, lest, if this fellow afterwards got into trouble, and I had been seen conversing with him, in so public a place, I might be suspected and thrown into difficulty. I did not however remain easy under the burden of such a secret, and consequently determined to consult a free man of colour named ——[1] and to ask his advice. On conferring with this friend,[2] he urged me with great earnestness to communicate what had passed between Mr. Paul's man and myself to my master, and not

---

[1] It would be a libel on the liberality and gratitude of this community to suppose that this man can be *overlooked* among those who are to be rewarded for their fidelity and principle.

[2] [According to the Charleston *Mercury*, Dec. 25, 1822, the legislature awarded the free Negro—named Pencell—$1,000 plus an exemption from taxes. Another informer, Scott, received $500 plus a tax exemption, while Colonel Prioleau's Peter Devany and Major Wilson's George were to be freed with the consent of their masters and awarded $50 each per annum for life. Peter's pension was raised to $200 per year in 1857—Ed.]

lose a moment in so doing. I took his advice and not waiting, even for the return of my master to town, I mentioned it to my mistress and young master—On the arrival of my master, he examined me as to what had passed, and I stated to him what I have mentioned to your-selves.

THE TRIALS

The Court organized for the trial of sundry Negroes apprehended and charged *"with attempting to raise an Insurrection amongst the Blacks against the Whites,"* and of such others as might be brought before them on the same charge, met on Wednesday, the 19th June, 1822, and consisted of the following Gentlemen, viz:

> Lionel H. Kennedy, Q. U.⎤
> Thomas Parker, J. P.   ⎦ *Magistrates.*
> William Drayton,   ⎤
> Nathan Heyward,   ⎟
> James R. Pringle,   ⎬ *Freeholders.*
> James Legare,   ⎟
> Robert J. Turnbull,   ⎦

The Trial of Rolla

The Trial of Rolla, a negro man, the slave of His Excellency, Governor Bennett—Jacob Axson, Esq. attending as Counsel for his owner.

Evidence

Witness No. 1 [3]—A negro man testified as follows:

I know Rolla, belonging to Mr. Thomas Bennett, we are intimate friends; all that I know of the intended Insurrection I got from him. About three months ago he asked me to join with him in slaying the whites, I asked him to give me time to consider of it; a week after he put the same question to me, and at the end of another week he again came to me on the same subject. I told him "take care, God says we must not kill;" you are a coward he said and laughed at me. He said he would tell me how it was to be done. There are said he, white men who have come from off, and who say that St. Domingo and Africa will assist us to get our liberty if we will only make the motion first.

[3] This witness came forward voluntarily, and gave information of the intended Insurrection, and of the places and those concerned, as far as his information ex-tended, *previously* to the appointed day, and only asked that his name would not be devulged, which the Court pledged themselves to conceal as far as it depended on them. His name is therefore suppressed—*He is in no way inculpated.*

I advised him to let it alone, and told him I would oppose them if they came to kill my owner, when he again laughed at me as a coward—He summoned me to go to their meetings where said he you will hear what is going on and be better informed; I told him yes, I would go —Friday night about three weeks ago he appointed to take me with him to their meeting; at that night he came to me and again summoned me to go to the meeting, I went away from him, I went out of his way. The next day he came to me and said the meeting had been expecting me and I must send my name to be put down as one of the Band—This thing has been going on for four months. He told me that at the meeting it was said that *some white men said Congress had set us free, and that our white people here would not let us be so,* and that St. Domingo and Africa would come over and cut up the white people if we only made the motion here first—that last Saturday night (the 15th June,) might be the last he had to live, as they were determined to break open the thing on Sunday night (the 16th June) —I told him it could not be done, it would not succeed, that our parents for generations back had been slaves, and we had better be contented—He desired me to tell—(Witness No. 2) to go up to him, that he wished to see him—No. 2 went in the evening—Rolla told No. 2 in my presence what he was going to do—No. 2 told him to let it alone, he would not succeed, and then turned away and wept— *Rolla replied 'tis now gone too far to stop it*—He told No. 2 to go out of town on Sunday night, as he did not wish him to be hurt—I told No. 2 to sound the alarm, and if he did not I would—I asked Rolla what was to be done with the women and children? he said, *"when we have done with the fellows, we know what to do with the wenches"*—He said *there are a great many involved in it in the country;* that Mungo from James' Island was to come over to Charleston with 4000 men, land on South-Bay, march up and seize the Arsenal by the Guard-House and kill all the City Guard; that another body was to seize upon the Powder Magazine, and another body to take the United States' Arsenal on the Neck, then march to town and destroy the Inhabitants, who could only escape by jumping into the river— *My Army he said will first fix my old buck and then the Intendant*— I asked him if he could bind his master or kill him; he laughed at me again; I then told him I would have nothing to do with him—He said he was going to John's Island to hasten down the country negroes, as he feared they would not come. I felt that it was a bad thing to disclose what a bosom friend had confided to me, and that it was wicked to betray him, and I suffered a great deal before I could bring myself to give information, but when I thought on the other hand that by doing so I would save so many lives *and prevent the horrible acts in contemplation,* 'twas overbalanced, and my duty was to inform—I refused to go to the meetings as Rolla wished, as I feared if I opposed them there, they might make away with me to prevent me from betraying them—I don't know where the meetings were held, but believe 'twas in Bull-street, in which street Denmark Vesey lives—Rolla said that Ned and Mathias were concerned—I am well acquainted with

Stephen, Mr. T. R. Smith's man; I believe him to be a worthy, good man, and in a conversation with him on this subject, he agreed with me that this was an abominable plot—I have not seen him for the last four weeks—I know Denmark Vesey—I was one day on horseback going to Market when I met him on foot; he asked me if I was satisfied in my present situation; if I remembered the fable of Hercules and the Waggoner whose waggon was stalled, and he began to pray, and Hercules said, you fool put your shoulders to the wheel, whip up the horses and your waggon will be pulled out; that if we did not put our hand to the work and deliver ourselves, we should never come out of slavery; *that Congress had made us free.* I know that he is intimately acquainted with Rolla—Rolla told me that there had been a sort of disagreement and confusion at their place of meeting, and that they meant to meet at Vesey's—Vesey told me that a large army from St. Domingo and Africa were coming to help us, and we must not stand with our hands in our pockets; he was bitter towards the whites. Sambo who lives on Mrs. La Roache's plantation (on John's Island) sent word down to Rolla that he would be in town on Sunday night last—Rolla said that they would have a countersign to be known to their friends, and in the action, those blacks who could not give it would be killed; that they would fire the town—Rolla's threats are that if any black person is found out giving information or evidence against them, they would be watched for day and night and be certainly killed—Even now the friends of those in prison are trying about the streets to find out who has given information—*If my name was known I would certainly be killed.* I advised Rolla to let it alone, but told him that if they persevered and commenced it, I had no arms, but that as they passed by my house, I would fall in behind with my fishing line and grains which was all that I had. Rolla did not tell to No. 2, all the particulars, but told him of the intended rising and the time.

Witness No. 2.[4] A negro man testified as follows:

The first I heard was from witness No. 1—he told me that such was the idea of the coloured people; that he was asked to join but that he asked for time to consider; that he was told to tell me to go out of town; that at 12 o'clock on Sunday (the 16th June,) the rising would take place.—I told him I would tell my master and he said he would do the same. On Friday (the 14th of June) witness No. 1, and myself told my master every thing. I went up to Rolla as he requested, and saw him, who complained of his hard living; I found that he was at something wrong and my heart got so full that I wept. Rolla never told me in express words that he was going to join in the rising to kill the whites. Witness No. 1, was present when Rolla and myself were speaking and heard most of what passed; Rolla's last words

[4] This witness as regards the concealment of his name, stands precisely in the same situation as No. 1.

were " *'tis gone too far now to be stopped.*" Though Rolla said nothing expressly to me about insurrection, yet we seemed to understand each other perfectly, and that such was in contemplation—Rolla told me that on Sunday evening I must go out of town as he did not wish me to be hurt; he said words to the effect that he was going to join in the rising; he said that on Sunday night at 12 o'clock such and such a thing would take place. Witness No. 1, said that Rolla had told him they were to join and take the Powder Magazine and the Arsenal on the Neck, and that an army of 4000 men from James' Island would land at South-Bay, march up and take the Laboratory in town and kill all the City Guard, and then they would kill the whites &c. Witness No. 1, and Stephen, Mr. T. R. Smith's man are truly good men. . . .

Witness No. 7, a negro man gave the following evidence:

I reside on John's Island. About a month ago Rolla advised me to join the blacks against the whites, I told him it was vain; he told me to come to town on Saturday week last (the 15th of June). He said he would let me know what day to be down and sent me word last Friday week not to come down on the Saturday as the thing had been found out. He said the plan was to take the Guard House and the Magazine and then get arms and ammunition: that a great many were concerned but no name was mentioned to me; I mentioned it to no one on the Island.

The voluntary confession of Rolla[5] *to the Court*, made after all the evidence had been heard, but before his conviction:

I know Denmark Vesey—On one occasion he asked me what news, I told him none; he replied we are free but the white people here won't let us be so, and the only way is to rise up and fight the whites. I went to his house one night to learn where the meetings were held. I never conversed on this subject with Batteau or Ned—Vesey told me he was the leader in this plot. I never conversed either with Peter or Mingo. Vesey induced me to join; when I went to Vesey's house there was a meeting there, the room was full of people, but none of them white. That night at Vesey's we determined to have arms made, and each man put in 12 1–2 cents towards that purpose. Though Vesey's room was full I did not know one individual there. At this meeting Vesey said we were to take the Guard-House and Magazine to get arms; that we ought to rise up and fight against the whites for our liberties; he was the first to rise up and speak, and he *read to us from the Bible, how the Children of Israel were delivered out of Egypt from bondage.* He said that the rising would take place, last Sunday night week, (the 16th June) and that Peter Poyas was one.

[5] Rolla on his arraignment and throughout his trial, until after the evidence closed denied his guilt, and pretended utter ignorance of the intended insurrection.

On behalf of Rolla, five witnesses were introduced and examined prior to his confession to the Court, with a view to impeach the credibility of witness No. 1, but they rather strengthened it. The owner of that witness, (No. 1,) who was introduced as a witness on behalf of Rolla, amongst other things creditable to that witness, stated, that since he had given information against Rolla, he had been distracted, that being the first day he seemed composed; that he thought and said he had acted like a traitor to his friend.

The Court *unanimously* found Rolla guilty—After sentence of death had been passed upon him, he made a confession in prison *to the Rev Dr. Hall,* who furnished the Court with it in writing, and in the following words:

> I was invited by Denmark Vesey to his house, where I found Ned Bennett, Peter Poyas, and others, some were strangers to me, *they said they were from the country.* Denmark told us, it was high time we had our liberty, and he could shew us how we might obtain it. He said, we must unite together as the St. Domingo people did, never to betray one another; and to die before we would tell upon one another. He also said, he expected the St. Domingo people would send some troops to help us—The best way, said he, for us to conquer the whites, is to set the town on fire in several places, at the Governor's Mills, and near the Docks, and for every servant in the yards to be ready with axes and knives and clubs, to kill every man, as he came out when the bells began to ring. *He then read in the Bible where God commanded, that all should be cut off, both men, women and children, and said, he believed, it was no sin for us to do so, for the Lord had commanded us to do it.* But if I had read these Psalms, Doctor, which I have read, since I have been in this prison, they would never have got me to join them—At another meeting, some of the company were opposed to killing the Ministers, and the women and children, but Denmark said, it was not safe to keep one alive, but to destroy them totally, for you see, said he, the Lord has commanded it—When I heard this, master Hall, my heart pained me within, and I said to myself, I cannot kill my master and mistress, for they use me, more like a son, than a slave—I then concluded in my mind, that I would go into the country, on Saturday evening, before they were to commence on Sunday, that I might not see it—Some of the company asked, if they were to stay in Charleston; he said no, as soon as they could get the money from the Banks, and the goods from the stores, they should hoist sail for Saint Domingo, for he expected some armed vessels would meet them to conduct and protect them. . . .

On the first day of July, the following letter was received from His Excellency Governor Bennett [in relation to the unanimous conviction by the court of his servant Batteau on June 28:]

Charleston, July 1st. 1822.

L. H. Kennedy, Esq. Q. U. ⎫   Presiding Magistrates
Thos. Parker, J. P.   ⎬   of the Court of Justices
and Freeholders organized for the trial of slaves charged with attempting to raise an insurrection:

Gentlemen,

After a very attentive consideration of the evidence yesterday presented, permit me to request that the case of Batteau may be reviewed with a view to the mitigation of his punishment; such a power is vested in the Court by the provisions of the act for the better ordering and governing of slaves.

If guilty of an attempt to raise an insurrection, it does not appear from the evidence to extend beyond an invitation to two boys to join in the project: from no part of the evidence does it appear that he is further implicated.

It is known that one of the boys referred to, was charged with using improper threats, and therefore supposed to be involved in the general plot, for which he was arrested. As he states that he had subsequently a communication with his brother, and they both testify to a simple insolated fact, collusion may be inferred. And even admitting the truth of their evidence, it would not appear that he is equally guilty with the others. If so the benignant provisions of that act would sanction the request made.

I ask this Gentlemen, as an individual incurring a severe and distressing loss.

I am very respectfully,
Your obedient serv't,

T HOMAS B ENNETT.

The Court agreeable to the request contained in the above letter, reviewed their decision, but after having sent for and again interrogated witness No. 3 and 4, came unanimously to the conclusion they had at first done. After his execution it was incidentally proved, in the course of the subsequent trials, that he attended the meetings of the conspirators at Vesey's. . . .

The Trial of Peter

The trial of Peter, a negro man the property of Mr. James Poyas. —Mr. Poyas with Robert Bentham, Esq. as his counsel attending.

Evidence

Witness No. 5,[6] a negro man, gave the following evidence:

[6] Against this witness the Court had not a tittle of testimony—he consented without hesitation to become a witness, and to give all the information he possessed, a pledge having been previously given him by the Court that he should not be prosecuted or his name revealed.

I know Peter, he belongs to Mr. James Poyas—in May last Peter and myself met in Legare street, at the corner of Lambol-street, when the following conversation took place—he asked me the news—I replied none that I know of—he said by George we can't live so—I replied how will we do—he said we can do very well; if you can find any one to assist us will you join—I asked him how do you mean—he said, why to break the yoke—I replied I don't know—he asked me suppose you were to hear that the whites were going to kill you would you defend yourself—I reply'd I'd try to escape—he asked have you lately seen *Denmark Vesey,* and has he spoken to you particularly—I said no —well then said he that's all now, but call at the shop tomorrow after knocking off work and I will tell you more—we then parted. I met him the next day according to appointment, when he said to me, we intend to see if we can't do something for ourselves, we can't live so—I asked him where he would get men—he said we'll find them fast enough, we have got enough—We expect *men from country and town.* But how said I will you manage it—why we will give them notice said he, and they will march down and camp round the city— but what said I will they do for arms—he answered they will find arms enough, they will bring down their hoes, axes, &c.—I said that won't do to fight with here—he said stop; let us get candidates from town with arms, and we will then take the Guard-House and Arsenal in town, the Arsenal on the Neck and the upper Guard-House, and supply the country people with arms—how said I will you approach these Arsenals &c. for they are guarded—yes said he, I know that, but what are those guards, one man here and one man there, we won't let a man pass before us—Well said I but how will the black people from the country and those from the Islands know when you are to begin; or how will you get the town people together—why said he we will have *prayer meetings at night and there notify them* when to start and as the clock strikes 12 all must move—But said I, the whites in the back country, Virginia, &c. when they hear the news will turn to and kill you all, and besides you may be betrayed—Well said he what of that, if one gets hanged we will rise at that minute— We then left his shop and walked towards Broad-street, when he said *I want you to take notice of all the Shops and Stores in town with arms in them, take down the numbers and give them to me*—I said I will see to it and then we parted—About the 1st June I saw in the public papers a statement that the white people were going to build Missionary Houses for the blacks, which I carried and shewed to Peter and said to him, you see the good they are going to do for us— when he said, what of that, have you not heard that on the 4th July the whites are going to create a false alarm of fire, and every black that comes out will be killed in order to thin them—Do you think that they would be so barbarous said I—Yes said he I do; I fear they have knowledge of an army from St. Domingo, and they would be right to do it, to prevent us from joining that army if it should march towards this land—I was then very much alarmed—we then parted and I saw no more of him 'till the Guards were very strict about a fortnight ago—at that time I saw Peter and Ned Bennett standing and talking together at the corner of Lambol and Legare-street—they crossed over and met me by Mrs. Myles, and Ned Bennet said to me, did you hear what those boys were taken up for the other day—I replied No, but some say 'twas for stealing—Ned asked me if I was sure I had never said any thing to the whites about what Peter Poyas had spoken to me about—I replied No—says Peter you never did—No I answered—says Ned to me how do you stand—at which I struck the tree box with my knuckles and said, as firm as this box, I'll never say one word against you—Ned then smiled and nodded his head and said, that will do, when we all separated—last Tuesday or Wednesday week Peter said to me you see my lad how the white people have got to windward of us—you won't said I be able to do any thing—O yes said he we will, by George we are obliged to—he said all down this way ought to meet and have a collection to purchase powder—what said I is the use of powder, the whites can fire three times to our once—he said but 'twill *be such a dead time of night they won't know what is the matter, and our Horse Companies will go about the streets and prevent the whites from assembling*—I asked him where will you get horses—why said he there are many butcher boys with horses, and there are the public Livery Stables, where we have several candidates and the waiting men belonging to the white people of the Horse Companies will be told to take away their master's horses—he asked me if my master was not a horseman—I said yes—has he not got arms in his house—I answered yes—can't they be got at—I said yes—then said he 'tis good to have them—I asked him what was the plan—why said he after we have taken the Arsenal and Guard Houses, then we will set the town on fire in different places, and as the whites come out we will slay them; if we were to set fire to the town first, the man in the steeple would give the alarm too soon—*I am the Captain said he, to take the lower Guard House and Arsenal*—But, I replied, when you are coming up the centinel will give the alarm—he said he would advance a little distance ahead, and if he could only get a *grip at his throat he was a gone man,* for his sword was very sharp; he had sharpened it and had made it so sharp it had cut his finger, which he shewed me—as to the Arsenal on the Neck he said that is gone as sure as fate, *Ned Bennett would manage that with the people from the country, and the people between Hibben's Ferry and Santee would land and take the upper Guard-House.*—I then said, then this thing seems true—My man, said he, God has a hand in it, we have been meeting for four years and are not yet betrayed—I told him I was afraid after all of the white people from the back country and Virginia, &c.—He said that the blacks would collect so numerous *from the country* we need not fear the whites from other parts, for when we have once got the city we can keep them all out—He asked if I had told my boys—I said no—then said he you should do it, for Ned Bennett has his people pretty well ranged; but said he take care and don't mention it to those waiting men who receive *presents of old coats &c. from their masters or they'll betray us;* I will speak to them.

We then parted and I have not since conversed with him—he said
the rising was to take place last Sunday night (16th June)—*that any of
the coloured people who said a word about this matter would be killed
by the others*—The little man who can't be killed, shot or taken is
named Jack, a Gullah negro—Peter said there was a French company
in town *of* 300 *men fully armed*—that he was to see Monday Gell
about expediting the rising. I know that Mingo went often to Mr.
Paul's to see Edwin, but don't know if he spoke with William—*Peter
said he had a sword* and I ought to get one—he said he had *a letter
from the country, I think from St. Thomas', from a negro man who
belonged to the Captain of a Militia Company, who said he could
easily get the key of the house where the Company's arms were put
after muster, and take them all out* and help in that way. This business originates altogether with the *African Congregation* in which Peter
is a leader. When Bennett's Ned asked about those taken up, he
alluded particularly to Mr. Paul's William, and asked me if I had
said any thing to him about it. . . .

William, a negro man belonging to Mr. Paul, testified as follows:

> Mr. Harth's negro man Mingo told me about the insurrection and
> referred me to Peter Poyas for further information, who he said had
> a list with 9,000 names upon it, and that he was still taking down
> names. On the week I was to see Peter I was apprehended. Mingo
> said that 600 men on the Bay were already down on the list in
> Peter's possession. I never had any conversation with Peter. Peter,
> Ned Bennett and Charles Shubrick are *class leaders in the African
> Church*. The African Association have also a Church in Anson-street
> and one in Cow-alley, where they have service. Mingo said that Peter
> would tell me when the rising would take place. He said that letters
> were passing between Peter Poyas and Ned Bennett and Charles Shu-
> brick, and that all the orders he got, he got from Peter. My fellow
> servant Edwin brought the first news of the rising into our yard. He
> has a wife at Mr. Parker's near the lines. One Monday morning when
> he came from his wife's he told me there would be something shortly
> 'twixt the blacks and the whites—that he knew the parties and that
> the thing was going on, and *all the African Church were engaged in it*,
> and in particular mentioned Peter Poyas and Ned Bennett. Edwin
> told me generally about the matter—that Peter knew all, and that all
> who wants to know goes to him.

. . . The Court *unanimously* found Peter guilty, and passed upon
him the sentence of death.

Subsequently to Peter's trial, a good deal of testimony was given
against him in the course of the succeeding trials. Amongst others, witness No. 10 testified that:

> Peter Poyas was the first man who spoke to me and asked me to
> join—I asked him what, the Church—he said no, have you not heard

that the blacks were joining to try to take the country—I asked him if he thought he had men enough to do it—he said yes, a plenty of men and the Society will contribute money with which a white man would purchase guns and powder for them—He said he would call back, and I must consider if I would join them—He called back and asked me if I was willing now—why Peter said I you have not got force enough—he said if I did not join he would turn all my country people against me—said I, if so, I'll join you, but you must not put my name down, when you come out if I find you strong enough I'll join you—well said he if you don't join you'll be killed—Peter and Harry Haig called on me afterwards—I was not at home. Peter Poyas told me also that they had force enough, that some would come from James' Island and Johns' Island, and some from Christ Church Parish, where he generally went over to a meeting to have a talk, and that he had some about and about in town, the number of which he would shew me from the Society Books if I would only come to the Society— he said they were to fight the whites and keep on fighting 'till the English came to help them—Harry Haig told me the same thing.

See also Frank Ferguson's testimony against Denmark Vesey, who told him that "himself, Ned, Peter and Monday Gell were the principal men, and himself the head man, &c. . . ."

The Trial of Jesse

The trial of Jesse, a Negro man, the slave of Mr. Thomas Blackwood.—His owner attending.

Evidence

Sally, a Negro woman, the slave of Mr. Alexander Howard, gave the following evidence:

I know Jesse and heard him speak several times about it—One day in particular he was anxious to see his brother who has my mother for his wife, and waited until he came, when they conversed together —Jesse said he had got a horse *to go into the country to bring down men* to fight the white people; that he was allowed to pass by two parties of the patrole on the road, but that a third party had brought him back and that if there were but five men like him they would destroy the city—this was on last Sunday week, (the 16th June)—he said that before 3 o'clock on that night all the white people would be killed—that if any person informed or would not join in the fight, such person would be killed or poisoned—he frequently came into the yard to see his brother, and I threatened to inform if he came there, and spoke in that way to get us all into trouble—We never had any quarrel.

Lot, a Negro man, the slave of Mr. Forrester, testified as follows:

> I know Jesse—he met me last Sunday week (16th June) at the corner of Boundary-street, as I was coming into town—he said he was going to get a horse *to go into the country*—From what my master had told me the Thursday before I distrusted his errand and gave him something of a caution when as I was going down into town towards Mr. Hibben's Ferry Slip, and conversing with him, he said *you shall see to night when I come down what I am going up for, and if my own father does not assist I will cut off his head*—He said he was going *as far as Goose Creek Bridge,* and would get him a horse if it cost him nine dollars—the church bells were then ringing, and at half past 10 o'clock the same day I saw him at Mr. Howard's, and afterwards *understood from Sally that he had set off for the country and had been brought down by the Patrole.*

Syke, a Negro man, the slave of Mr. Waring, gave the following testimony:

> Jesse asked me on Sunday week last, (16th June) before breakfast, where he could get a horse to go a little way *into the country with*— I told him I did not know—he then went away and did not return before 9 o'clock that night—he had a wife at Mr. Waring's.

Frank, Mrs. Ferguson's slave, testified as follows:

> On the 15th of June, Vesey gave to Jesse $2 to hire a horse *to go into the country to my Mistress' plantation in St. John's, to inform the people to be down* on the night of the 16th. Myself and Adam put in 25 cents each for it. Vesey told Jesse, if he could not go, he must send some one else.

The voluntary confession of Jesse *to the Court,* made after all the evidence had been heard, but before his conviction.

> I have had several conversations with Denmark Vesey, the first about four weeks ago (about 1st June) he asked me if I had heard about the rising, &c. and did I know that the coloured people were going to try to get their liberty—I then could stop no longer and he asked me to call and see him—I afterwards met him on Wednesday previous to the Sunday (16th of June) that the rising was to take place—we walked up St. Phillip-street and were joined by Frank Ferguson opposite Liberty-street, and we all three walked up to Vesey's house. Says Frank I am just from the country—well says Vesey and what success —says Frank I have got two fine men for our purpose on my Mistress' plantation, who must be sent up to and informed when the people are wanted in town—Vesey asked me if I would be the man to go—I

said yes, but I don't know the way—says Vesey, Frank will tell you—Frank then told me how to go to Mrs. Ferguson's plantation, and that I must ask for John O and Pompey and gave me other directions—Vesey then gave me $2 to hire a horse and Frank and Adam threw down on the table 25 cents each, I dont know what for —this was about 1 o'clock P. M. on Saturday before last (15th June) —I promised to go that night. On Sunday I met Lot who betrayed me; the same day I told Vesey I had started but that the patrol turned me back; in fact I had not started and only told him so to deceive him—the same day I met Charles Drayton at Vesey's who said the business was postponed—Vesey asked Charles how he knew the business was postponed—Charles said Ned Bennett and Monday Gell told him so. But said Vesey, how could they know it was postponed as they have not seen me—Says Charles they said they had seen you and that you had told them so. Now, said I to Vesey, you see there, suppose I had gone into the country and brought those people down to night, we should all have been destroyed. As far as I know, I believe *Denmark Vesey and Monday Gell were the chief men.*

The Court *unanimously* found Jesse guilty, and passed upon him the sentence of death.

Subsequently to his conviction, he made the following confession in prison *to the Rev. Dr. Hall:*

I was invited to Denmark Vesey's house, and when I went, I found several men met together, among whom was Ned Bennett, Peter Poyas, and others, whom I did not know. Denmark opened the meeting by saying, he had an important secret to communicate to us, which we must not disclose to any one, and if we did, we should be put to instant death. He said, we were deprived of our rights and privileges by the white people, and that our Church was shut up, so that we could not use it, and that it was high time for us to seek for our rights, and that we were fully able to conquer the whites, if we were only unanimous and courageous, as the St. Domingo people were— He then proceeded to explain his plan, by saying, that they intended to make the attack by setting the Governor's Mills on fire, and also some houses near the water, and as soon as the bells began to ring for fire, that they should kill every man as he came out of his door, and that the servants in the yard should do it, and that it should be done with axes and clubs, and afterwards they should murder the women and children, for he said, God had so commanded it in the scriptures— At another meeting at Denmark's, Ned Bennett and Peter Poyas, and several others were present, in conversation, some said they thought it was cruel to kill the ministers, and the women and children, but Denmark Vesey said, *he thought it was for our safety not to spare one white skin alive, for this was the plan they pursued in St. Domingo—* He then said to me, Jesse, I want you to go into the country to enlist as many of the country negroes as possible, to be in readiness to come down to assist us—I told him I had no horse and no money to hire one; he then took out two dollars, and gave them to me to hire a horse, and told me to enlist as many as possible. I got the horse the next Sabbath, and started, but the guard was so strict, I could not pass them without being taken up; so I returned, and told Denmark, at which he expressed his sorrow, and said, the business was urgent, for they wanted the country people to be armed, that they might attack the Forts, at the same time, and also to take every ship and vessel in the harbour, and to put every man to death, except the Captains. For said he, it will not be safe to stay in Charleston, for as soon, as they had got all the money out of the Banks, and the goods out of the stores on board, they intended to sail for Saint Domingo, for he had a promise that they would receive and protect them. This Jesse asserted to me, was the truth, whilst the tears were running down his cheeks, and he appeared truly penitent, and I have reason to hope, that he obtained pardon from God, through the merits of Christ, and was prepared to meet his fate with confidence and that he was accepted of God—At 4 o'clock, on the morning of the execution, I visited all the prisoners condemned, and found Jesse at prayers—he told me, his mind was placid and calm; he then assured me, that what he had told me was the truth, and that he was prepared to meet his God.[7]

The Trial of Denmark Vesey

The trial of Denmark Vesey,[8] a free black man—Col. G. W. Cross attending as his Counsel.

[7] The Court considered Jesse's confession good evidence, because it was voluntarily made under the conviction of approaching death, and because the court did not think the principle of the common law relative to the testimony of a convicted prisoner to be applicable to an individual in the situation of this witness. Moreover, the confession of Jesse and Rolla to the Court were made before conviction.

[8] The following sketch of his life is copied from the account of the intended Insurrection published by the authority of the Corporation of Charleston.

"As Denmark Vesey has occupied so large a place in the conspiracy, a brief notice of him will, perhaps, be not devoid of interest. The following anecdote will shew how near he was to the chance of being distinguished in the bloody events of San Domingo. During the revolutionary war, Captain Vesey, now an old resident of this city, commanded a ship that traded between St. Thomas' and Cape Francais (San Domingo.) He was engaged in supplying the French of that Island with Slaves. In the year 1781, he took on board at St. Thomas' 390 slaves and sailed for the Cape; on the passage, he and his officers were struck with the beauty, alertness and intelligence of a boy about 14 years of age, whom they made a pet of, by taking him into the cabin, changing his apparel, and calling him by way of distinction *Telemaque*, (which appellation has since, by gradual corruption, among the negroes, been changed to *Denmark*, or sometimes *Telmak*.) On the arrival, however, of the ship at the Cape, Captain Vesey, having no use for the boy, sold him among his other slaves, and returned to St. Thomas'. On his next voyage to the Cape, he was surprised to learn from his consignee that Telemaque would be returned on his hands, as the planter, who had purchased him, represented him unsound, and subject to epilectic fits. According to the custom of trade in that place, the boy was placed in the hands of the king's physician, who decided that he was

Evidence

William, the slave of Mr. Paul, testified as follows:

> Mingo Harth told me *that Denmark Vesey was the chiefest man, and more concerned than any one else*—Denmark Vesey is an old man in whose yard my master's negro woman Sarah cooks—he was her father in law, having married her mother Beck, and though they have been parted some time, yet he visited her at her house near the Intendant's, (Major Hamilton) where I have often heard him speak of the rising—*He said he would not like to have a white man in his presence—that he had a great hatred for the whites,* and that if all were like him they would resist the whites—he studies all he can to put it into the heads of the blacks to have a rising against the whites, and tried to induce me to join—he tries to induce all his acquaintances —this has been his chief study and delight for a considerable time— my last conversation with him was in April—he studies the Bible a great deal and tries to prove from it that slavery and bondage is against the Bible. I am persuaded that Denmark Vesey was chiefly concerned in business.

See [testimony of Witness No. 1 and] the confession of Rolla.
Frank, Mrs. Ferguson's slave, gave the following evidence:

> I know Denmark Vesey and have been to his house—I have heard him say that the negroe's situation was so bad he did not know how they could endure it, and was astonished they did not rise and fend for themselves, and he advised me to join and rise—he said he was going about to see different people, and mentioned the names of Ned Bennett and Peter Poyas as concerned with him—that he had spoken to

unsound, and Captain Vesey was compelled to take him back, of which he had no occasion to repent, as Denmark proved, for 20 years a most faithful slave. In 1800, Denmark drew a prize of $1500 in the East-Bay-Street Lottery, with which he purchased his freedom from his master, at six hundred dollars, much less than his real value. From that period to the day of his apprehension he has been working as a carpenter in this city, distinguished for great strength and activity. Among his colour he was always looked up to with awe and respect. His temper was impetuous and domineering in the extreme, qualifying him for the despotic rule, of which he was ambitious. All his passions were ungovernable and savage; and, to his numerous wives and children, he displayed the haughty and capricious cruelty of an Eastern Bashaw. He had nearly effected his escape, after information had been lodged against him. For three days the town was searched for him without success. As early as Monday, the 17th, he had concealed himself. It was not until the night of the 22d of June, during a perfect tempest, that he was found secreted in the house of one of his wives. It is to the uncommon efforts and vigilance of Mr. Wesner, and Capt. Dove, of the City Guard, (the latter of whom seized him) that public justice received its necessary tribute, in the execution of this man. If the party had been one moment later, he would, in all probability, have effected his escape the next day in some outward bound vessel."

Ned and Peter on this subject; and that they were to go about and tell the blacks that they were free, and must rise and *fight for themselves*—that they would take the Magazines and Guard-Houses, and the city and be free—that he was going to send *into the country* to inform the people there too—he said he wanted me to join them—I said I could not answer—he said if I would not go into the country for him he could get others—he said himself, Ned Bennet, Peter Poyas and Monday Gell were the principal men and himself the head man. He said they were the principal men to go about and inform the people and fix them, &c. that *one party would land on South-Bay, one about Wappoo, and about the farms*—that the party which was to land on South-Bay was to take the Guard-House and get arms and then they would be able to go on—that the attack was to commence about 12 o'clock at night—*that great numbers would come from all about,* and it must succeed as so many were engaged in it—that they would kill all the whites—that they would leave their master's houses and assemble together near the lines, march down and meet the party which would land on South-Bay —that he was going to *send a man into the country* on a horse *to bring down the country people* and that he would pay for the horse. He gave $2 to Jesee to get the horse on Saturday week last, (15th June) about 1 o'clock in the day, and myself and No. 8, also put in 25 cents a piece, and he told Jesse, if he could not go he must send some one else. I have seen Ned Bennett at Vesey's—I one night met at Vesey's a great number of men, and as they came in each handed him some money. Vesey said there was a *little man named Jack,* who could not be killed, and who would furnish them with arms, he had a charm and he would lead them—that Charles Drayton had promised to be engaged with them— Vesey said the negroes were living such an abominable life, they ought to rise. I said I was living well—he said though I was, others were not and that 'twas such fools as I, that were in the way and would not help them, and that after all things were well he would mark me. He said he did not go with *Creighton to Africa, because he had not a will, he wanted to stay and see what he could do* for his fellow-creatures—I met Ned, Monday and others at Denmark Vesey's where they were talking about the business. The first time I spoke with Monday Gell 'twas one night at Denmark Vesey's house, where I heard Vesey tell Monday that he must *send some one into the country to bring the people down*— Monday said *he had sent up Jack* and told him *to tell the people to come down and join in the fight* against the whites and also to ascertain and inform him how many people he could get. A few days after I met Vesey, Monday and Jack, in the streets, under Mr. Duncan's trees at night, where *Jack stated that he had been into the country round by Goose-Creek and Dorchester,* and that he had spoken to 6,600 persons who had agreed to join. Monday said to Vesey, that if Jack had so many men they had better wait no longer but begin the business at once, and others would join. The first time I saw Monday at Vesey's, he was going away early, when Vesey asked him to stay, to which Monday replied, he expected that night a meeting at his house to fix upon and mature the plan, &c. and that he could stay no longer—I afterwards conversed with Monday in his shop, where he asked me if I had heard that Bennett's and Poyas' people were taken up, that 'twas a great pity—he said he had joined in the business—I told him to take care he was not taken up. Whenever I talked with Vesey, he always spoke of Monday Gell as being his principal and active man in the business. . . . I heard Gullah Jack say, he would pay no more wages, he was too busy in seeing about this insurrection; besides what would the white people want with wages they would soon be no more—Monday Gell said to Vesey, that if Jack had so many men they had better wait no longer, but begin the business at once and others would join.

Adam, a Negro man belonging to Mr. Ferguson, testified as follows:

Denmark Vesey one day asked me to walk to his house, and there asked me for 25 cents to hire a horse to send up into the country—I put down the money on the table and asked what he was going to send into the country for—he said 'twould be for my benefit—as he would tell me no more I took up the money and put it back into my pocket again—I afterwards met the man who was to go into the country, who told me he had set off, but had been brought back by the patrole; *that he was going up to bring down the black people to take this country from the whites*—I have been at Vesey's house and there it was I met the man who was to go into the country, he was a yellowish man—the witness pointing at Jesse said, that is the man who was to go into the country.

See the confession of Jesse to the Court . . .

Benjamin Ford, a white lad, about 15 or 16 years of age, deposed as follows:

Denmark Vesey frequently came into our shop which is near his house, and always complained of the hardships of the blacks—he said the laws were very rigid and strict and that the blacks had not their rights—that every one had his time, and that his would come round too—*his general conversation was about religion which he would apply to slavery,* as for instance, he would speak of the creation of the world, in which he would say all men had equal rights, blacks as well as whites, &c. *all his religious remarks were mingled with slavery.*

The Court *unanimously* found Denmark Vesey guilty, and passed upon him the sentence of Death. After his conviction, a good deal of testimony was given against him during the succeeding trials.—Amongst others

Witness No. 9, a negro man testified as follows:

Denmark Vesey has frequently spoken to me about the intended insurrection, and endeavoured to persuade me to join them—He enquired of me *if my master had not arms in his house, and tried to per-*

suade me to get them for him. The blacks stand in great fear of him, and I so much so, that I always endeavoured to avoid him. . . .

Sentence on Denmark Vesey

Sentence on Denmark Vesey, a free black man.

Denmark Vesey——The Court, on mature consideration, have pronounced you guilty—You have enjoyed the advantage of able Counsel, and were also heard in your own defence, in which you endeavored, with great art and plausibility, to impress a belief of your innocence. After the most patient deliberation, however, the Court were not only satisfied of your guilt, but that you were the author, and original instigator of this diabolical plot. Your professed design was to trample on all laws, human and divine; to riot in blood, outrage, rapine, and conflagration, and to introduce anarchy and confusion in their most horrid forms. Your life has become, therefore, a just and necessary sacrifice, at the shrine of indignant Justice. It is difficult to imagine what *infatuation* could have prompted you to attempt an enterprize so wild and visionary. You were a free man; were comparatively wealthy; and enjoyed every comfort, compatible with your situation. You had, therefore, much to risk, and little to gain. From your age and experience, you *ought* to have known, that success was impracticable.

A moment's reflection must have convinced you, that the ruin of *your race,* would have been the probable result, and that years' would have rolled away, before they could have recovered that confidence, which, they once enjoyed in this community. The only reparation in your power, is a full disclosure of the truth. In addition to treason, you have committed the grossest impiety, in attempting to pervert the sacred words of God into a sanction for crimes of the blackest hue. It is evident, that you are totally insensible of the divine influence of that Gospel, "all whose paths are peace." It was to reconcile us to our destinies on earth, and to enable us to discharge with fidelity, all the duties of life, that those holy precepts were imparted by Heaven to fallen man.

If you had searched them with sincerity, you would have discovered instructions, immediately applicable to the deluded victims of your artful wiles—*"Servants' (says Saint Paul) obey in all things your masters'; according to the flesh, not with eye-service, as men-pleasers, but in singleness of heart, fearing God."* And again *"Servants' (says Saint Peter) be subject to your masters' with all fear, not only to the good and gentle, but also to the froward."*

On such texts comment is unnecessary.

Your "lamp of life" is nearly extinguished; your race is run; and you must shortly pass "from time to eternity." Let me then conjure you to devote the remnant of your existence in solemn preparation for the awful doom, that awaits you. Your situation is deplorable, but not destitute of spiritual consolation. To that Almighty Being alone, whose Holy Ordinances, you have trampled in the dust, can you now look for mercy, and although "your sins be as scarlet," the tears of sincere penitence may obtain forgiveness at the "Throne of Grace." You cannot have forgotten the history of the malefactor on the Cross, who, like yourself, was the wretched and deluded victim of offended justice. His conscience was awakened in the pangs of dissolution, and yet there is reason to believe, that his spirit was received into the realms of bliss. May *you* imitate his example, and may *your* last moments prove like his!

The Trial of Monday

The trial of Monday,[9] a Negro man, the slave of Mr. John Gell. Col. Wm. Rouse as his friend, and Jacob Axon, Esq. Counsel for his owner attending.

Evidence

[See testimony of Frank, belonging to Mrs. Ferguson, and Edwin's testimony:] . . .

Witness No. 10, a Negro Man, gave the evidence following:

I saw Charles Drayton before the 16th at Monday Gell's—I was going to Market and Charles called to me—as I was crossing the street Joe who has a wife at Mr. Remoussin's, asked me if I did not know that Monday was at the head of the Ebo Company who are going to fight the white people—Monday is an Ebo—I asked Joe if he was one of that Company—he said yes he was—I asked him what he could do as he was an invalid—he said he would take Remoussin's sword and gun and tell him to lay down in his bed and be quiet—We parted.—Previous to the 16th of June, Monday Gell called me into his shop—I went in and said to him, I heard he was Captain of his countrymen's company the Ebo's—he said he was a sort of a one—I bid him good morning, when he said when you want to hear the news come here—I never saw him afterwards.—Monday and Charles were very often together.

See the *latter part* of Jesse's confession. . . .

[9] James Hamilton, Jr., *An Account of the Late Intended Insurrection Among A Portion of the Blacks of This City* . . . (Charleston, 1822), p. 21: "*Monday Gell* is very well known in this city. He is a most excellent harness-maker, and kept his shop in Meeting-street. It would be difficult to name any individual more actively engaged in the plot than himself, or more able to aid Denmark Vesey, from his uncommon sagacity and knowledge. He reads and writes with great and equal facility, and obviously seems to have been the individual who held the pen, at all the meetings. At which he wrote more than *one* letter to San Domingo, for succors. His own situation afforded no excuse for the effort in which he was engaged, as he enjoyed all the substantial comforts of a free-man; much indulged and trusted by his master, his time and a large proportion of the profits of his labour were at his own disposal. He even kept his master's *arms* and sometimes his money. Monday is an *Ebo,* and is now in the prime of life, having been in the country 15 or 20 years."

The Court *unanimously* found Monday guilty, and passed upon him the sentence of death; after which he made the following confession:

Confession of Monday Gell

I come out as a man who knows he is about to die—some time after Christmas Vesey passed my door, he called in and said to me, that he was trying to gather the blacks to try and see if any thing could be done to overcome the whites; he asked me to join; I asked him his plan and his numbers; he said he had Peter Poyas, Ned Bennett, and Jack Purcell; he asked me to join; I said no; he left me and I saw him not for sometime—About four or five weeks ago as I went up Wentworth-street, Frank Ferguson met me, and said he had four plantation's of people who he was to go for on Saturday, 15th June. How, said I, will you bring them down; he said through the woods; he asked me if I was going towards Vesey's to ask Vesey to be at home that evening, and he would be there to tell me his success. I asked Jack Purcell to carry this message, he said he would; that same evening at my house I met Vesey's mulatto boy, he told me Vesey wished to see me, I went with him; when I went in to Vesey's I met Ned Bennett, Peter Poyas and Frank Ferguson, and Adam, and Gullah Jack; they were consulting about the plan; Frank told Vesey on Saturday 15th, he would go and bring down the people and lodge them near town in the woods; the plan was to arm themselves by breaking open the stores with arms. I then told Vesey I would join them, after sometime I told them I had some business of my own and asked them to excuse me, I went away, and only then was I ever there. One evening, Perault Strohecker, and Bacchus Hammet brought to my shop a keg, and asked me to let it stay there till they sent for it; I said yes, but did not know the contents; the next evening Gullah Jack came and took away the keg, this was before the 16th June; since I have been in prison I learnt that the keg contained powder.

Pharo Thompson is concerned, and he told me a day or two after Ned and Peter were taken up, if he could get a fifty dollar bill, he would run away; about two Sunday's before I was brought here, he asked me, in Archdale-street, when shall we be like those white people in the Church; I said when it pleased God; Sunday before I was taken up, he met me as I came out of Archdale Church, and took me into a stable in said street, and told me he told his master, who had asked him, that he had nothing to do in this affair; which was a lie. William Colcock came to my shop once and said a brother told him that five hundred men were making up for the same purpose. Frank said he was to send to Hell-Hole Swamp to get men.

Perault Strohecker is engaged; he used to go of a Sunday on horse back up the road to a man he knows on the same errand. One Sunday he asked me to go with him; I went and Smart Anderson; we went to a small house a little way from the road after you turn into the ship yard road, on its left hand; they two went into the stable with an old man that lived there, I remained in the yard; they remained in the stable about half an hour; as soon as they came out, I and Perault started to town to go to Church, and left Smart there; I was told by Denbow Martin, who has a wife in Mr. Smith's house, that Stephen Smith belonged to some of the gangs.

Saby Gailliard is concerned, he met me on the Bay, before the 16th June and gave me a piece of paper from his pocket; this paper was about the battle that Boyer had in St. Domingo; in a day or two he called on me and asked if I had read it, and said if he had as many men he would do the same too, as he could whip ten white men himself; he frequently came to me to speak about this matter, and at last I had to insult him out of the shop; he and Paris Ball was often together. A week before I was taken up, Paris told me that my name was called.

Billy Palmer and Vesey were constantly together; there was once in my shop a long talk between them about this same matter; I begged them to stop it; Vesey told him to try to get as many as he could; he said he would.

John Vincent told me that Edward Johnson, a free man, had said, as he was a free man he would have nothing to do with slaves, but the night they began he would join them.

I told Charles Drayton what uproar there was about this business, and since we have been here we have talked together.

Albert Inglis came to me and asked if I knew any thing about it; I said yes. He asked me if I had joined; I said yes; he said he was one also: he said Adam, a free man wanted to see me, I went with him one night; Adam asked me how many men had joined; I told him what Frank Ferguson had said; he asked me if I believed it; I said yes; he said if he could only find men behind him he would go before. Previous to the 16th, Albert said to me quit the business; I told him I was too far into it, so I must stick to it.

I never wrote to St. Domingo[10] or any where else on this subject, nor kept a list or books, nor saw any such things, but heard that Paul's William had a list, nor did I hear any thing about arms being in possession of the blacks. I don't know that Tom Russell made pikes, nor that Gullah Jack had any of them.

Lewis Remoussin called at my shop and asked me to call at his house, he had something to tell me, but I did not go; Jack Glen told me he was engaged.

I met Scipio Sims one Sunday, coming from the country, who said he had been near the Savannah's to Mr. Middleton's place; I heard afterwards that his errand was on this business.

I know John the cooper, who said he was engaged too in this business.

---

[10] According to James Hamilton, Jr., *An Account,* p. 41 note: "Perault unhesitatingly stated to Monday's face, that he had written two letters to St. Domingo, and that he (Perault) had gone to Vanderhorst's wharf with him, in April or May last, to give them in charge of a black cook on board of a schooner bound to that island. After Monday was so charged, he confessed that the fact was so, and that he had been induced to conceal it under an apprehension that if it were known he had been guilty of such an act all chance of mercy would be denied him."

William Garner said he was engaged in it and had got twelve or thirteen draymen to join.

Sandy Vesey told me he belonged to it too.

At Vesey's house, Frank told Gullah Jack, to put one ball and three buck shot in each cartridge.

Mingo Harth acknowledged to me that he had joined, and Peter Poyas told me so too; he, Mingo, told me so several times; Mingo said he was to have his master's horse on the night of the 16th.

Lot Forrester told me frequently that he was one of the company, and I know that he had joined in the business myself. Isaac Harth told me once that he had joined, he knew I was in the business.

Morris Brown knew nothing of it, and we agreed not to let him, Harry Drayton, or Charles Corr, know any thing about it. —— —— told me in my store that he was to get some powder from his master and give it to Peter Poyas; he seemed to have been a long time engaged in it, and to know a great deal—Joe Jore acknowledged to me once or twice that he had joined, he said he knew some of the Frenchmen concerned; he knew I was in it.

Subsequently to this confession, Monday was examined as a witness in a number of cases, during which, he stated many things he had not mentioned in his confession. The Court conceiving it all important to obtain from Monday, all the information he possessed, (believing him to possess more information on this subject than any man then alive) offered to recommend him to the Governor for a conditional pardon, or commutation of his punishment to banishment, if he would reveal all he knew in relation to this plot. He promised to do so, and made this second confession:

The first time I heard of the intended insurrection, was about last Christmas, from Denmark Vesey, who called at my shop, and informed me of it. Vesey said he was satisfied with his own condition, being free, but as all his children were slaves, he wished to see what could be done for them. He asked me to join, but I then positively refused to do so—I inquired of him, how many he had enlisted, and he mentioned the names of Peter Poyas, Ned Bennett, Rolla Bennett, and Jack Purcell. I inquired if those were all and he replied "yes." He then departed, and had no further correspondence with me until about three months ago—I was then walking in Wentworth-street on my way to a man named Peet-Smith, up King-street, and was accosted by Frank Ferguson, who told me, he had just returned from the country, and had *collected four plantations of Negroes.* He requested me to inform Vesey, that he would call on him that evening, and give him an account of his *operations in the country.*—I went to Jack Purcell and requested him to carry the message for me, being busy—On my return home, in the evening, I met Vesey's Son-in-law, at my door, who said, that Vesey wished to see me—I accompanied him to

Vesey's, and there found Peter Poyas, Ned Bennett, Gullah Jack, Frank and his fellow servant, Adam Ferguson. Frank then informed Vesey, he had collected four plantations of negroes, and said he would start on Saturday the 15th of June, to bring them to town, on the 16th. He said, he would conduct them into the woods, and place them, about three miles from town, until Sunday night. Vesey then again urged me to join, and I consented. This was about three months prior to the 16th of June. Vesey, from that time continued to visit the shop, in which I worked. Peter, Ned, Vesey, Frank, Rolla, Adam, Gullah Jack, Jack Purcell and myself were the party at Vesey's, and there agreed to enlist as many men as we could. Vesey *even ceased working himself at his trade, and employed himself exclusively in enlisting men,* and continued to do so until he was apprehended. Shortly afterwards Vesey said he would endeavour to open a correspondence with Port-au-Prince, in St. Domingo, to ascertain whether the inhabitants there would assist us. He said he would send letters there and I advised him to do so, if he could. Some time after this he brought a letter to me, which was directed to President Boyer, and was enclosed in a cover, which was directed to the uncle of the cook of the vessel by which it was sent. The name of this cook was William— His uncle was to open the envelope, and present the letter to Boyer— this vessel, a schooner, had been repaired at the ship-yard, at Gadsden's Wharf, and was afterwards brought to Vanderhorst's wharf, where she was then lying—I walked with Vesey to the wharf—Pierault was in company with us, at the time—Vesey asked William the cook, if he would carry the letter for him, and he consented to do so—We then returned, each of us to his respective home—nothing extraordinary took place after this, and I met no other band or association after this time, but Vesey's particular company—*Bacchus Hammett brought a keg of Powder to my shop, and said he would procure five hundred (500) muskets from his master's store on the night of the 16th June—* Bacchus also told me, that he could procure *more Powder,* but did not say where—the plan was to break open all the Stores where Arms were deposited, and seize them, after they had procured the five hundred muskets above mentioned—Vesey said he would appoint his leaders, and places of meeting, about one week before the 16th of June, but the meeting for this purpose was prevented by the capture of some of the principals before that period—Vesey determined to kill both women and children, but I opposed him and offended him in doing so—Peter and the rest agreed to the opinion of Vesey in the murder of all—some time before any discoveries or apprehensions were made, myself and Pierault wished to drop the business, but thought we had gone too far to retreat—I knew personally of no arms, except six pikes, shewn to me by Gullah Jack, which were made by Tom Russell—I knew of no lists except the one which I kept, containing about forty names, and which, I destroyed after the first interruption and alarm—It was said that William Paul had a list, but I never saw it—William Garner told me that he was to command the Draymen, and that he had procured twelve or thirteen horses—Jack Purcell told me that *Scipio Sims had been at the Savannah's, in the neighbourhood of Bacon's Bridge, to obtain men*—Denbo Martin belonged to the party, and informed me that Stephen Smith acknowledged that he was one.

Charles Drayton and Perault have both seen Denbo at my shop— *Vesey originally proposed the second Sunday, or the 14th of July, as the day for rising,* but afterwards changed it to the 16th of June. After the plot was discovered, Vesey said, it was all over unless an attempt was made to *rescue those who might be condemned,* by rushing on the people, and saving the prisoners, or all dying together. Vesey said, that as Peter and Ned were accustomed to go into the country they must go there and recruit men. Vesey was in the habit of going to Bulkley's farm—*William Palmer and Vesey were very intimate*—Jack Purcell knew of this conspiracy before myself—I do not recollect any person who refused when I applied to him. Some took time to consider, but they all finally agreed. Vesey was considered by the whole party, as a man of great capacity, and was also thought to possess a bloody disposition—He had, I am told, in the course of his life, seven wives, and had travelled through almost every part of the world, with his former master Captain Vesey, and spoke French with fluency— Morris Brown, Harry Drayton, and Charles Corr, and other influential leaders of the African Church, were never consulted on this subject, for fear they would betray us to the whites—Vesey had many years ago a pamphlet on the slave trade—Vesey said that his eldest step son was engaged in this affair.[11]

The Court had, previously to this confession, twice applied for and obtained from the Governor a respite for Monday, Charles Drayton and Harry Haig, with a view to obtain from them the testimony and information they appeared willing to give. On the 24th day of July, after Monday had made his last confession, they addressed the following letter to the Governor.

[11] The [second] Court [which assembled August 3–8] at the commencement of their investigations determined thoroughly to examine into the degree of credit to be attached to the witnesses, and were very particular in their enquiries in respect to the two principal witnesses, *Monday Gell* and *Perault*. It appeared that the character of these men for veracity and honesty, had been unexceptional through life—Monday indeed seemed to have been distinguished for the candour, sobriety, and integrity of his life, and of Perault, his master declared that his only fault was "that he was sometimes so blunt and free spoken, as to approach to rudeness." The Court were finally of opinion that entire reliance could be placed on these two witnesses, and that every word which came from Monday could be implicitly relied on—Several circumstances occurred during the trials to confirm the favourable impressions of the Court with respect to these witnesses—one or two of them will be here stated. The witnesses were not permitted to have any communications with each other, and they were never informed of the particular prisoner against whom they were to appear. They were brought forth separately and examined. Their *concurrence,* under such circumstances certainly afforded strong evidence of their truth.

Charleston, 24th July, 1822.

Sir,

We recommend that Monday Gell, Charles Drayton, and Harry Haig should be pardoned upon condition that they be sent out of the limits of the United States. We feel it our duty to state to your Excellency the reasons which have influenced us in this measure. These men are unquestionably guilty of the offences with which they have been charged, but under the impression that they would ultimately have their lives spared they have made to us disclosures not only important in the detection of the general plan of the conspiracy, but enabling the Court to convict a number of the principal offenders. Having used these individuals as witnesses and obtained from them the knowledge they could communicate, we deemed it unnecessarily harsh and amounting almost to treachery afterwards to sacrifice their lives. In addition to this inducement, we regard it to be politic that the Negroes should know that even their principal advisers and ringleaders cannot be confided in, and that under the temptation of exemption from capital punishment they will betray the common cause.

On the next day they received an answer, in which the Governor declines pardoning conditionally, Monday, Charles and Harry, and says, "the cases of Monday Gell, Charles Drayton and Harry Haig, would produce me considerable embarrassment, were you not clothed with authority to carry your recommendation into full effect."

The Court then resolved to *reconsider the sentence* they had passed on Monday, Charles and Harry, *unanimously altered* their sentence, and passed upon them the following—"That they be imprisoned in the Work-House of Charleston, until their masters, under the direction of the City Council of Charleston, shall send them out of the limits of the United States, into which they are not to return under penalty of death."

The Trial of Gullah Jack

The trial of Gullah Jack, a Negro man, belonging to Mr. Pritchard—His owner attending.

Evidence

Witness No. 10, testified as follows:

Jack Pritchard also called on me about this business—he is sometimes called Gullah Jack, sometimes Cooter Jack; he gave me some dry food, consisting of parched corn and ground nuts, and said eat that and nothing else on the morning it breaks out, and when you join us as we pass put into your mouth this crab-claw and you can't then be wounded, and said he, I give the same to the rest of my troops—if you drop the large crab-claw out of your mouth, then put in the small one—said I, when do you break out and have you got arms—he said a plenty, but they are over Boundary-street, we can't get at them now, but as soon as the patrol was slack they could get them—this was previous to the 16th June, on which day he said they were to break out—On that day he came to me and said they would not break out that night as the patrol was too strong—he said he would let me know when they were ready—that Sunday fortnight, the 30th June, he came to me and said I must lay by still, they would not break out then, that he had been round to all his company and found them cowards. I said thank God then—he said give me back my corn and cullah (that is crab-claw) I said I would not and upbraided him for having deluded so many. He said all his country born promised to join because he was a doctor (that is a conjurer)—He said the white people were looking for him and he was afraid of being taken; that two men came to his master's wharf and asked him if he knew Gullah Jack, and that he told them no—*he said his charms would not protect him from the treachery of his own colour.*—He went away and I have not seen him since. On the 16th June, Jack requested me to let twelve men sleep at my wife's, as they were to break out that night and he wanted them to be near Boundary-street, near to which in King-street my wife lives—on being refused he departed in anger and reproached me. Geo. Vanderhorst called on me yesterday morning and asked if I knew that Charles Drayton was taken up, and said he was afraid Charles would name him, not because he was on his list, for he had joined Jack's Company, but because Charles had met him at Gullah Jack's when they were consulting on the subject—that if he could hear that Charles had named him he would run off—on Monday, 1st July, Charles Drayton told me that there would be an Insurrection on the *morning of the 6th July, as soon as the Guards turned in*—he *said he commended the country born company*—Jack told me on the 1st July the same thing, and in addition that they were to rush with their dirks, guns and swords, &c. they had got, kill the City Guard, and take all the arms in the Arsenal—he also said there were some arms in King-street beyond Boundary-street, in the possession of a white man which they intended to take—(alluding to the arms of the Charleston Neck Company, deposited at Mr. Wharton's in King-street.)

The blacks would have risen on the night of the 16th June, had the Guards not been so strong—this I know from Gullah Jack and Harry Haig, who said, that if the Guards were not too strong they would get the arms near the Lines, but if the Guards were out, they could not get them to break out with—("Jack is a little man, a Gullah Negro, with small hands and feet and large whiskers, and belongs to Mr. Pritchard," was the discription given of him by this witness, and by which Jack was apprehended.)

Gullah Jack when apprehended denied to the Court that he ever wore whiskers, although the map of a large pair of them was plainly discernable on his face, and continued to deny it stoutly until confronted with his owner—he also positively denied that he ever pretended to be a Doctor or Conjurer.

Mr. Paul Pritchard deposed as follows:

> My Slave Jack always wore a very large pair of whiskers which he prized very much, and which nothing could induce him to cut off, and which I often threatened to shave off as a punishment when he misbehaved—These whiskers I found he had cut off to my great surprise about three days ago, and wondered at the cause of it, little dreaming that it was to prevent his being apprehended by a description of him—I did hear some years ago that Jack was a Doctor or Conjurer—he is called Gullah Jack and Cootter Jack.

George, Mr. Vanderhorst's slave, gave the testimony following:

> Gullah Jack is an enemy of the white people. I attended a meeting of several at his house, and he was the head man there—all present agreed to join & come against the whites—Jack was my leader—he is the head of the Gullah Company—I heard that amongst them they had charms—Jack said if any man betrayed them, they would injure him, and I was afraid to inform—the little man standing before me is Gullah Jack, who had large black whiskers, which he has cut since I saw him last—If I am accepted as a witness and my life spared, I must beg the Court to send me away from this place, *as I consider my life in great danger from having given testimony.* I have heard it said all about the streets, generally, I can't name any one in particular, that whoever is the white man's friend, God help them; from which I understood they would be killed—I was afraid of Gullah Jack as a conjurer. . . .[12]

Sentence on Gullah Jack

Sentence on Jack, *a slave belonging to Paul Pritchard, commonly called* Gullah Jack, *and sometimes* Couter Jack.

> Gullah Jack—The Court after deliberately considering all the circumstances of your case, are perfectly satisfied of your guilt. In the prosecution of your wicked designs, you were not satisfied with resorting to natural and ordinary means, but endeavoured to enlist on your behalf, all the powers of darkness, and employed for that purpose, the most disgusting mummery and superstition. You represented yourself as invulnerable; that you could neither be taken nor destroyed, and that all who fought under your banners would be invincible. While such

[12] When this witness was about to be examined in the presence of Gullah Jack, it was not without considerable difficulty that the Court satisfied him that he need no longer fear Jacks *conjurations,* (as he called them.) It was in the course of this witness' evidence that Jack laid aside the character of the fool he was counterfeiting, and shewed his real character.

wretched expedients are calculated to excite the confidence, or to alarm the fears of the ignorant and credulous, they produce no other emotion in the minds of the intelligent and enlightened, but contempt and disgust. Your boasted charms have not preserved yourself, and of course could not protect others.—"Your Altars and your Gods have sunk together in the dust." The airy spectres, conjured by you, have been chased away by the superior light of Truth, and you stand exposed, the miserable and deluded victim of offended Justice. Your days are literally numbered. You will shortly be consigned to the cold and silent grave; and all the Powers of Darkness cannot rescue you from your approaching Fate!—Let me then, conjure you to devote the remnant of your miserable existence, in fleeing from the *"wrath to come."* This can only be done by a full disclosure of the truth. The Court are willing to afford you all the aid in their power, and to permit any Minister of the Gospel, whom you may select to have free access to you. To him you may unburthen your guilty conscience. Neglect not the opportunity, for there is "no device nor art in the grave," to which you must shortly be consigned.

The Trial of Harry

The trial of Harry, a Negro man belonging to Mr. David Haig. —James Haig, Esq. attending as Counsel for his owner.

Evidence

Witness No. 10, testified as follows:

> After Peter Poyas had twice called on me about this business, he and Harry Haig called on me. I was not at home, but the next morning I met Harry who asked me for my name—I refused it—he said I would be killed if I did not join—I said I would join when they came out, if they were stronger than the whites—Harry called on me again, and asked me if I was willing, that the thing would break out soon—I asked him where he would begin—he said in Boundary-street—at what hour—he said at 12 o'clock at night or early in the morning as soon as the guard were discharged. Harry Haig has since seen me several times, and told me to hold myself ready—I said I'm ready when called on. He said all the draymen came to his master's Cooper-yard, and said they were ready, but he told them he was waiting for Gullah Jack—he said he would tell me when they were ready, that they were only waiting for the head man, who was a white man; but he, although asked, would neither tell me the white man's name, nor where the powder and arms were—this was last Tuesday, the very day six negroes were hanged, about 6 o'clock, A. M.—This was the last time we spoke though I have seen him since. . . .

The court *unanimously* found Harry guilty and passed upon him the sentence of death.

Subsequently to [Gullah Jack's] conviction, Harry Haig, who received sentence of death at the same time that he did, made the following confession:

> Julius Forrest and myself always worked together—Gullah Jack calls himself a Doctor Negro—he induced Julius and myself to join at last, but at first we refused—before the 16th of June, Jack appointed to meet us at Bulkley's farm—when we got there Jack was not there, but Peter Poyas came—we broke up at day light. Not quite a month before the 16th of June, Jack met us and talked about war—I asked Jack how he would do for arms—bye and bye, said Jack, we will have arms—he said he would have some arms made at the blacksmith's— Jack was going to give me.   *   *   *   *
>
> *   *   *   *   *   *   *   *   *
>
> *   *   *   *   *   *   *
>
> I refused to do this as I considered it murder, and that God would never pardon me for it; 'twas not like fair fighting. Until Jack was taken up and condemned to death, I felt as if I was bound up, and had not the power to speak one word about it—Jack charmed Julius and myself at last, and we then consented to join—Tom Russel the Blacksmith and Jack are partners, (in conjuring) Jack learnt him to be a Doctor. Tom talked to Jack about the fighting and agreed to join, and those two brought Julius and myself to agree to it. Jack said Tom was his second and "when you don't see me, and see Tom, you see me." Jack said Tom was making arms for the black people—Jack said he could not be killed, nor could a white man take him." [13]

The reasons which induced the Court to alter the sentence passed on Monday [and Charles] to transportation, induced them to alter Harry's to the same.

The Trial of Mingo

The trial of Mingo, a Negro man, the property of Mr. William Harth—His owner attending.

Evidence

. . . William, a negro man belonging to Mr. John Paul testified as follows:

> I have heard something about an insurrection of the blacks, but was not concerned in it—Mr. William Harth's Negro man Mingo told

[13] . . . On the 13th of July, Mr. James Legare, from feeble health and great exhaustion during the previous sittings of the Court, asked, and obtained, leave to withdraw; whereupon Mr. Henry Deas, was summoned by the Magistrates, who took his seat and served until the adjournment of the Court.

me about it, and referred me to Peter Poyas for further information, who he said had a list with 9,000 names upon it, and that he was still taking down names—on the week I was to see Peter I was apprehended. Mingo said that 600 men on the Bay was already down on the list in Peter's possession—Mingo would not before the Wardens own what he told me—I never had any conversation with Peter—Mingo said his name was not yet down, and he would not put it down 'till he knew all that was to be done—that Ned Bennett knew all about it, and told it to all Mr. Bennett's people, and that letters were passing between those concerned—I can read and count printed characters but not written. On a Saturday night Mingo told me as we were going towards his wife's house, that every day at 2 o'clock Peter went to Mr. Harth's lumber yard and talked to the other men about this matter, to make them sensible of the plan. At Mingo's house I took up the Bible and read two chapters from the prophet Tobit—Mingo said that *all those belonging to the African Church are engaged in the insurrection, from the country to the town—that there is a little man amongst them who can't be shot, killed or caught, who was to be their general, and who would provide them with arms—that some arms were provided but he did not tell me where they were,* and he also said that Ned Bennett and Charles Shubrick are officers. Peter, Ned and Charles I know to be class leaders in the African Church—The African Association have also a Church in Anson-street near Boundary-street, and one in Cow-alley, where they have service. I believe that Mingo was endeavouring to get me to join them in the rising, and from his conversation I have no doubt but that he was engaged in the conspiracy, and that all he said to me was to get me to join them. *It was also told to me that our colour from the North to the South had combined together to fight against New-Orleans.* Mingo was no doubt satisfied that I would join— I never had any conversation with any one about the rising but with Mingo and Col. Prioleau's man—Mingo said that Peter Poyas would tell me when the rising would take place—that Mr. Bennett's Ned was one of them—*that Denmark Vesey was the chief man and more concerned than any one else.* I beg you won't take up Sarah, for no woman knows any thing about it—Mingo said that letters were passing between Peter Poyas, Ned Bennett and Charles Shubrick. I am persuaded that Denmark Vesey was chiefly concerned in this business— Mingo said that the country places were engaged in the plot, and also the Islands—that he knows the little man who can't be shot, who told him that there was a *Gullah Society* going on which met once a month—that all the orders he got he got from Peter—Mingo always denied that he was engaged, and yet always talked to me as if he wanted me to join. Mingo said they would get horses, which were engaged at one, two or three *Livery Stables from the Stable Boys; two Stables he named in particular, viz:* Mr. Billing's and the one behind the old Church—Mingo said a brown man, the steward of the cutter, had stolen some of the arms, and that Jim, a blacksmith of Mr. Bennett made arms. . . .

The court *unanimously* found Mingo guilty, and passed upon him the sentence of death.

The Trial of Jack

The trial of Jack, a Mulatto man, belonging to Mrs. Purcell— Mr. Thomas Smith, the brother of his owner attending.

Evidence

Monday testified as follows:

> I have seen Jack and Vesey talking together before my door—he told me that he was one of those to rise against the whites, and Vesey told me so before—the message that Frank Ferguson gave to me to give to Vesey, I got Jack to carry to Vesey for me—the message was, that he had just come from the country, that he had there got four plantations of men to join—and to go to Vesey and ask him to be at home to night, as he would call on him—I know he carried it, because Vesey told me so that night—he came to my shop afterwards and said to me he was looking for Vesey, and be sure that I called no name.

Frank testified as follows:

> I know Jack Purcell, but don't know that he is concerned in this business—I did give to Monday Gell a message for Vesey.

Charles gave the following evidence:

> Jack told me he had been at his Mistress' Plantation and tried to get down the people to join in this business—but could not go again— he said he had joined, and asked me where Lot Forrester lived, that he was the proper person to go into the country to bring the people down.

The prisoner asked permission to cross examine Charles, which was granted; but his questions were such, that no one could well answer them but himself. In the course of this examination he admitted, that a large meeting had been called on Stono by Lot, and that considerable preparations were made to receive him, but that Lot did not attend, and he was requested to reprove him for not doing so.

The Court *unanimously* found Jack guilty, and passed upon him the sentence of death.—A few moments preceding his execution, he made the following confession to the Intendant of Charleston:

> If it had not been for the cunning of that old villain Vesey, I should not now be in my present situation. He employed every

stratagem to induce me to join him. He was in the habit of reading to me all the passages in the newspapers that related to St. Domingo, and apparently every pamphlet he could lay his hands on, that had any connection with slavery. He one day brought me a speech which he told me had been delivered in Congress by a *Mr. King* on the subject of slavery; he told me this Mr. King was the black man's friend, that he Mr. King had declared he would continue to speak, write and publish pamphlets against slavery the longest day he lived, until the Southern States consented to emancipate their slaves, for that slavery was a disgrace to the country.

The Trial of Smart

The trial of Smart, a Negro man, the slave of Mr. Robert Anderson—His owner and M. King, Esq. his Counsel attending.

Evidence

. . . Monday gave the following evidence:

I saw Smart at Vesey's in the day—Perault and Peter Cooper were also there—I have often conversed with him on this business, and he seemed to be as much in it as possible—I never asked this man to join—Vesey brought all of us into it—he belongs to the same gang that I did.

Cross-Examined by Mr. King:

I was not the first man who spoke to him—I first saw him at Vesey's—he was very much attached to me and called me Pa, and my wife Ma—I don't know that he ever got any one to join, and think he would have told me if he had—he was just such another as myself—I had a list with about forty on it, *but tore it up on the first discovery*— he belongs to the African Church.

Perault [,a Negro man belonging to Mr. J. Strohecker,][14] gave the testimony following:

[14] Upon the testimony of this witness, the Court placed great reliance. His open, frank and blunt manner convinced every one who heard him that he was incapable of uttering a falsehood, and that he possessed many fine traits of character.—The following account of his life was politely furnished by his owner. Perault was born at Jumba in Africa, about a weeks travel from Goree. Mamadu his father, who is wealthy and owns about 60 working hands, trades to Hassou with Tobacco and Salt, in exchange for which he receives Gold; to which place Perault accompanied him six times. Perault was engaged in three battles against the people of Hassou, who do not cultivate their lands, but make predatory incursions into the cultivated territories of their neighbours. Perault also fought twice against the people of Darah, but in the second battle he was taken prisoner and carried to that place. Here his brother-in-law saw him, and offered to the Captain of a Brig three

Smart is a Drayman, and engaged in this business and in the same company, and confessed the same to me—I have met him at Vesey's and at Bulkley's Farm—I met him at Vesey's on Sunday in the day, and there was Monday Gell also, where we talked about the rising— the second time I met him at Bulkley's Farm where were thirteen in all—Smart and I have often spoken and promised to fight by one another against the white people—On Saturday the 15th June, Smart got two *muskets from Mr. Fordham's shop to carry up to Gadsden's Wharf,* they were shortly after taken away from Smart's dray, on which he was carrying them—and he made off with himself—I was present, *one was for me, one for Smart*—we borrowed the muskets from my brother.

. . . The court *unanimously* found Smart guilty, and passed upon him the sentence of death.

When Smart was arraigned he pleaded Guilty to the charge, and his Counsel handed to the Court his confession in writing; but the Court advising that the plea of Guilty should be withdrawn, his Counsel did so and pleaded Not Guilty. The confession handed to the Court was not used against him, but is now given to the public.

Monday Gell invited me to go up the road to Mr. Bulkley's Farm, on Sunday about three months ago, where there were upwards of thirty persons present, and among them Bulkley's man Billy—I said I would not trust countrymen—I believe Denmark Vesey was there, but did not see him. About four months ago, or going on four months, William Garner, drayman, told me, he expected people from St. Domingo; white people would kill as many as they could. I call Monday Gell Pa, and his wife Ma—About three weeks before going up to the farm, Monday Gell asked me to join him, by telling me that they were in servitude, kicked and cuffed and abused, &c. &c. He spoke to me about St. Domingo people turn and fight the white people. I said we can't do that, but Gell said we could make a contrivance to do it. Monday Gell told me that Gullah wanted to begin when the Negroes of the African Church were taken up in 1818— that if I told any thing they would kill me, and made me hold up my hand and swear not to tell any thing.

I asked when they intended to rise, he said on Saturday night previous to the death of Dr. M'Call. Monday told me the old man said we must begin to night about 10 o'clock—I said to Monday, he must

---

slaves for him if he would wait his return from Jumba. The Captain, however, could not delay his voyage, and Perault was brought to Charleston in a Brig belonging to Mr. Delaire, who kept him for his own service. In 1814, he was purchased by his present owner, who is satisfied with his conduct since he bought him. His master stated that he is very tenacious, whenever he conceives that he is right, and that he believes he would rather suffer death than deviate from the truth— that those who are not accustomed to his mode of expressing himself would be affronted by his bluntness, but that he does not mean to offend.

stop it, that Monday must send word to the old man to stop it, that it was a great sin.

I meet at Monday Gell a black man named Jack Glen, a painter.

When at the Farm of Mr. Bulkley, we meet a snake at the gate, which the old man Vesey killed, and one of them says, that's the way we would do them. I seen Monday, and he says, they had better begin about eight o'clock, before the Guard meet, and if they don't do that, meet away on the Green, some where by the lines, march down through the streets, come down to the Guard-House—Monday told me there were three or four gangs—I asked him some questions about the mode of attack, which I consented to—Monday told me that they would have a meeting, or setting up at night, and begin then.

I did not agree to have a fire in the city—At a meeting at Monday Gell's house, Denmark Vesey present, I asked him if he was going to kill the women and children—Denmark answered, what was the use of killing the louse and leaving the nit. I said my God what a sin—Denmark Vesey told me I had not a man's heart, and that I was a friend to Buckra—Monday Gell told me that they sent to several places in the country.

Jack Glen, a black man wanted to borrow my horse to go up the country—I said I had not one to lend—he said he must go in the country that day Sunday, to Goose Creek.

The time I was at the farm they told me they had long things like my arm to put handles to, that they would make contrivance.

Vesey told me one day, after they had taken the place, they would take the money, and he would go in a vessel and put as many as he could, and go back to his own country.

Vesey told me that all the powder was about three miles out of town, and they must take it—could easily get it; and they knew about a place in Queen-street, opposite the Planters' Hotel, where there was arms, &c. The old man, Denmark Vesey, said that they were to attack the Guard House, in three or four ways, and then they would get all the arms.

I never heard about sending the two persons to St. Domingo.

Monday told me they were about to engage some draymen in it, but did not know how to trust them.

Monday told me that they meet every other night, and he would to tell me more about it, when he saw me again. The old man, (meaning Vesey) told me to get some draymen who had horses, and if I was a good rider he would make me a captain of a troop.

When they meet they did not pray at the meeting in the kitchen. I was only at the Neck meeting about one hour—Peter Poyas was not at that meeting. I told Monday not to put my name on the list that they had—Peter was not at that meeting, but was to go with us.— Monday said he expected Peter there. I have no knowledge of any deposit of arms, ammunition or powder—I did not promise to any particular act in the business, or know of any other persons engaged in the business than those I have already mentioned—I never asked any person to join.

The Trial of Bacchus

The trial of Bacchus, a Negro man, belonging to Mr. Benjamin Hammet—Francis S. Belzer, Esq. his owner's Counsel attending.

. . . [After taking evidence] the Court *unanimously* found Bacchus guilty, and passed upon him the sentence of death.

Mr. Hammet, whilst he was not desirous that Bacchus should escape punishment, yet was anxious to save his life, and previously to his trial handed to the Court in writing a confession which Bacchus had made to him, and stated, that he came forward with this candid confession of Bacchus, in hopes of saving his life thereby; but that if the Court thought his case did not admit of a less punishment than death, he then requested that his confession should not be used against him. The Court after consultation determined to proceed to his trial. —The following confession though not used against Bacchus is now given to the public:

Perault, when hauling cotton from my master's store, told me in the yard, secretly, that he wanted me to go to Society with him. I asked what Society? He told me, never mind what Society, and said he would call for me that night—he did call and I went with him. Perault carried me to Denmark Vesey's house, by Bennett's mill—there I met about twelve men, among whom was Monday Gell, and Smart Anderson. After I got in they fastened the gate—it was before nine o'clock— Denmark and Perault took me to one side, Perault told me they were going to tell me something; this was in another room, not before the gang—Denmark and Perault said that they were going to turn to and fight the white people, and take the country, and that New-Orleans was taken. I considered a long while, and they found me considering, and at last I said to Perault I was very sorry he brought me there, I did not wish to belong to such a Society—Denmark Vesey said to me before Perault, that the one that did not wish to join the Society must be put to death as an enemy—he told all the gang so after he went back with me into the room. Denmark told the gang, that they must meet at his house that night next week. Perault told me to try and get powder, that the gang would *throw in and make it up to me.* They all threw in the night of meeting 12 1-2 cents each, and I also. This money was thrown in to give a man to go into the country and bring down the country negroes when they are all ready. When I asked about arms, and where they were, Denmark recommended to them to look thro' the town for the stores that had the most guns. Perault then jumped up and said "Bacchus don't you know where Capt. Martindale's arms is," I said, yes, my man, but you can't get them, and you had better drop this thing altogether. About two or three days after this last affair, Perault came to me and told me that they had caught Denmark, and carried me down to Monday Gell. Monday and Perault told me that Denmark said that if they caught him, he would tell no body's name, and that I must not tell his, Perault's name, nor Monday's, and they would not mention mine. I took the keg of powder out of the back store of my master, and carried it in a bag to Denmark, with a man belonging to Mr. Bennett which I believe is a blacksmith—Bennett's man met me at my master's gate—I suppose Pritchard's Gullah Jack and Perault carried the powder to Monday from Denmark's house. In company with Denmark Vesey and Perault, Denmark told me to get what arms I could—I said I could get one horseman's sword in a scabbard, which I took to Denmark's house. I also said I could get a pistol, but was afraid my master would miss it—Perault told me never mind he could make me easy about it—I did take the pistol to Denmark's house with the sword, on Sunday night the 16th June. Denmark told me previously, I must not go home—this Denmark told at the meeting previous, and said they were to go up the road and meet the country negroes. Last night, when I was put in the room in the Work-House with Perault, he told me Gullah Jack had buried the powder, and I think Perault knows where it is. All the negroes engaged in the plot were ordered by Denmark to leave their masters and go up the road.—The night they carried me to Denmark, I was so frightened that I was obliged to say yes; for they threatened to kill every one that did not wish to join. A large book like a Bible was open before them at Denmark's house; but I do not know whether it was to sign names in, or what purpose. At the first meeting at Denmark's, they asked me my name, and Perault answered my name was Bacchus, belonging to Mr. Hammet—Denmark asked me which Hammet? I said Benjamin Hammet, the gentleman who sued Lorenzo Dow.

The week after Denmark was dead, Perault told me to mind and keep myself ready, that they intended to come up at the corner where the arms of the Neck Company is kept; and I said very well; they were to take the arms, and I was to assist them, they were to break open the door—Monday Gell can tell who is at the head of this last arrangement—I believe Perault knows all about it—Gullah Jack was to distribute the Powder amongst us—Perault told me that they had a Blacksmith to make daggers for this party, and that they had made some. On Sunday, 16th June, he told me, *they had three or four hundred daggers*—he told me on the 11th July, the night I was committed, that I must not tell his name or any thing about it—This was the reason I was afraid to tell or make a confession to my master, Mr. Hammet, on this morning, the 12th July—Perault is the fellow that has brought me into this scrape—A fellow about my size, a dark black skin negro, who I believe is called *Charles,* took me up the road just before you come to the forks of the road, on the Meeting-street road, to a Farm— the House on the Farm *has a Piazza on the top;* Charles told the negro man on the Farm, mind next Sunday the business is to be done; meaning to kill the white people; and that the negroes from the country were to stop at this Farm—Denmark Vesey and his party from town was to go there to the Farm to meet the negroes from the country—I solemnly declare as to being brought into this scrape; and that Perault is the one who enticed me into it—At the first meeting at Denmark Vesey's house, on the breaking up of the meeting Denmark said—"Friends you all throw in seven pence a piece, those who have got it, it is to make up for a friend to pay his wages to his master, before he went into the country to bring the people down."

At the meeting at Denmark Vesey's the first time I was there, I saw a fat black fellow whom I think was Denmark's son, as he looked very much like Denmark, had a full face, that he could read, as he shewed Monday Gell the large book on the table, and said to Monday, shewing him some of the leaf of the book, "see here, they are making real game at we" and Monday looked at the book and said nothing—Denmark took me a one side and said, "we shan't be slaves to these damn rascals any longer. We must kill every one that we can get hold of, and drive the rest out of the city." No one was with me when I was requested by Charles (whom he calls Charles Drayton now) to go to the Farm at the Forks of the Roads; when Charles set out to go there, he came from Monday Gell's house, met me, and carried me to Monday's—Monday was to go with Charles to the Farm, but put it off on account of having a hog to kill, and said to Charles, let this friend go with you; and I and Charles went to the Farm—when we went to the Farm, Charles asked a negro woman on the Farm, if the old daddy was home, and she called him—this old daddy is an African, marked on both sides of his face—Charles took him in the stable, and also myself, and told him about the country negroes coming there, &c. The fellow who helped me to carry the powder belonged to Bennett I think, because I have seen this man in Bennett's Blacksmith shop at the mill, years before this; Perault told me that they had *two or three hundred bayonets made already*—Perault is a Blacksmith—I believe *Monday* knows as well as Perault where the arms and bayonets are—Monday said they were to have mounted horsemen—that many Draymen belonged to it who had horses—at Denmark's house they all rose up and swore, lifting up the right hand, saying, "we will not tell if we are found out, and if they kill us we will not tell on any one." Denmark said they must all say so, and that they did say so. Denmark told me that he gave the sword to Perault, and Perault gave it to a man named Cæsar—I know no other Cæsar but a Drayman named Cæsar—Smith a tall negro, an African, who is an intimate acquaintance of Perault's, and who is often at the stable where Perault keeps his horses—Perault told me that French negroes were amongst them—Denmark said country born, Africans and all kinds joined—Monday and Perault appeared to be the intimate friends of Denmark, he thought a heap of them—Denmark took the pistol for himself, it was given to him in his own hand—Those meetings were held at Denmark's house, where he had a black wife—two or three women were at the house ironing.

John, a Negro man, the slave of Mr. J. L. Enslow, pleaded guilty.—

His owner, who was present, stated to the Court, that John was willing to make the only reparation in his power, for his conduct, and would reveal all the information he was in possesion of relative to the insurrection. The Court informed John that he might state whatever he had to say, but as they would not make him any promise, he must not make confessions in hopes of pardon.—John said he would state all he knew of the intended insurrection, and proceeded to make the following confession:

Monday Gell led me into it, and took me to Vesey's—There was a large meeting—Vesey told the people, the meeting was to rise up and fight the white people for their liberty—we always went to Monday's house afterwards—Monday did all the writing. I heard that they were trying all round the country *from Georgetown and Santee, round about to Combahee,* to get people. Peter Poyas was also there, he was one— Peter named Poyas' plantation where he went to meet—Bellisle Yates I have seen at the meetings, and Adam Yates, and Naphur Yates, and Dean Mitchell, and Cæsar Smith, and George a Stevidore—At Vesey's they wanted to make a collection to make pikes for the country people, but the men had then no money—Monday Gell said Perault was one to get horses to send men into the country—I heard that a Blacksmith was to make pikes—Jack M'Neil is engaged—I have seen them all at Monday's—Jack said he was one and would try to get men—The plan was to take the Arsenal and Guard Houses for arms, and not to fire the town unless they failed—Monday was writing a letter to St. Domingo[15] to go by a vessel lying at Gibb's and Harper's Wharf—the letter was about the sufferings of the blacks, and to know if the people of St. Domingo would help them if they made an effort to free themselves—he was writing this letter in March, I am not certain of the time—Perault was present when Monday wrote the letter, and also a Painter named Prince Righton—I have seen Pompey Haig at Monday's, but he neither assented or dissented—Jerry Cohen was at Vesey's, and said to me he was one—I heard from Vesey and Monday that they had engaged men from the country—Peter Poyas said he had sent into the country to his brother to engage men who would send him an answer—A party was to attack the Guard-House and Arsenal— another the Arsenal on the Neck—another to attack the Naval Store on Mey's Wharf—another to attack the Magazine—another to meet at Lightwood's Alley, and then try to cut off the Companies from meeting at their places of rendezvous—I belong to the African Congregation—On Saturday, the 15th June, a man was to be sent into the country to bring down the people, and Rolla was to command (the country people from Ashley River) at the Bridge—Ned Bennett and John Horry to meet at Mr. Horry's corner, and Batteau to come down with Vesey's party.

[15] [For further testimony concerning St. Domingo, see original *Report*, pp. 125, 153—Ed.]

The Court having used John as a witness in the subsequent trials, passed upon him the following sentence. "That he be imprisoned in the Work-House of Charleston, until his master, under the direction of the City Council of Charleston shall send him out of the limits of the United States, into which he is not to return under penalty of Death." . . .

Sentence of Ten of the Criminals

The Court, on mature deliberation, have pronounced you guilty; the punishment of that guilt is death. Your conduct, on the present occasion, exhibits a degree of depravity and extravagance, rarely paralleled. Your professed objects were to trample not only on the laws of this state, but on those of humanity; to commit murder, outrage and plunder, and to substitute for the blessings we enjoy, anarchy and confusion in their most odious forms. The beauties of nature and of art, would have fallen victims to your relentless fury; and even the decrepitude of age and the innocence of childhood, would have found no other refuge than the grave!

Surely nothing but infatuation could have prompted you to enter into a plot so wild and diabolical.—A moment's reflection would have convinced you, that disgrace and ruin must have been its consequence, and that it would have probably resulted in the destruction and extermination of *your race*. But if, even complete success had crowned your efforts, what were the golden visions which you anticipated?— Such men as you, are in general, as ignorant as you are vicious, without any settled principles, and possessing but few of the virtues of civilized life; you would soon, therefore, have degenerated into a horde of barbarians, incapable of any government. But admitting that a different result might have taken place, it is natural to enquire, what are the miseries of which you complain?—That we should all earn our bread by the sweat of our brow, is the decree which God pronounced at the fall of man. It extended alike to the master and the slave; to the cottage and the throne. Every one is more or less subject to control; and the most exalted, as well as the humblest individual, must bow with deference to the laws of that community, in which he is placed by Providence. Your situation, therefore, was neither extraordinary nor unnatural. Servitude has existed under various forms, from the deluge to the present time, and in no age or country has the condition of slaves been milder or more humane than your own. You are, with few exceptions, treated with kindness, and enjoy every comfort compatible with your situation. You are exempt from many of the miseries, to which *the poor* are subject throughout the world. In many countries the life of the slave is at the disposal of his master; here you have always been under the protection of the law.

The tribunal which now imposes this sentence through its humble organ, affords a strong exemplification of the truth of these remarks. In the discharge of the painful duties which have devolved on them the members of this Court have been as anxious to acquit the innocent as determined to condemn the guilty.

In addition to the crime of treason, you have on the present occasion, displayed the vilest ingratitude. It is a melancholy truth, that those servants in whom was reposed the most unlimitted confidence, have been the principal actors in this wicked scheme. Reared by the hand of kindness, and fostered by a master who assumed many of the duties of a parent—you have realized the fable of the Frozen Serpent, and attempted to destroy the bosom that sheltered and protected you.

You have moreover committed the grossest impiety: you have perverted the sacred words of God, and attempted to torture them into a sanction for crimes, at the bare imagination of which, humanity shudders. Are you incapable of the Heavenly influence of that Gospel, all whose "paths are peace?" It was to reconcile us to our destiny on earth, and to enable us to discharge with fidelity all our duties, whether as master or servant, that those inspired precepts were imparted by Heaven to fallen man.—There is no condition of life which is not embraced by them; and if you had searched them, *in the spirit of truth,* you would have discovered instructions peculiarly applicable to yourselves—*"Servants (says St. Paul) be obedient to them that are your masters according to the flesh, with fear and trembling, in singleness of your heart, as unto Christ; not with eye-service as men pleasers, but as the servants of Christ, doing the will of God from the heart."* Had you listened with sincerity to such doctrines, you would not have been arrested by an ignominious death.

Your days on earth are near their close and you now stand upon the confines of eternity. While you linger on this side of the grave, permit me to exhort you, in the name of the everliving God, whose holy ordinances you have violated; to devote most earnestly the remnant of your days, in penitence and preparation for that tribunal, whose sentence, whether pronounced in anger or in mercy, is eternal.[16]

Charleston, 24th July, 1822.

Sir:

In deciding on the numerous cases submitted to us, we thought it proper to distinguish between the degrees of guilt of the different offenders and to distribute them into two classes. Under the first were comprehended those who exhibited peculiar energy and activity: under the second, those who did little (if any more) than yield their acquiescence to the proposal to enter into the Plot . . . and therefore recommend to your Excellency that they should be pardoned upon condition that they be transported out of the limits of the United States. The terror of example we thought would be sufficiently operative by the number of criminals sentenced to death; and therefore without any

---

[16] [From South Carolina House of Representatives Records, Governor's Message No. 2, 1822, Document F, p. 2 (South Carolina Department of Archives and History, Columbia, S.C.)—ED.]

injury to the community that a measure might be adopted by us which would save the necessity of more numerous executions than policy required.

We remain very respectfully

Yr. Excellency's Obdt. Servts.

Lionel H. Kennedy
Thomas Parker
Wm. Drayton
Nathl. Heyward
J. R. Pringle
H. Deas
Robert J. Turnbull

His Excellency
Thomas Bennett

On Friday the 25th July the Court Adjourned, *sine die,* having disposed of every case before them after a session of nearly six weeks.[17]

APPENDIX

At a Court of Sessions

Held at Charleston, on the 7th October, 1822, before his honor Judge Bay, four [white] men were tried and convicted of *"a Misdemeanor in inciting Slaves to Insurrection."*

These cases created much interest, in consequence of their connection with the late attempt made by the slaves, to raise an Insurrection in this state. It did not appear that the prisoners were actually concerned in the insurrection, any further than in exciting the Slaves. The plot certainly did not originate with white persons, nor was it ever communicated by any person concerned in it, to a single white man, until the information was given which led to the developement of the scheme.

It has appeared, however, that as soon as *rumours of a Negro Plot went abroad,* some white men of the lowest characters, determined to avail themselves of the occasion, and by exciting the slaves, to hasten an event, which however calamitous to the rest of the community, they vainly imagined might be beneficial to themselves. Whether any of these men would actually have taken part with the slaves in the conduct of the insurrection, and whether the slaves themselves would have permitted white men to act in their ranks cannot be now ascertained. It is presumed that *plunder, and indemnity to their own persons,* were the objects sought for by these offenders. Only four individuals have been detected and brought to punishment for the crime of "inciting slaves to insurrection."—Against these, the testimony of

[17] [Another court heard several cases from August 1 through 8—Ed.]

white persons was obtained; but when the nature of the crime, the secrecy that would naturally have been observed, and the incompetency of slaves to give evidence, are duly considered, there is every reason to believe that many other cases (perhaps more aggravated) have existed, and which still remain undiscovered. It cannot be doubted, that there are to be found in the city of Charleston, desperate men, (outcasts from countries from which they have been banished for crimes,) who hold themselves in readiness at a moment's warning, to engage in any enterprise of blood and ruin, from which plunder may be gained. It will be the part of wisdom *to mark and profit by,* every fact and circumstance connected with the late Conspiracy. The indictment and conviction of the persons hereinafter named, is an incident in the late transactions in this city, too important to be overlooked; a brief report of their cases is therefore annexed.

The State of South-Carolina,
vs.
William Allen.
} Indictment for a Misdemeanor, in inciting slaves to insurrection.

This was a tall, stout, fine looking sailor, a Scotchman by birth, about forty-five years of age, and who had recently arrived in Charleston. It appeared that having fallen in company with a free man of color, named *Scott,* at the time when the city was much agitated by the rumors of the late intended insurrection, he enquired of Scott concerning it; and not only urged the execution of the plan, but stated his willingness to be concerned in it. Scott immediately gave information to John Stoney, Esq. an eminent merchant of this city, who directed him to assume an apparent willingness to engage in the plot, and see to what extent Allen would go. In order to identify the man, Scott led him into the store of William E. Snowden, Esq. on the pretence of business, by whom his person was marked. Several interviews took place between Scott and Allen, at all of which he held the same language; and it was finally agreed between them, that they should meet at night, at the house of a free negro man named Joe, the father in law of Scott, where the subject was to be fully considered. Hitherto the evidence against Allen was not such as could have led to his conviction; but arrangements were now made to obtain full information, and decisive evidence of the nature and extent of his guilt. Information having been given to his Honor James Hamilton, jun. Intendant of the City of Charleston, of the contemplated meeting, he summoned Richard W. Cogdell, Esq. one of the Wardens, to his assistance, and they repaired to the house of the negro Joe, and concealed themselves in a small upper room, which was so darkened that they could distinctly see and hear every thing which passed below, without being themselves observed. Allen soon after entered with Scott, and was introduced to Joe. No other persons were present in the room below. As soon as Allen entered the room, he expressed apprehensions that he might be overheard—examined the room, and caused the windows and doors to be carefully closed. He stated also, that he was armed, and threatened vengeance if betrayed. The Negroes soon succeeded, however, in removing his apprehensions—some brandy was produced, and the three sat down together at a table, and entered upon the business of the meeting. During a conversation which lasted nearly two hours, Allen expressed his approbation of the scheme of attempting an insurrection—urged the usual arguments in justification of such a measure, and explicitly declared that he would take part in it. He furnished ready answers to every objection that was urged, and endeavored to remove all the difficulties that were suggested. In doing this, he certainly made *false statements,* intended, however, to give confidence to the blacks. He pretended, for instance, to be acquainted with the plans, & spoke of large parcels of arms secreted near the city. In speaking of the plan of operations, he declared "that it would take 400 men to make the grand stand," and added, "that he would head them as soon as that number was obtained. He added, however, that he knew a Captain of a vessel, whom he named, (who then resided in Elliott-street) who had been *a Pirate for 15 years,* and was in all respects qualified to be the leader of the expedition.[18] He insisted that this man should be obtained, and that he (Allen) would serve under him. He spoke freely of the operations, and declared it to be his opinion, *"that there ought to be an indiscriminate destruction of all the whites, men, women and children."* In the course of the interview, it was objected by the Negroes, that he (Allen) being a white man, could not be safely trusted by them. To this he replied, that "though he had a white face, he was a negro in heart." As the party below stairs continued to drink, Allen, before the end of the interview, became somewhat intoxicated, though he had been sober at the commencement. The Intendant and Mr. Cogdell, from their place of concealment, had a distinct view of every thing which was passing in the room below, and expecting opposition, and finding that Allen was a strong, stout man, and probably armed, they made their arrangements for overcoming him. Allen finally rose to depart, and being immediately followed by the gentlemen above mentioned, was seized in the street by them, and taken to the guard-house. He made no resistance, and seemed so completely subdued by his fears, that no doubt could be entertained that he was by no means qualified on the score of courage, to conduct a dangerous enterprise. In the course of the interview, Allen explicitly declared, that he looked for a *handsome pecuniary reward* for the

---

[18] The individual named by Allen, was known in this city. He was certainly well qualified on the score of courage and talent, for any desperate enterprise; no reason exists, however, to support that he would have engaged in one of a criminal nature.

services he was to render, and hinted that *the freedom of the blacks was an object of no importance to him.*

From this circumstance, and his making false statements in relation to the arms, and pretending that he was one of the initiated, it is clear that Allen was not actually engaged in the conspiracy; that his object was money, and that he would probably have been content in urging on the ignorant blacks to an attempt, which in any event, must have produced the most lamentable consequences. At his trial, Allen made no defence, though his ingenious counsel urged some points of law to the court, as to the legal character of the offence. The Jury found him guilty without hesitation. He was sentenced to be imprisoned twelve months; to pay a fine of one thousand dollars, and to find security for his good behavior for five years after his liberation. This sentence, unless modified by a pardon, will doubtless amount to imprisonment for life, since the circumstances and character of the prisoner will effectually prevent him from paying the fine, or giving the security. After the sentence was passed, Allen addressed the Court in a clear, distinct voice, and with considerable ingenuity. He gave a brief history of his life, and stated that he had served on board of two American privateers during the late war, and also in the navy of the U.S.—that he had been in several severe actions, and was a pensioner of war in England. His strong Scottish dialect, however, might lead us to doubt his having been so long in this country. Certain it is, that he had never been a resident in Charleston, and had very recently arrived here before the disclosure of the late insurrectionary movements. . . .

RECAPITULATION OF SENTENCES

Number of Blacks found guilty and executed 35
  "   " " " , sentenced to death, but pardoned upon the condition that they be transported out of the limits of the United States 12
  "   " " " and sentenced to be transported beyond the limits of the United States by their owners, under the direction of the City Council . . 19
  "   " " " and sentenced to be transported out of the state of South Carolina . . . 1
  "   " found not guilty, but suggested to owners to transport beyond the limits of the United States 11
  "   " found not guilty and discharged . . 15
  "   " arrested, not tried, and discharged . 38
Number of Whites convicted and imprisoned 4
Whole Number Arrested 135

2

Original Confessions of Bacchus Hammet and John Enslow

> *Despite the Magistrates' claim that the printed evidence was "in most cases preserved, as it was originally taken, without even changing the phraseology, which was generally in the very words used by the witnesses," original manuscript sources reveal that this was not so in some important instances. For example, the manuscript confessions of Bacchus Hammet differ substantially from the printed record, and those of John Enslow include testimony not contained in the* Official Report.[1] *However, the way in which the confessions were extracted and the court record was edited may account for the discrepancies.*

Confession of Bacchus, the Slave of Mr. Hammet

Bacchus stated that *Perault*, (Stroekers man) on or about the 2nd May, whilst hauling cotton to the wharf, persuaded him to go to a Society; that he enquired of Perault what society it was, and was told never to mind but pressed earnestly to go. That Perault would call for him that night, which he did.[2] That they went together to Denmark Vesey's house near Bennets Mills. that they were recd by Denmark when they went into his yard at his house door, and the gate locked upon them. That Denmark after ascertaining it was Perault & another man (as Perault said to D) he went with them into the house. In a

---

[1] From the William and Benjamin Hammet Papers (Durham, N.C.: Duke University Library). Used with permission of the Duke University Library.

[2] About this time Perault was discovered one evening by Bacchus's master as wishing to get into his gate; who on enquiry found that Perault wanted to see B and when asked *what for*, after much hesitancy, stated, "he wanted to give Bacchus a little Bit of Religion, that Bacchus was a very wicked boy, and he wanted to get him to try to serve God, and try and save his soul and be a better servant to his master." Mr. H. questioned him as to the liberty he took in attempting such a thing with his servant, and enquired of Perault if he did not belong to the African Church. He said: "Yes" and when warned about leading his Boy in to such Society as Mr. H thought them great rascals Perault replied, He was sorry but he thought them as good as any other people: Bacchus no doubt went with him as he was absent at 12 o'Clock at night.

large room I seen ten or a dozen men, a table in the midst of the room and a large Book open on it, probably the Bible. Denmark asked me who I belonged to and my name, Perault immediately answered "Bacchus belonging to Mr. Hammet," Denmark asked me which Hammet, I said Mr. Benjamin Hammet, the gentleman who put old Lorenzo Dow in jail; and is an officer in Capt. Martindale's company. Perault and Denmark then took me in a side room; and Perault says to me, "Bacchus I have some particular thing to say to you; I asked what it was he said "that they were going to have war and fight the white people" and that I must join them. I said "Perault I am sorry you brought me into this business and you better let it alone," and I considered some time; at last Perault says *"Bacchus you need not fret, you may as well join us."* Denmark then said *"any person who don't join us must be treated as an enemy and put to death";* and I said *if that is the case, well I will join you.* We all three then went into the large room, and there I seen Rolla Bennet, Monday Gell, Charles Drayton & Smart Anderson and another who I believe is Denmark Veseys son. They had the large Book open and something like a letter in it, which *believe come from some free Country off, may be St. Domingo:* and Denmarks son says to Monday, shewing him something in the letter, "look here Monday see how they are making fun of we," meaning the people off in the free country. That Denmark said, "Friends we have a friend who is to go into the Country to raise the country negroes to come down, all who can *must* put in money to raise a sum *to pay his master wages while he is gone.*" That they all put in, and I and Perault put in seven pence. Denmark then said they must all swear, that *they all held up their right hand and swore,* and said after Denmark: *"We will not tell on one another, we will not tell on any body, We will not tell if taken by the whites, nor will we tell if we are to be put to death."* that under the sanctity of this Oath he never told his master. This was the first meeting—Denmark told me and the rest that night the next week, we were to meet again at his House, I believe it was Thursday: at the next meeting, I was asked by Denmark *if I could get any arms,* I told him may be *an old sword;* and he said no matter *any arms* I can get to bring them to him. Perault told me to try and get arms and powder. I said *my master has pistols, but I am afraid to take them,* and Perault said never mind We *will satisfy your master*[3] on that subject. *That I did at the middle of the day steal out of the Back store of my master when the clerks were busy and the store open one Keg of powder and old horsemans sword.*—that when busy in the house, *I did steal my masters pistol out of the closet of one of the rooms.* That (Ned Bennet) one of Bennetts men came and waited in the street that

---

[3] No doubt by a murdering argument, as a small Hatchet, with a long handle is in possession of the master; a very useful and deadly weapon it is. The Horseman's sword was considered of little value and lay in the Back Store.

night until I came out to assist me in carrying the powder to Denmark's. we carried it in a bag and I gave the sword and pistol & powder to him. He afterwards told me he gave the sword to Perault, and Perault gave it to Caesar Smith.[4] The powder was carried to Monday Gells house by Perault, where Gullah Jack came and got it. Denmark told me, that on Sunday 16th, June we must not go home, that every one must stay out, and go up the road to a farm on meeting street road, as soon as we hear the noise, and there meet the country negroes under him, and another. that *I must not join the people where my master lived but join another Gang,* and *he would send a Gang to take my Master, and to take Capt. Martindale*[5]—every one who could was to come out. That morning I went to Monday Gells (the 9th June) and there I met Charles Drayton who was going with Monday to the farm; but Monday seeing me said "Charles here is a friend he will go with you, I have a hog to kill, and can't go. he will go." I went up to a farm on Meeting Street road with a House having a balcony at the top is on it—Here Charles Drayton called for the old Daddy and some two Women came to the gate and went back and called him. He came and Charles, and myself, went into the stable with him, and Charles told him, that he must be in readiness as the Country Negroes would be down next Sunday, and he must receive them. We then came away——
On the next Sunday the 16th June, Gullah Jack came to Monday Gell, where I was and Charles Drayton, and said you can't go up to the farm, I have been up the road and just come down, and the negroes can't go up *as the Patrol* [6] *is out quite strong—That I was to help to get the arms of the Neck Company*—That Monday Gell told me when the Negroes was taken up (for holding meeting in Anson Street) in 1820, *that the African Church was the people, and that they met for this very purpose but that business put them back, and now they had began again to try it*—After Denmark was taken, Perault came and told me, and said Denmark said nobody must tell any thing—That Perault said never mind keep yourself in readiness, and when you hear the noise in the street you must come out and help us to *get the Arms of the Neck Company* (6th July) that Gullah Jack was to head this party and then to fight the white people with them. The General plan was to fight the white people and them that were not killed to be driven out of the City— (That when in prison[7] *Perault told me not to tell as I was put in the same room with him—He told me when I asked where the powder was that it was buried by Gullah Jack.*) That Perault told me, *"we have a Blacksmith who is making Baynets or something to stick*

---

[4] Caesar Smith. Hung 26 July.

[5] Capt. M & Mr. H. were to be tortured.

[6] The Charleston Neck patrol no doubt prevented an assemblage that day, and consequently much alarm. Yet Council arrogates all the whole and sole praise.

[7] Perault never began to confess until the day he found Bacchus had told something.

with, we have already 2 or 300 Baynets and 3 or 400 (hundred) men— Monday said "We are 2000 (thousand) strong." When I asked Denmark about how they would be able to do this thing without arms— he said, every one must look out for the different stores that had arms such as guns &c, and take notice to them.—He told me also that all the Ministers[8] were to be killed except a few who were to be saved and showed the different passages in the Bible from which Denmark preached (& the rest) and they were to be asked Why they did not preach up this thing (meaning the passages[9] on liberty &c) to them before and that they were to be made to tell—

Notwithstanding the evidence of guilt against this fellow & from his own confession, yet he went to the Gallows, *laughing and bidding his acquaintances in the streets "good bye."* On being hung, owing to some mismanagement in the fall of the trap, he was not thrown off, but as the board canted he slipped; yet he was so hardened, that *he threw himself forward, and as he swung back he lifted his feet, so that his knees might not touch the Board!*—In prison he was considered very hardened. He told a clergyman the evening before his execution, that *"He never had* any goodness in him, and that Hell was his portion." He was well-used, and had many privileges allowed him—So Hardened was he in fact, that he was seen to laugh a moment or two before the cap was drawn over his eyes.

The following is furnished by a friend of the owner who obtained it from the Revd Mr. Backman.

That Revd Gentleman was in the habit of visiting the prisoners; on a visit of this kind he happened to step into the room where Bacchus was and found him very dejected, apparently in a deep study. He enquired how it was with him, meaning his future state & hopes, Bacchus replied "bad enough," and said "he would go to Hell"; indeed that is bad enough said the clergyman; Bacchus replied *"he was thinking if he ever did a good action,"* and found he never had. He told the clergyman, *"that he was the Devil amongst the women,"* that he believed he would go to Hell, "that his master thought he was a good servant and he had been a very bad boy." He also stated how he was carried to Veseys by Perault, How Vesey sat him along side of him, and when he found he——[torn] to join him He asked him seven queries such as— *"Did His master use him Well—Yes he believed so, Did He eat the same* as his master, Yes sometimes not always as well as his master— *Did his master not sleep on a soft bed,* Yes. *Did he Bacchus sleep on as soft a Bed as his master—No—Who made his master—God—Who made you—God—And then ar'nt you as good as your master if God made him & you, ar'nt you as free,* Yes, *Then why don't you join and*

---

[8] Corroborated by the Testimony of Jessee Blackwood.

[9] The Passages alluded to were Exodus 1st. Chap. & 21 st. Chap. & the 16th verse. also 19th Chap. Isaiah, and 14 Zachariah 1 & 3 Verses &c.

fight your master. Does your master use you well, Yes I believe so, *Does he whip you when you do wrong,* Yes sometimes, *Then why dont you as you are as free as your master, turn about and fight for yourself.* Upon this delusive reasoning he joined, and then stated how his name was put down and the mode of swearing &c &c &c already described. After joining (with such delusions) he said would have went as far as any of them in the Business. . . .

The Confession of Mr. Enslows Boy John

The Plan was that every Black man who was attached to them was to come out and assemble where the Beat companies meet. Others had their positions assigned to them, to push for the different magazines and Guard Houses. The House servants were to Kill their Masters, with whatever instruments they had or could obtain, it was thought that the House servants would do most mischief at the commencement. There was to be no signal, because Denmark and the principal leaders said it would excite alarm, but at 12 O'Clock at Night, they must take their stations & act their part. The people up the road to take the Magazine then push for Town, and spare nothing that obstructed them. The Country people was to push for Meys Wharf & take the U States Navy Yd. on Meys Wharf (to be commanded by Gullah Jack). Rolla Bennett, to command the Country people who cross the Bridge on Ashly River. Ned Bennet, to meet in Mr. Elias Horry's house and collect a number (assisted by John Horry & push for the Guard House) the corner of Meeting & Broad Streets, and join those from the road. Negroes would be supplied with arms, from this source, (who had not been provided) if successful,—Monday & denmark to have strongest force, and come to town, when they had succeeded up town, and Peter Poyas was to have command along East & South Bay and try to capture the shipping. This was considered the most active station, as he would prevent the escape of the whites if they conquered. The Resolve was if they did not succeed in town they would fire it and retreat to the Lines and there fight man for man and if defeated go to the woods and do all the harm they could. I have spoken myself to Denmark & Peter about the people in the Country and know they went into the country often and told me they had communications in all the Islands—also in Columbia, Santee, and different places, in that direction. I also heard them say they were well informed in Georgetown. That they would let the principal Men know the time of attack, being a short distance from Charleston would commence a day or two before. Kill all the whites between there and Charleston. make their way thro' the woods and be in time to assist their people in town. It is also said by them that the Population in Georgetown could be killed in one half hour. They would capture all the Boats &c and get a great many arms, from that place. Master I tell you candidly the thing was general and known.

Denmark read at the meeting different Chapters from the Old Testament, but most generally read the whole of the 21. Chap. Exodus & spoke and exorted from the 16 Verse the words "and He that stealeth a man" &c He read frequently in a Book about the complexion of people and said it was the climate of Africa made them Black but were not inferior to Whites on that account. Monday Gell also wrote letters to St. Domingo by the steward of a Brig lying at Gibbes & Harpers Wharf. It was understood that they would obtain assistance from St. Domingo and the North—because Monday Gell read several speeches, and pamphlets, and said that the *Northern Brothers* would assist them and if they failed would be no disgrace. Monday Gell is the first person who spoke to me, and told me he expected a number at that time (Feby) to join him for he had spoken to a considerable number. Denmark, Peter Poyas, Rolla, Ned, Garner, John Vincent & others have spoken to many particularly the first six who were hung; but in consequence of their deaths the names of a number remain secret as they spoke to them individually. Billy Palmer was also considered an active man. I was not at the last meeting but understood they had determined to Kill Men, Women & Children. I believe the report true for at the Meeting before the last, Denmark & Peter Poyas said if you Kill the *Lice,* you must Kill the *Nits.*

Master having read this over to me I do swear it is true and some facts left out, of which I will remind him (because I was at all their meetings,) and was considered an active man. there was a quantity of Arms, of different Kinds furnished, for Denmark told me in March, he was getting Arms fast, about 150 to 200 pikes made, and there was a great deal of money placed in his hands for the purpose. they must have been sent in the Country by Rolla, Ned, Peter, Denmark, and Batteau.

AMERICANS REACT TO THE PLOT

3

Justice William Johnson Doubts the Extensiveness of the Plot, Warns Against Mass Hysteria, and Is Rebuked by the Court

The Charlestonian William Johnson (appointed Associate Justice of the United States Supreme Court by President Thomas Jefferson in 1804 and married to Governor Thomas Bennett's sister) in an anonymous communication to the respectable Charleston Courier *on June 21, warned against the undesirable effects of public hysteria. Privately, Johnson protested, along with Bennett, that the Vesey conspirators were not getting fair trials. Johnson related how, a dozen years before, panic over a suspected slave rebellion had seized the white population of the state and a black man was executed without receiving a hearing.[1] As a result of his communication, Johnson was severely rebuked by the court, and the editor of the* Courier *apologized for ever having printed Johnson's letter. Johnson then requested readers to suspend judgment and on July 4, issued a short pamphlet* To the Public of Charleston *(Charleston, C. C. Sebring, 1822) in which he defended his views. However, neither he nor his brother-in-law ever came to believe that the conspiracy was as deep as portrayed by the court, nor that the authorities had handled the affair equitably. Johnson expressed these views later in letters to Thomas Jefferson and John Quincy Adams, and Bennett criticized the court and others in his Message No. 2 to the state legislature on November 28—a document which Johnson probably helped write. On August 7, 1823, Johnson, sitting as a federal circuit court judge upheld federal control of commerce and opposed the doctrine of secession in a case involving the Ne-*

---

[1] From the Charleston *Courier*, June 21 and June 29, 1822.

gro Seamen Act passed by the South Carolina Assembly in December, 1822, partly in response to the Vesey plot. Later, in 1832, Johnson strongly opposed nullification of the tariff laws by South Carolina. For these opinions he was ostracized in his home state and soon moved to Pennsylvania, where he died in 1834.

MELANCHOLY EFFECT OF POPULAR EXCITEMENT

The following anecdote may be relied on as a simple narrative of facts, which actually occurred within the recollection of thousands.

In the year 1810 or 1811, Mr. Blount being Governor of North Carolina, Mr. Milledge of Georgia, and Mr. Drayton of South Carolina, the two latter states were thrown into great alarm by a letter transmitted from Gov. Blount to Gov. Milledge, and by the latter despatched by express to Gov. Drayton. The militia of the two states, in the counties adjacent to Augusta, were ordered to be held in readiness for action, *en masse,* and Guards and Patrols to scour the country. The sufferings of the inhabitants, particularly the females, from apprehensions painfully excited, induced a gentleman of this city, then a resident near Augusta, to call on the Governor, then residing near that place, and request a sight of the letter. At the first glance of the eye he pronounced it a hoax: for it bore date on the 1*st April.* And had been picked up in one of the country towns in North Carolina, where it had in fact been dropped by some thoughtless schoolboys. On the face of it also it bore such evidence of its origin, as must have struck any observer whose vision was not distorted by alarm. For it was dated Augusta, signed "Your loving brother Captain Jack," and purported to be directed to an associate, in Lewisville, North Carolina. But it was in vain that these suggestions were made. The Governor of Georgia could not brook the mortifying discovery of his having been duped, and the whole country, on the designated night was kept in agitated motion.

Happy had it terminated in nothing more than the suffering and disturbance communicated to the people of both states, and the useless expenditure of some thousands of public money. But another hoax gave it a most tragical termination.

The trumpeter of the Augusta Cavalry resided in the opposite district of Edgefield, and orders had been issued to him to attend the company that night. By some accident these orders did not reach him in time to make Augusta that evening, and he halted at Moore's mills, on Chever's creek, in South Carolina. Here he and a companion were shown into a garret, where they were amusing themselves over their pint of whiskey, when the continual passing and repassing of the mounted militia drew their attention; and the half intoxicated bugle-man resolved to try the effect of a blast of his music upon the fears of a party just gone by. The effect was electrical; it was deemed the expected signal; the detachments gallopped off in all directions in quest of the offender, and towards morning returned with a single poor half-witted negro, who had been taken crossing a field on his way home, without instrument of war or of music. But none else could be found, and he alone could have given the significant blast, which so many had heard. It was in vain that he denied it: he was first whipped severely to extort a confession, and then, with his eyes bound, commanded to prepare for instant death from a sabre, which a horseman was in the act of sharpening beside him.

He now recollected that a man named Billy, belonging to Capt. Key, had one of those long tubes which boatmen use on our rivers, and declared that he had sounded the horn, and done it at the command of Capt. Key's men; but still denied all sort of combination, and affirmed the innocence of the act.

An armed force was immediately detached to the house of Billy, and there found him quietly sleeping in the midst of a large family, in a degree of comfort very unusual for a slave—for Billy was a blacksmith, a fellow of uncommon worth, and indulged in such privileges by his master as his fidelity justly merited.

But in one corner of his house, exposed to the view of every one, was found the terrific horn, and he was hurried away to be tried for his life. The Court of Magistrates and Freeholders was selected from men of the first respectability in the neighborhood; and yet it is a fact, although no evidence was given whatever as to a motive for sounding the horn, and the horn was actually found covered and even filled with cobwebs, they condemned that man to die the next day!—and, what will scarcely be believed, they actually received evidence of his having been once charged with stealing a pig, to substantiate the charge upon which he then stood on trial. Respectable bystanders have declared, that his guilt or innocence as to the pig soon took the lead of every other question on the trial.—The owner, one of the worthiest men in all that country, thunderstruck at the sentence, entreated a more deliberate hearing; but not being listened to, hastened away to his friends, and among them a judicial character in the neighborhood, to unite their entreaties with his. They promptly attended to his solicitations, procured a meeting of the court, and earnestly pressed the injustice and precipitation of the sentence, and their right to time to solicit a pardon, but in vain. The presiding magistrate actually conceived his dignity attacked, and threatened impeachment against the judge, who, as an individual, had interfered only to prevent a legal murder; and interferred upon the witness, retracting all he had testified to.

Billy was hung amidst crowds of execrating spectators;—and such appeared to be the popular demand for a victim, that it is not certain a pardon could have saved him.

COMMUNICATION

The Members of a Court now assembled, upon a very painful occasion, are compelled to notice a publication which appeared in the *Courier,* on the 21st inst. headed *"Melancholy effect of popular excitement."* This piece, in their own opinions, and of all with whom they have conversed relative to it (the number of whom is very great,) contained an insinuation, that the Court, under the influence of popular prejudice, was capable of committing perjury and murder, and implied that the author of it possessed sounder judgment, deeper penetration, and firmer nerves, than the rest of his fellow citizens. The individuals constituting this humble tribunal, relying upon the purity of their motives, and their conduct through life, had hoped to have pursued their labors, important to the state and distressing to themselves, unassailed by suspicion or malevolence; and, notwithstanding the publication they have adverted to, they would never have addressed their fellow citizens, if the person who caused its insertion, had declared in the gazette, as he was required to do, that he "did not mean to imply any thing disrespectful towards the court, much less to insinuate that, under the influence of popular excitement, or of any other inducement, they were capable of departing from the course which was prescribed to them by their oaths and by their consciences." But this requisition, after first promising to comply with, he afterwards refused to perform.

Injured and defamed as the Court considers itself to be, they nevertheless owe it to themselves and to the community, not to degrade themselves by the use of epithets and expressions which the occasion would seem to require: they, therefore, leave it to the public to make their comments—and to the individual they will only say, that they are at a loss how to reconcile his conduct with that which ought to influence a gentleman respecting his solemn promise, and sensible of the obligations of decency and propriety.

4

Southerners Privately Ponder the Meaning of the Conspiracy

Private reactions to the conspiracy are extremely rare, and only a few personal letters survive to give some indication of the confusion, hysteria, and fear which gripped white Charlestonians and others in the vicinity of the plot. In June and July, Miss Anna Hayes Johnson wrote several confidential letters from Charleston to her cousin in Raleigh, N.C., which demonstrate the sexual fears associated with slave rebellions that plagued the minds of southern whites. About twenty years old, Anna was the daughter of United States Supreme Court Justice William Johnson, who on June 21 had questioned whether the conspiracy was as extensive as the court maintained.

Meanwhile, John Potter, a Charleston financial agent, wrote to South Carolinian Langdon Cheves, then residing in Philadelphia as director of the Bank of the United States, detailing the events of the plot and the reactions of Charlestonians. Similarly, State Chancellor Henry W. Desaussure wrote to Joel R. Poinsett blaming the conspiracy on West Indian blacks.

One hundred and twenty-five miles south in Savannah, Georgia, Mrs. Martha Proctor Richardson composed a series of letters to her nephew, then traveling in Europe, which revealed the excitement sweeping that town during the summer months. Quoting interesting passages from private letters by Charleston Intendant James Hamilton, Jr., and Chancellor Henry William Dessaussure, Mrs. Richardson alluded to Judge Johnson's dissent and seemed confused that privileged slaves would actually conspire to revolt.

Joel R. Poinsett, a member of the second court from August 3–8, a United States Congressman from 1821–25, a close friend of Andrew Jackson, and the leader of South Carolina Unionists during the Nullification Crisis of 1828–33, wrote to President James Monroe after the trials, convinced that the Missouri debates were responsible for deluding the insurrectionists. Finally, in December of 1822, and again in July of 1824, William Johnson reiterated his views of the conspiracy in private letters to former Presi-

dent Thomas Jefferson and to Secretary of State John Quincy Adams.

ANNA HAYES JOHNSON TO HER COUSIN [1]

Charleston, June 23, 1822

. . . And now my dear Betsy "I will a tale unfold" whose lightest word—Would harrow up thy soul; freeze thy young blood
Make thy two eyes like stars start from thy spheres
Thy knotted and combined locks to part
Like quills upon the fretful porcupine—list list oh list
In sober phrase, our city is now in the most fearful state.
Gracious Heaven when I think what I have escaped & what I may yet suffer my blood curdles—Alas' Sterne too truly said that "Slavery was a bitter draught"—Our slaves have revolted and the plot was only found out by the noble interposition of a negro whom they invited to join them   he instantly with the subtlety of his class drew from his acquaintance the design plan time &ca and then with trembling anxiety inform'd his master who instantly informed the Intendant & my uncle who is fortunately Governour and by them every means was taken to protect the city—for the information was given only a few days before the insurrection was to have taken place—since which a court of enquiry has been instituted of the most impartial and honourable men of our city who have been sitting now more than a week and the number implicated is incredible—and I blush to own that it has been traced to the whites for this day one or two white men have been taken up and the proofs are so strong as to hang them—for some intelligent negro who acts as a spy for the court found where their nightly meetings were held and carried our Intendant and one or two others there who saw and heard scenes of rapine & murder talked of with the coolness of demons—Their plans were simply these—they were to have set fire to the town and while the whites were endeavouring to out it they were to have commenced their horrid depredations —It seems that the Governour Intendant and my poor father were to be the three first victims—the men & Black [sic] Women were to have been indiscriminately murdered—& we poor devils were to have been reserved to fill their Harams—horrible—I have a very beautiful cousin who was set apart for the wife or more properly the "light of the Haram" of one of their Chiefts—and the old and infirm women were to have shared the fate of our fathers—It is true that in our city the white & Black population are equal 16,000 each but about George-

[1] From the Ernest Haywood Papers, Southern Historical Collection (Chapel Hill, N.C.: University of North Carolina). Used with permission of the director of the Southern Historical Collection.

town the odds is fearful—16,000 B—to 150 W—I do not know the estimate of the black population thro' the state but I know that it is very great—I am told that the number in the plot is computed to be about 3000—The children were to have been spiked murdered &ca and I am told that the observation heard from the man taken up to day was this—I feel a little sorry for the children, but they must go, as to those already condemned it is no matter some must die for the cause—you have still many brave spirits among you—go on [torn] *booty Beauty & Glory*—This from a free born American—Oh my cousin I thought not to have found such a villain breaking the pure air of free born America—Six of the Chiefts are to be hung the 2 July. . . .

God bless you

A H J

Charleston, July 18th, 1822

My dear Cousin,

. . . I suppose that by this time you are anxious to hear more about the unhappy business which has fulled with consternation all our city and nothing but the merciful interposition of our God has saved us from horror equal if not superior to the scenes acted in St Domingo— The catalogue is not filled up for we thought that it was ended and that the execution of six of the chiefts would suffice. The court had been dismissed and the town was again sinking into its wanted security when information was given that another attempt would be made at such a time, and the states witness gave information of such a nature as to induce the city council to recall the court, and since that period the alarm has spread most widely, and there are now between 50 & 60 of the leaders in our jail—It is said that twenty of them have been convicted & sentenced, and in all probability the execution will not end under 100, but I was told yesterday that the prisoners had been heard to say that even should there be 500 executed there would be still enough to carry the work into execution. Denmark Vesey one of those already executed and who was the instigator of the whole plot acknowledged that he had been nine years endeavouring to effect the diabolical scheme, how far the mischief has extended heaven only knows—I never heard in my life more deep laid plots or plots more likely to succeed, indeed "t'was a plot a good plot—an excellent plot"

But t'was a plot that had it succeeded would have told to after ages a most fearful tale—It would be absurd in me to attempt a detail of all the circumstances real or imaginary which I have heard—this much is all that I know of that bears the stamp of truth: that their intention was to take the city and keep it as long as possible and then carry *us* & the common negro's to St D there to be sold as slaves with as much plunder as they could find   it seems that this Vesey had been to St D and made an agreement that at such a time so many Vessels should be here to assist—it would have been a complete scene of desolation—as yet thank God none of our slaves have been found in the plot, tho' there are 20 of them in [———?] in the yard

   . . . Farewell God Bless you

Anna

Charleston, July 27th 1822

My dear Coz

   . . . We had yesterday the most aweful tragidy acted in this devoted city that comes within the recollection of man—22 unfortunate wretches were at one fatal moment sent to render up their dread account. 29 had been sentenced but 7 had their sentence commuted to perpetual banishment—but on Tuesday 6 more are to be executed—Gracious Heaven to what will all this lead—certainly it will throw our city back at least ten years—30 have already been executed, and I am told that there are an aweful number yet to be tried, I wish I could act for myself   I would not stay in this city another day for my feelings have been so lacerated of late that I can hardly think speak or act   there is a look of horror in every countenance—I wish I was with you, at least I should experience comparative happiness tho' even there what I have seen would pursue me—Do not think I saw them hung, I would as leave be hung my self—tho' it was within sight of our house—But I can imagine & feel. . . . Remember me to all my kith & kin—Yours—most sincerely

Anna

Charleston, S.C., July 24, 1822

My dear Betsy

   . . . On Friday 29 of the unfortunate creatures are to be hung—it is most horrible—it makes my blood curdle when I think of it but they are guilty most certainly. . . .

Yours Affcly—

Anna

JOHN POTTER TO LANGDON CHEVES [2]

private)   Charleston 29th June 1822

My Dear Sir,

   I wrote you a few lines by James who sailed home for New York—last monday and where I hope he has arrived—I adverted to a subject which he could better explain that I could do it by letter—a circumstance which has caused much agitation and extreme feeling in the public mind—as such reports ever will keenly produce among us—

   A court of the most respectable individuals in the City have been

[2] From the Langdon Cheves Papers (Charleston, S.C.: South Carolina Historical Society). Used with permission of the South Carolina Historical Society.

patiently and laborously investigating this business, for 10 or 12 days past—and you will perceive by the news papers I send you that six wretches are to pay the forfeit of their worthless lives on tuesday—the plot was deeply laid, and a plan of insurrection (which a member of the court told me yesterday) was organized with an address & cunning, as he said would much surprise the community. At first Governor Bennett could not believe that his own negroes were implicated—but the subsequent investigation proved a scene of guilt, and murder, to be intended, unparallel'd even exceeding if possible, the *Demons*, of St. Domingo!!!

His excellency it is said was to be the first victim by his favorite servant Rolla—and his reward was to be Miss B. the Governor's daughter—the very thought makes my blood recoil in my veins. I believe the plan was that the white males were all to be cut off—!!

Their meetings commenced, and were held under the perfidious cover of religion—and I cannot doubt that they were aided by the black missionaries from your City!

Judge Wm. Johnson put in the Courier of yesterday [a] week a piece of as much independent tendency as ever a man in his sober senses could write—it was a severe reflection on the court composed of members as highly respectable as he was—The Intendent Mr Hamilton, in behalf of the wardens, made a reply on saturday this days week—both of which you can see published in the papers I now send you—You will see a severe recrimination on the Judge, by the members of the Court, (in which the whole community seems to concur) and his short reply!!! I believe he thought that Bennett's negroes were innocent & possibly his publication was intended to have a bearing on this supposition—a moments reflection must have shown it would & must have had a contrary tendency—

A white villain was apprehended the night before last—(a fellow lately tryed for piracy)—he had been endeavouring [to] suborn a free negro into a plot, all he wanted he said was 400 such fellows to effect his purposes: the negro deceived and induced this fellow to come at night & develop all his plans where Major Hamilton the Intendant & a warden had been secreted & heard all that passed—when the meeting broke up & the fellow was going off the Intendant clapped a pistol to his breast, when he was easily led to Jail & I hope will receive the gallows as he deserves—no doubt others are implicated in this plot which will be constantly in agitation if we do not get rid of the *poison* that has been too deeply & I fear successfully introduced into this place—You are free from these unpleasant feelings   I wished most that my wife & daughter would have gone with James but it would not be listened to with them

I am always Yrs truly

J: Potter

private   Charleston, 5th July, 1822
My Dear Sir,

Since I wrote you our situation here—and investigation made by the Court, which has again been constituted by the same gentlemen, and are still proceeding in their enquiries—altho' many are implicated in the crime, for which six have already suffered—I do not know whether more lives will attone for their plans of deep laid treachery and murder.

I fear it will have a sad effect on this kind of property, much depends on what is now adopted for our future safety, and laws that may be adopted at the ensuing meeting of our legislature—

I do not recollect whether I mentioned the circumstance of *Vesey* (the Chief who was hanged) and others, had wigs and whiskers made, to wear on the occasion—this wretch denied the fact, never had seen the french man who had made them, when confronted together, until this man took one of the wigs from his pocket, and asked him if he knew that [?] when the villian was abashed—I believe for the first time—as he had denied it totally before—I hear Major Willsons servant (Gibbs' son in law) was the person who first discovered and developed the plot of murder which his mind could not submit to—

I must confess, if one of these fellows had made his way into my bed room, in the dead of night, dressed out in his *wig, whiskers,* and a *whitened face*—that I might have been appaled, not being aware of the circumstance—but possibly these precious few would have had enough to do out of doors—and the trifling [?] business of *taking care* of *the males* would have fallen to other agents, with the servants of the family, many of whom, who are not yet known I fear, would have turned traitors on the Occasion—Certainly this discovery has awakened unpleasant feelings, tho' I firmly believe all such danger is over for the present—this however my friend is more than I durst own before my family who have been more alarmed than I have ever seen before—nor can I deem it surprising from the horrid aspect of the transaction and consequences which might have followed in the event taking place—attended with the smallest success—tho' in the end they could not have succeeded at all—

I have already mentioned how Judge Johnson was implicated in foolish, illtimed publications—the minds of the people were exceedingly irritated against him.

Inclosed is his justification which came out yesterday—but which somehow has not given much relief or satisfaction to the public mind —and his pushing it on Willington, the printer [of the *Courier*]— will only involve, I fear, more recriminations.

For a man so well informed, it is surprising he does so many I may say weak imprudent acts—certainly the ancedote he first gave the public (as he calls it) was at any time improper and a libel on his

Country—but particularly at such a moment, doubly improper, and unguarded—the Union Bank gives 175—and planters 87 ½ cents per share—shall I sell the remainder of your shares in the fall—

Yrs, ever truly

John Potter

(Confidential)   Charleston 10th July 1822
My Dear Sir

. . . Since I last wrote you about this most diabolical plot which the mercy of God prevented on the very eve & very day of distruction —the public mind has been very much agitated—the first court resumed its labors, and every step they advanced it was found that the Conspiracy had spread wider and wider—Confessions were made more freely and a vast number of slaves were taken up; on yesterday 5 more wretches were condemned to death to be hung on friday next—1 belonged to Gill, who kept the stables, 1 to Paul Pritchard (who was the "wizzard"), one to John Drayton his cook who had hitherto behaved well—1 to David Haig & a favourite servant of *Elias Horry's*— I believe his coachman!! Indeed it is now well ascertained that most of the coachmen & favourite servants in the City knew of it even if they had not participated in the intentions & plans proposed—

Mrs. Bryans coachman—as well as Mrs. Fergusons—knew all— but when it came to the murder of their masters (young Bryan & Ferguson) the mind revolted they say—but as Rolla who is hung told his master the governor—tho' he would not have done the deed —another had undertaken the Office—it seems—or as reports give it—that Peter Smiths house [———?] alas a house newly built opposite Judge Johnson's, R. Cunningham's & several others most conspicuous, at the opposite corner—were to be fired on the night of the 16th ult. when as the white males were to appear—even before they could leave their own doors, the indiscriminate massacre was to take place —the females were to be reserved *for worse than death*. It is believed that Vesey's plans when this had been completed [were] to have forced the Banks and carried off as much plunder as he could to St. Domingo—and leave his blind agents behind (as all could not go) [to] perish for their crimes—

When your kind, and *tender hearted Philadelphians,* as *well as Quakers* preach up emancipation—let them *ponder* on the deeds of darkness & misery that would have taken place had this plot even in part succeeded—but such evils are disregarded if their favourite plan of *philanthropy* had been successful—God in his mercy reward them for it!!! this is the spot from whence our evils spring!! we will throw back on them all these black free incendiaries—where the wretches who are implicated in consenting to the deed will go, I cannot yet say, but here they cannot remain—a high & steady hand will go forth, where the laws cannot reach—*Your Branch here* would no doubt have had the *first preference* of *plunder*—this is a risk you had not I suppose contemplated!! Our best respects to all your family & friends—always yrs

J: Potter

My dear Sir   Charleston 16th July 1822
. . . As yet, I have sold no further of your stock. 60 & 30 is the utmost talked of, and sales made at those prices—I have always found before that stocks rated as high after a few weeks—as they had sold before the dividend—but in fact nothing is doing, the sensations on peoples minds seem to occupy their whole attention. As for *negroes* I do not believe they would bring any price at present—I have not heard of the proceedings of the court yesterday, but they are proceeding with a firm step, and I apprehend many more will forfeit their lives. new incidents are appearing every day—some pike handles were found at Buckley's farm, and the pike maker is safely housed—but the pikes are not found yet, I believe, as well as powder & arms that are known to have been within possession—the Charleston Neck Company had always left their arms and accoutrements at Wharton's on the King St. Road and placed in the back store. his negro, or else one he hired, had got the key and agreed to deliver them at the moment agreed on—Mr. Chanet had a quantity of new Guns for sale—who lives near the inspection, which were to have been seized also. You cannot think how cunningly devised the scheme was—and had the execution been as well supported, many of us this day would not have been left, to tell the tale, if it had not been providentially discovered in time—The french negroes it seems had joined them— a french negro—a matrass maker (and the very last that could have been suspected) was apprehended on friday or saturday evening— apparently a quiet & most innofensive creature—above all, a fellow of Mrs. Colcocks, a very pattern of good behaviour, has been apprehended & many such are now coming forward!!! Our best regards to all your family, I am always Yr obt. friend

J: Potter

My Dear Sir—
P:S: Since writing the above I was told by the Intendant Mr. Hamilton that 3 butcher negroes have been apprehended and many more of that class *suspected*—Dr. Haig's *Harry* who is under condemnation & respited a week to give information—says that *Gullah Jack* who was hanged last friday wished him to *poison his master's well*—which was it is supposed to have been general!! Good God, what have we come to. Mr. Hamilton says 50 or 60 more will have to be tried for their lives.
   29 & 59 Cannot be had for Bank Stocks. . . .

Charleston 20th July 1822

My Dear Sir

Your esteemed favors of the 11th & 12th Inst. were received yesterday—by which mail I sent you a news paper, detailing the sentence of the court, of the day preceeding—and from the numerous arrests daily, there is no knowing how many more will suffer. poor Robertson has three condemned, as you would see—whilst those fellows belonged to us jointly, I never had a complaint of them for 10 years—one had *then,* a wife in my yard, and when I left the City, I always directed him to sleep in the yard, which I thought safe under his charge—

Bennett did the same with Rolla, who had indeed the safety of his family entrusted to him, whilst absent in Columbia—

This cunningly and deeply devised plot was much more extensive than you had any idea of, when you wrote on the 11th: nothing could be better arranged and would have done credit to a better cause & other means—

all the arms on the Neck were deposited in one place—to which a negro had access and was to deliver the key—700 stand of muskets would also [——?] been in their power— & there was enough powder ready at hand—and when the guard was overpowered—and arsenal taken, the torch was to give the signal of murder and blood—all those who were to go out on the cry of fire, which was to be multiplied, would meet their fate—the draymen, carters, and coachmen to act as Cavalry and secure the streets, when the confidential servants in the plot indoors were to murder every white male master of an adult age—many I hope were not implicated, I have no reason to suppose any of my house servants were guilty, but there were enough to commence with, and but anyway successfull even for a moment all, or nearly all, would have joined!

it is said by a fellow in his confession that when *Vesey* was inducing him to murder his master, he hesitated—but at length assented—then, what says he, will be done with the children? what says this *arch villain,* kill the *Lice* and let the *nitts* remain—no—no—never!!! Dr. Haig's Harry was pressed by Gulla Jack to poison his masters well—but he says he refused to do that deed, but assented to all the rest—had it taken place two weeks sooner, as the condemned wretch *Peter Poyas* wished, the result probably would have been dreadful—we were then all unprepared, completely so—this is all private & confidential. . . .

the weather is very pleasant, so much so that we have had no inclinations to go to the Islands as yet, & quite healthy—with our best respects to all your family & friends—always Yrs.

J: Potter

HENRY W. DESAUSSURE TO JOEL R. POINSETT [3]

Columbia [S.C] 6th July 1822

My dear Sir

On my return home from a long, a hot, & a busy circuit, I had the pleasure of receiving your favor of the 20th June. . . .

We have been much shocked & grieved here, to learn that the suspicion of Insurrectionary movements among the Blacks were but too true: and that there has been a necessity to resort to measures of severity. I fear this kind of property is fast losing its value on the Sea Coast; for its vicinity to the W.I. Islands, & the great intercourse with them, must introduce among our people many of those who have been engaged in Scenes of blood in the West Indies, who will beguile our Slaves into rebellion with false hopes & idle expectations. We had no indications of any combinations here, tho' the negroes were well apprized of what was passing in Charleston, certainly as soon as we were, if not sooner—

Hamilton & the Council have acted with discretion & firmness, as far as I have learnt; & are entitled to the thanks of the Country— The Court was wisely selected from among the best informed, most reasonable & firm of the Community; men neither to be misled by violent popular rumors, nor deterred from the performance of painful duties, by a false humanity—may God in mercy extinguish this rebellious temper. . . .

I am sorry to see Judge Wm. J. has been drawn into an unpleasant controversy, on the subject of your distressing events. He certainly meant well, but was indiscreet. . . .

Your affecte friend

Henry W. DeSaussure

Honble Joel R. Poinsett, Charleston

MRS. MARTHA PROCTOR RICHARDSON TO HER NEPHEW [4]

Savannah 6th July 1822

My Dear James,

. . . The people of Charleston have been for some time past in aweful commotion. they had received information that an insurection was in contemplation, the 16th July the day fixed on for its com-

---

[3] From the Joel R. Poinsett Papers (Philadelphia: Historical Society of Pennsylvania). Used with permission of the director of the Historical Society of Pennsylvania.

[4] From the Arnold-Screven Papers, Southern Historical Collection (Chapel Hill, N.C.: University of North Carolina Library). Used with permission of the director of the Southern Historical Collection.

mencement—the city was to have been set fire to—in forty different
places—the whites murdered as they left their dwellings—the arsenal
to be seized on—the negroes from the country were then to join them
—and the shipping in the harbour was to be also taken possession of
—this information it is said was given by the coachman of Doctor
Simons—the city council were called together and sat in judgment
on those suspected—Six were condemned & exicuted on the 2d July
—it is said that the leaders in this conspiracy were class leaders of
religious societies—you recollect that in Carolina the blacks are not
allowed to preach in congregations of their own—they *must* associate
with the white people in the different churches—God knows how all
this will end—but I fear such an attempt will one day be made—and of
what consequence will it be to those who are killed by them whether
they succeed or not—Mr Harris has just called   he brought a
letter from Major Hamilton the Intendant of Charleston   I will
copy the part relating to this unfortunate business as it will enable
you to understand it better than I related it—"you may feel some
solicitude to learn something of the late threaten'd insurrection in
this city—a few of the prominent particulars of which I will relate to
you—This plot had its origin among the Black Class leaders of some
of the different religious associations of this city—and altho' its
causes may be in some degree referable to the temporal inconveniences
& suffering unavoidable incident to a state of slavery there are mainly
to be attributed to religious Fanaticism—The ring leaders of the
conspiracy were all of them Class Leaders or Deacons—Six of whom
were yesterday executed, and who met their fate with the heroic forti-
tude of Martyrs—They have been for some time engaged in their
preparations for the explosion, which was to have been consummated
on the night of the 16th—Their plan denoted a fine Military *Tact*
and admirable combination. Their forces were to have been divided
into three columes.—The first and most important was to carry the
main Guard House & Arsenal—this was to have been concentrated at
south Bay & to have been composed of the Male Negroes from James
Island, led by a determined fellow, full of courage & sagacity.—This
body were to have been supplied with arms sufficient to effect their
purpose and were to have formed in the centre of the city a junction
with the two other divisions from the West & North—on which the
Town was to have been fired in Forty different places and the house-
holders murdered at their doors on coming out—This conflagration
was to be a signal to the negroes from the country to flock in & join
their associates in arms in the city.—The discovery of their designs
was made by the fidelity of a favorite slave to his master—We have
been thus far very successful in our developments & have proceeded
with great activity & perseverance—I am happy amidst all this excitement to say to you that no excesses of popular feelings & preju-

dices have disgraced the character of our city—& that a remarkably respectable court has conducted its deliberations with humanity to the accused but with great energy as it regards the public safety—I am sorry to say that our friend judge Johnson has involved himself in an unpleasant controversy with the public authorities & court, by volunteering a very unreasonable & unnecessary admonition by which a great ferment has been excited against him."—In this place every suspicion appears at rest—and I trust there is no cause for alarm—but I am of opinion that the Blacks knew of this business long before it was known by us— . . .

Your affectionate Aunt

M. Richardson

Savannah 7th August 1822—

My Dear James,

. . . Charleston has undergone a dreadful state of things—in my last I gave you an account of what had come to our knowledge of this intended insurrection—it proves to be much more extensive than was at first suspected—Six of the insurgents had suffered when I wrote last—since then, 26 have been hung—and many ordered for transportation out of the limits of the United States—not to return on pain of death—the first court which sat five weeks, had retired from the painful duty—& a new one instituted—they are still going on with trials—The Mail carrier had been fired on in the neighborhood of Parkers ferry by 4 negroes—three of them were executed—we are now fearful some accident has occurred as it is stated in the papers that the mail carrier was persued by 12 armed negroes on Tuesday last, near salt catcher—since wednesday we have had no mail from Charleston, this is sunday—there may be other reasons—such as bad roads—sickness & c but I always dread the worst that may happen—one white man was found aiding & abetting the negroes—he has been a pirate—Judge Johnson has published his vindication but it is very lame—in my poor opinion I should pronounce the writer humbled—at any rate it was too serious a business for jesting—and at his age evinced a degree of levity which takes from the character of a person in his dignified station—we cannot put any other motive on his conduct, than a vanity to appear more wise & resolute than his neighbors—but he should have reflected that strong nerves do not belong to everyone any more than rectitude & dignity of conduct—the negroes too who were first convicted belonged to his Brother in law Bennet—therefore delicacy should have kept him silent—It is impossible for me to give a correct account of the proceedings in Charleston—every thing has been kept a profound secret—for reasons which will occur to every one—still enough has transpired to convince us that they had too much cause for alarm—for four years has this business been in agitation—still so secret were they—and prudent also—that no suspicion from their conduct could be entertained—You may judge of their secrecy by what I am going to relate—two negroes belonging to the same Master—both working in the same mill—were ignorant that either was engaged in the plot until they met in jail—when the constables went into Mr. Horry's yard to take up his waiting man— he assured them they were mistaken, he could answer for his inno- cence—he would as soon suspect himself—he accompanied him on his trial convinced still he could not be guilty—on hearing the evidence—he turned round to his man—tell me, are you guilty? for I cannot believe unless I hear you say so—yes replied the negro— what were your intentions?—to kill you, rip open your belly & throw your guts in your face—It is said they were true warriors—not a single woman knew a word of their plans—In the course of time the whole proceedings will be published—never told—our journals are preferred for an account of the wildest plans engendered by religious enthusiasm and a [w]rong conception of the Bible—so true it is, "a little learning is a dangerous thing"—I am very fearful this business will not rest there, however we may hope it—and dreadful must be the state of our city when all confidence is lost in our servants—it is to be regretted that almost in every instance, the condemned slaves belonged to the most humane & indulgent owners—some plan must be adopted to subdue them—however repugnant to the feelings—their situation when compared with the poor of other countries was certainly happy —they are clothed, fed & taken care of when sick—and I may venture to say the house servants are not half-worked—had they been more employed they would have wanted time to plan mischief—I hope the laws will now force every family to keep but a certain number about them and oblige all useless ones to be sent into the country—Huxters, day labourers, draymen & all that useless class of servants who are only a tax to their owners & a nuisance to the city—. . . . believe me always your affectionate parent

M. Richardson

P.S. I am happy to say that the mails have been detained by the Fish Pond bridge falling in—

Savannah 16th Sept—1822—

My Dear James

. . . The insurrection in Charleston (the intended one I should have said) has been happily terminated—I will give you an extract from a letter I received last week from Mr Desaussure   "I receive Dear Madam your kind congratulations at the successful termination of the recent disturbances in Charleston with much sensibility—The hand of providence was singularly visible in the discovery & develop- ment of the plot, & our gratitude should be commensurate with it—

I do not think that the object could have been accomplished to any save a very limited extent, but probably many valuable lives would have been sacrificed before order was re-established—our examples have been written in Blood, but policy & perhaps humanity rendered them indispensible—& will perhaps deter similar efforts for 20 or 30 years"—32 of the poor wreches were hung & some shipt for Africa— The trials have been published in a small pamphlet which I have read—it is a history of the wildest plans—engendered by superstition and ignorance—most of the ringleaders were of the Gullah tribe mechanic's and draymen—of the Methodist religion—you may hear that an attempt has been in agitation here—but it is without foundation—some few have been tried for an attempt to poison their Master —Flourinoy—but they have not as yet been sentenced or it is supposed the evidence will be sufficient [sic] to criminate them. . . .

your affectionate parent
M. Richardson

JOEL R. POINSETT TO JAMES MONROE [5]

Charleston 13 th Augt. 1822

Dear Sir

. . . Our City is again restored to order and tranquillity and the trials of the miserable deluded conspirators are over. The discussion of the Missouri question at Washington, among other evils, produced this plot. It was considered by this unfortunate half instructed people as one of emancipation. . . .

With sincere regard and the highest
respect, I am dear sir, Yours
J. R. Poinsett

WILLIAM JOHNSON TO THOMAS JEFFERSON [6]

Charleston, Dec. 10, 1822

My dear Sir. . . .

I have now passed my half-century, and begin to feel lonely among the men of the present day. And I am sorry to tell you, particularly so in this place. This last summer has furnished but too much cause for shame and anguish. I have lived to see what I really never believed it possible I should see,—courts held with closed doors, and men dying by scores who had never seen the faces nor heard the voices of their accusers. I see that your governor has noticed the alarm of insurrection

[5] From the James Monroe Papers (Washington, D.C.: Library of Congress).
[6] From the Thomas Jefferson Papers (Washington, D.C.: Library of Congress). Quoted in Donald G. Morgan, *Justice William Johnson, The First Dissenter* (Columbia, S.C.: University of South Carolina Press, 1954), p. 138.

which prevailed in this place some months since. But be assured it was nothing in comparison with what it was magnified to. But you know the best way in the world to make them tractable is to frighten them to death; and to magnify danger is to magnify the claims of those who arrest it. Incalculable are the evils which have resulted from the exaggerated accounts circulated respecting that affair. Our property is reduced to nothing—strangers are alarmed at coming near us; our slaves rendered uneasy; the confidence between us and our domestics destroyed—and all this because of a trifling cabal of a few ignorant pennyless unarmed uncombined fanatics, and which certainly would have blown over without an explosion had it never come to light.

When the Court of Magistrates and Freeholders who tried the slaves implicated, were pursuing that course of sitting in conclave and convicting them upon the secret ex parte examination of slaves without oath, whose names were not I believe revealed even to the owners of the accused, the governor, whose feeling revolted at this unprecedented & I say, illegal mode of trial, consulted the attorney general . . . on the legality of their proceedings, and you will be astonished to hear that he gave a direct opinion in favour of it. If such be the law of this country, this shall not long be my country. But I will first endeavour to correct the evil.

Yr friend
Wm. Johnson

WILLIAM JOHNSON TO SECRETARY OF STATE JOHN QUINCY ADAMS [7]

Charleston, July 3, 1824

. . . I do not hesitate to express the opinion, that the whole of the alarm of 1822 was founded in causes that were infinitely exaggerated. A few timid and precipitate men managed to disseminate their fears and their feelings, and you know that popular panics spread with the expansive force of vapor.

I remain,
William Johnson

[7] From *House Reports,* No. 80, 27th Cong., 3rd sess., 1843, pp. 14–15.

5

Southern and Northern Newspapers Editorialize on the Conspiracy

Southern newspapers suppressed news of the conspiracy for several weeks, and then only gave notice of the number of rebels executed. Soon, northern editors began to speculate as to what was transpiring in Charleston. Many northern newspapers accepted or approved of the punishments meted out to the conspirators, but others questioned the severity of the retribution. At least one New York paper condemned slavery in broad, humanitarian terms, and denounced the "bloody sacrifice" of the rebel leaders.

As they came under criticism South Carolina newspapers defended the "humanity, justice, and wisdom" of the trials, requested God's blessings, and reminded Northerners of their own severe repression of slave revolts in the past. In addition, Carolinians pointed to the poor treatment of free blacks in the North, and held the Missouri debates and the Haitian Revolution responsible for the unrest in the South. Neither side seemed willing to compromise, as the sectional conflict implicit in the editorial debates began to surface.

BALTIMORE, *NILES' WEEKLY REGISTER*, VOL. 22 (JULY 13, 1822) 320

The design [in South Carolina] appears to have been a pretty formidable one. Three of them (the blacks) were slaves of the governor of the state, and one of these was to have had his daughter, a beautiful young lady, as part of his share of the spoils on the destruction of her father and the whites.

NEW YORK *NATIONAL ADVOCATE*, QUOTED IN THE WASHINGTON, D.C., *NATIONAL INTELLIGENCER*, JULY 20, 1822

This is a rigid but necessary punishment. The safety of families, from plots thus formed, requires the strong arm of authority. Misguided persons, thus plotting the work of murder and conflagration, may give a fatal blow to a portion of our country. Whatever we may think of slavery, it is not to be denied that the domestics in the South work less and live better than many poor free white men of the north. They are a lazy pampered race, and if they meditate murder when thus indulged they must suffer for it.

CHARLESTON *MERCURY,* JULY 29, 1822

The Court adjourned, *sine die,* on Friday, having no further business before them.—They have deserved and they receive the grateful thanks of their fellow citizens for their labours. Their humanity has equalled their justice, and their perseverance was not exceeded by their wisdom. Patient, inquiring and firm in the fulfilment of the duties that have devolved upon them, they have discharged their high trust in the spirit of enlightened gentlemen and conscientious Christians. The stream of justice would never be polluted if it always flowed in the channel to which it would be directed by such a tribunal.

The public spirit and well directed zeal of the Intendant and Council, during the late agitation, call likewise for the thanks of the community. After a whole month's incessant vigilance, they at length have reached a period of comparative repose. May the sweets of their labours be found in the satisfaction that exertions like theirs, happily but seldom required, have secured the safety of the city, and the lasting gratitude of its inhabitants!

NEW YORK *DAILY ADVERTISER,* JULY 31, 1822

Insurrection Among the Blacks

. . . It ought to excite no astonishment with those who boast of freedom themselves, if they should occasionally hear of plots and desertion among those who are held in perpetual bondage. Human beings, who once breathed the air of freedom on their own mountains and in their own valleys, but who have been kidnapped by white men and dragged into endless slavery, cannot be expected to be contented with their situation. White men, too, would engender plots and escape from their imprisonment were they situated as are these miserable children of Africa.

AUGUST 5, 1822

The Bloody Sacrifice

. . . Twenty-two human beings, blacks, were executed at Charleston on the morning of the 26th ult.

AUGUST 6, 1822

Insurrection at Charleston

. . . As yet nothing has appeared that has met our view to justify the great sacrifice of human lives that has taken place. . . . How many more of these miserable wretches are to pay the forfeit of their lives for an attempt to free themselves from bondage we are yet to learn. How far the destruction of so many lives as have already been taken can be justified in the eyes of a christian world, if it can be justified at all, must depend upon what is hereafter to be disclosed. Certain it is that neither the spirit nor letter of the law under which these executions have taken place, sanctions the enormous sacrifice.

CHARLESTON *COURIER,* AUGUST 12, 1822

We are happy to state that the tranquillity of the city is now restored. The legal investigations of crime have ceased. The melancholy requisitions of Justice, as painful to those who inflicted, as to those who suffered them, have been complied with; and an awful but a necessary, and, it is hoped, an effectual example has been afforded to deter from further occasions of offence and punishment.

We have not been inattentive, in this distressing period, to the notice which might be taken of our situation by the journals in our sister states. It is grateful in the extreme to mark the tenderness and sympathy which, with the exception of one solitary print in New-York, have been universally manifested towards us. We are not in a state of mind to use language of acrimonious asperity. We regard with pity the individual who could deliberately sneer at our misfortunes—we leave him to the consolations of his conscience—his nightly dreams on his pillow—and hope he may always enjoy that security, which he so much rejoices that our city has been deprived of.

Yet, as an historical fact, worthy to be remembered, particularly at this time, and which Mr. STONE, of the N. York *Commercial Advertiser,* appears to have forgotten, we would remind him, as we had occasion once before to remind another editor of New-York, that in the year 1741, in the city of New-York, *thirteen Negroes were* BURNT ALIVE *for insurrectionary efforts.*

During the whole of this momentous inquiry, the utmost confidence has been felt in the State and City authorities, and in the two successive Courts organized to award justice, and acting under the most painful responsibilities. The Militia have with alacrity performed the unusual and laborious duties assigned them;—and now let us hope that the God of goodness and of mercy, who has guarded and protected us in the hour of peril, will continue to us his benevolent care, and frustrate always the evil designs of our enemies, and of those who conspire alike against our happiness and their own.

CHARLESTON *CITY GAZETTE*, AUGUST 14, 1822

In the opinion of the community of Charleston . . . the *Blue-light* editor of *The New York Daily Advertiser* might invent some other way of edifying his readers than in groaning over the execution of a score of Culprits upon whose fate Justice and Humanity alike pronounced the sentence. The "bloody sacrifice" of which he so insolently speaks, might have been prevented by a few peace offerings of such lambs as he and his faction can produce.

They talk of philanthropy, but the Missouri poison is still garnered in their bosoms; and although they may never have dreamed of the awful consequences of the wild and foolish doctrines which have gone abroad—they begin already to feel in New York, Philadelphia, and Boston, how very agreeable is the extension of the rights of Citizenship to those whom they pretend to regard as equals. We say pretend, for the Blacks in those cities are neither citizens nor aliens. There are few or no places where they are admitted to amusements or instruction; little or no moral education by which they can be rendered virtuous members of society; little or no interest in their spiritual happiness; no master or patron by whom they are protected, as was the case of the Freedman in ancient Rome, and as is frequently exhibited in South Carolina.

BOSTON *EVENING GAZETTE*, QUOTED IN THE CHARLESTON *MERCURY*, AUGUST 26, 1822

Strictly speaking, nobody can blame the servile part of the population (the blacks) for attempting to escape from bondage, however their delusion may be regretted.

CAMDEN, N.J., *STAR*, QUOTED IN *IBID*.

We by no means would be understood to justify ANY attempts in slaves to regain their liberty in any other mode than by manumission. We warn them of the awful consequences inseparably connected with an enterprise which would in all probability produce a war of extermination against them in this country, or at least be the means of rivetting the galling fetters ten-fold more firmly on the unhappy captives. If ever their emancipation be effected, it must be through the Divine agency of the light of reason, not by the sword, bloodshed, and rapine.

WASHINGTON, D.C., *NATIONAL INTELLIGENCER*, AUGUST 31, 1822

We are sorry to see that a discussion of the hateful "Missouri question" is likely to be revived, in consequence of the allusion to its supposed effect in promoting the servile insurrection in South Carolina. In a spirit of amity to all parties, we venture to recommend that it be suffered to sleep. It appears to us, that the fact disclosed from Charleston, could not well have been suppressed, though the *name* might and perhaps should have been, and that the disclosure of the fact ought not to be offensive. No one ever supposed, nor have the public authorities or prints of Charleston most remotely suggested, that the speeches in Congress were *intended* to produce such an effect. We cannot therefore see any cause for irritation on either side; whilst we see on all hands powerful reasons for avoiding further controversy on the subject.

COLUMBIA, *SOUTH CAROLINA STATE GAZETTE*, SEPTEMBER 7, 1822

We are sincerely averse to mentioning the name of Mr. King, [antislavery Congressman from New York] as connected with this affair; but as the Bible has been profaned in the service of guilt, where is there anything improbable, or even remarkable in the fact that extracts of speeches on the Missouri question were calculated to promote Insurrection. "The Devil can quote scripture"—and propositions about liberty and equality (particularly when made to bear upon a particular class) suited exactly the ends of those who grasped at the brightest names, and even tore the inspiration page, to sanction deeds of darkness. . . .

CHARLESTON *CITY GAZETTE*, SEPTEMBER 20, 1822

When we think of the murder and violence and destruction of property which those deluded wretches might have committed, we cannot but be grateful to the Negro who gave the information. We do not doubt but his reward will be commensurated to the services he rendered, while we shudder at the scenes which might have been acted, and contemplate its origin and progress in a society, we cannot but hope that our Southern fellow citizens will hereafter be permitted to manage their own concerns in their own way. They have as much humanity and intellect, and more experience on this subject, than the people of the non-slave holding states can be supposed to have.

SALEM, MASS., *GAZETTE*, JANUARY 10, 1823

While slavery exists, the fearful apprehension of massacre and Insurrection will be inevitable; and for the causes of which our brethren need not look to the North, but nearer home, at their door. The household slaves, who are numerous, are treated with kindness and familiarity, and from their association acquire much knowledge, and of course a relish for the sweets of liberty, and an abhorrence for their servile condition. Some of them are intelligent, as well as enterprising and fearless . . . In a free community the slaves are bound to imbibe notions of liberty. From the household slaves the contagion of liberty is spread to the plantations . . . Unless the masters seal up the avenues of knowledge among the blacks, unless they close their eyes that they see not, and stop their ears that they hear not, they certainly will be prone to fancy that liberty is a blessing worth the hazard of their lives to obtain.

6

Governor Bennett Explains the Circumstances of the Conspiracy

Throughout June, July, and much of August, 1822, neither South Carolinians nor American citizens generally had received any official word on the nature of the slave conspiracy or the trial proceedings. Finally, on August 10, apparently in order to dispel false rumors which continued to circulate, Governor Thomas Bennett issued the following letter in the form of a printed circular for general distribution to the press. It was reprinted by the Washington, D.C., National Intelligencer *on August 24 and by* Niles' Weekly Register *on September 7. Bennett's disagreements with the court's procedures and his doubts over the extent of the plot are revealed in his unprinted Message No. 2 to the state legislature, November 28, 1822, in the South Carolina Department of Archives and History, Columbia.*

Executive Department, *Charleston, August 10, 1822.*

SIR: After a prolonged and almost uninterrupted session of six weeks, the first court organized for the trial of slaves charged with an attempt to raise an insurrection in this city, was dissolved on the 20th ult. Another court was subsequently convened, and, after a session of three days, closed the unpleasant investigation with which it was charged, and adjourned on the 8th instant, *sine die.*

During the interesting period occupied by the court first organized, the public mind was agitated by a variety of rumors, calculated to produce great excitement and alarm. These had their origin in the nature of the transaction, and the secrecy and seclusion observed in the incipient stages of the inquiry; as but few of the circumstances were known to the community, and the number apprehended and sentenced to the severest punishment, beyond any former example. Certainty gave place to exaggeration, and the general impression sustained the rumor of a very extensive conspiracy.

The effects resulting from these reports, if uncontrolled by an exhibition of facts, are too obvious to require comment. The reputation of the state must suffer abroad, and a rapid deterioration of property occur within; while suspicion and anxiety will continue long to mar the public tranquility. It becomes, therefore, a duty imperiously obligatory on me, to represent the occurrences as they have transpired, and thus evidence to you that the attempt has not only been greatly magnified, but as soon as discovered it ceased to be dangerous. . . .

Having established the existence of a plot, and the places of rendezvous, all that was deemed requisite for conviction was to prove an association with the ringleaders, and an expression of their assent to the measure. On such, generally, the sentence of death has been executed. Others who, without actually combining, were proved to have known of the conspiracy, and to have given their sanction by any act, have been sentenced to die, and their punishment commuted to banishment from the United States; or sentenced, in the first instance to banishment from this state or from the United States. In this manner, the whole number, seventy-two, have been disposed of; thirty-five executed, and thirty-seven sentenced to banishment. With these we may reasonably conclude that we have reached the extremities of this conspiracy, and this opinion, if not conclusive, is entitled to great weight, when we advert to the extraordinary measures pursued to effect the object and the motives which influenced the accused.

No means which experience or ingenuity could devise were left unessayed, to eviscerate the plot. In the labors of investigation, the court was preceded by a committee formed by the city council, whose intelligence, activity, and zeal, were well adapted to the arduous duties of their appointment. Their assiduity, aided by the various sentiments which influenced the prisoners, produced a rapid development of the plot. Several of the conspirators had entered into solemn pledges to partake of a common destiny, and one, at least, was found, who, after his arrest, felt no repugnance to enforce the obligation, by surrendering the names of his associates. A spirit of retaliation and revenge produced a similar effect with others, who suspected that they were the victims of treachery; and this principle operated with full effect, as the hope or expectation of pardon predominated. To the last hour of the existence of several, who appeared to be conspicuous actors in this drama, they were pressingly importuned to make further confessions. . . .

From such means and such sources of information, it cannot be doubted that all who were actually concerned, have been brought to justice. There is no exception within my knowledge; it has, however, been stated, that a plantation in St. John's was infected, but I do not know on what authority.

This plain detail of the principal incidents in this transaction, will satisfy you that the scheme has not been general nor alarmingly extensive. And it furnishes a cause for much satisfaction, that, although religion, superstition, fear, and almost every passion that sways the human mind, have been artfully used by the wicked instigators of this design, so few have been seduced from a course of propriety and obedience. Those who associated were unprovided with the means of attack or resistance. No weapons (if we except thirteen hoop-poles) have been discovered; nor any testimony received but of six pikes, that such preparations were actually made. The witnesses generally agree in one fact, that the attempt was to have taken place on Sunday night the 16th June, differing a little as to the precise time; 12 o'clock appears to have been the hour.

From the various conflicting statements made during the trials, it is difficult to form a plausible conjecture of their ultimate plans of opperation; no two agreeing on general definite principles. That the first essay would be made with clubs against the state arsinal is inferrible, from their being unprovided with arms, and the concurrence of several witnesses. But whether the attack would be made simultaneously by various detachments, or whether the whole, embodied at a particular spot, would proceed to the accomplishment of their object, is very uncertain. Upon the whole, it is manifest that if any plan had been organized, it was never communicated by the principal conspirator to the leaders or the men, as they were wholly ignorant even of the places of rendezvous; although within two days of the time appointed, and but one man arrested prior to the day fixed on for the attempt.

When we contrast the numbers engaged with the magnitude of the enterprize, the imputation of egregious folly or madness is irresistible: and supposing the attempt to have been predicated on the probability, that partial success would augment their numbers, the utmost presumption would scarcely have hazarded the result. Servility long continued, debases the mind and abstracts it from that energy of character, which is fitted to great exploits. It cannot be supposed, therefore, without a violation of the immutable laws of nature, that a transition from slavery and degradation to authority and power, could instantly occur. Great and general excitement may produce extensive and alarming effects; but the various passions which operate with powerful effect on this class of persons, impart a confident assurance of detection and defeat to every similar design. While the event is remote, they may listen with credulity to the artful tale of the instigator, and concur in its plausibility; but the approach of danger will invariably produce treachery, the concomitant of dastardly dispositions. In the fidelity and attachment of a numerous class of these persons, we have other sources of security and early information; from both of which, it is reasonable to conclude, that, in proportion to the number engaged, will be the certainty of detection; and that an extensive conspiracy cannot be matured in this state.

I have entered with much reluctance on this detail, nor would it have been considered requisite, but to counteract the number of gross and idle reports, actively and extensively circulated, and producing a general anxiety and alarm. And, although their authors may have no evil design, and may really be under the delusion, it is easy to perceive what pernicious consequences may ensue from not applying the proper corrective. Every individual in the state is interested, whether in relation to his own property, or the reputation of the state, in giving no more importance to the transaction than it justly merits. The legislature has wisely provided the means of efficient protection. If the citizens will faithfully perform the duty enjoined on them by the patrol laws, I fear not that we shall continue in the enjoyment of as much tranquility and safety as any state in the union.

I have the honor to be, very respectfully, sir, your obedient servant,

THO. BENNETT.

7

Statement by the Mayor of Charleston

On August 13, the Charleston City Council resolved "that the Intendant be requested to prepare for publication, an account of the late intended Insurrection in this City, with a Statement of the Trials and such other facts in connexion with the same as may be deemed of public interest." Consequently, on August 16, James Hamilton, Jr. (who was soon elected to the United States Congress, 1822–29 and then served as the nullificationist governor, 1830–33), issued a forty-seven page report.[1] Including a brief narrative of events and extracts from the court record, the report began with the following statement "To the Public," which was indicative of the intense emotional feelings still current after the trials:

In complying with the objects of the above Resolution, I have not been insensible to the difficulties and embarrassments necessarily incident to the subject, as to what it might be politic either to publish or suppress. With the advice, however, of the Corporation, I have deemed a full publication of the prominent circumstances of the late commotion the most judicious course, as suppression might assume the appearance of timidity or injustice. Whilst such a Statement is due to the character of our community, and justification of our laws, there can be no harm in the salutary inculcation of one lesson, among a *certain* portion of our population, that there is nothing they are bad enough to do, that we are not powerful enough to punish. . . .

These trials, together with some private arrangements, made with their owners, in reference to the banishment of several slaves, in cases where their guilt was clear, but not of the first degree, have at length closed the anxious and irksome labours of the corporation, after an examination of little less than two months.

It will be seen . . . that one hundred and thirty-one were com-

---

[1] From James Hamilton, Jr., Intendant, *An Account of the Late Intended Insurrection Among A Portion of the Blacks of This City.* . . . (Charleston, S.C.: A. E. Miller, 1822).

mitted; thirty-five have suffered death, and thirty-seven have been sentenced to banishment. The most important object to be obtained in uprooting a conspiracy, we have fully accomplished, by bringing to punishment the whole of the ringleaders. . . .

We, moreover, believe, that all who were active agents (though not ringleaders) in the conspiracy, have expiated their crimes, or are about to do so, by an eternal exile from our shores. It may be mentioned, in confirmation of this belief, that Monday Gell, from memory, made out a list of forty-two names, of those who were in the habit of visiting his shop, for the purpose of combining and confederating in the intended insurrection, whom he called his company; every one of whom have been apprehended, and disposed of. We cannot venture to say, to how many the knowledge of the intended effort, was communicated, who, without signifying their assent, or attending any of the meetings, were yet prepared to profit by events. That there are many who would not have permitted the enterprize to have failed at a *critical moment,* for the want of their co-operation, we have the best reasons for believing.

Before we conclude, some notice of the probable causes of this conspiracy may be expected. As this is a matter of speculation, we shall not speak without reserve. Of the motives of Vesey, we cannot sit in judgment; they have been scanned by a power who can do higher justice than ourselves. But as they are explained by his character and conduct, during the combinations of the plot, they are only to be referred to a malignant hatred of the whites, and inordinate lust of power and booty. Indeed, the belief is altogether justifiable, that his end would have been answered, if, after laying our city in ashes, and moistening its cinders with blood, he could have embarked with a part of the pillage of our banks for San Domingo; leaving a large proportion of his deluded followers to the exterminating desolation of that justice, which would have awaited, in the end, a transient success. His followers were slaves, and for them it would not be so difficult to assign a motive, if it had not been distinctly proved, that without scarcely an exception, they had no individual hardship to complain of, and were among the most humanely treated negroes in our city. The facilities for combining and confederating in such a scheme, were amply afforded, by the extreme indulgence and kindness, which characterises the domestic treatment of our slaves. Many slave owners among us, not satisfied with ministering to the wants of their domestics, by all the comforts of abundant food, and excellent clothing, with a misguided benevolence, have not only permitted their instruction, but lent to such efforts their approbation and applause.

Religious fanaticism has not been without its effect on this project, and as auxilliary to these sentiments, the secession of a large body of blacks from the white Methodist Church, with feelings of irritation and disappointment, formed a hot-bed, in which the germ might well be expected to spring into life and vigour. Among the conspirators *a majority* of them belonged to the *African Church*,[2] and among those executed were several who had been Class Leaders. It is, however, due to the late head of their church (for since the late events the association has been voluntarily dissolved) and their deacons, to say, that after the most diligent search and scrutiny, no evidence entitled to belief, has been discovered against them. A hearsay rumour, in relation to *Morris Brown,* was traced far enough to end in its complete falsification.

That the course which certain discussions assumed in Congress were likewise efficacious in producing both discontent and delusion, is sufficiently apparent. Jack Purcell's confession . . . will show to what a purpose Vesey applied those beautiful propositions of civil and natural freedom, which were sported with a wanton recklessness of their consequences, as applied to the condition of a certain portion of our common country.

It is consoling to every individual, who is proud of the character of his country, in the late unhappy events, to be able to say, that, within the limits of the City of Charleston, in a period of great and unprecedented excitement, the laws, without even one violation, have ruled with uninterrupted sway—that no cruel vindictive or barbarous modes of punishment have been resorted to—that justice has been blended with an enlightened humanity, in according to those who had meted out for us murder, rapine and conflagration, in their most savage forms—trials, which, for the wisdom, impartiality and moderation that governed them, are even superior to those which the ordinary modes of judicature would have afforded ourselves.

With little to fear, and nothing to reproach ourselves we may, without shrinking, submit our conduct to the award of posterity, and ourselves to the protection of the Supreme Ruler of Events.

[2] An appellation, the seceders assumed after their leaving the white Methodist Church.

8

The Court Releases Its Explanation of the Causes of the Plot

As a preface to the trial record, Kennedy and Parker's Official Report *contained the following "Narrative of the Conspiracy and Intended Insurrection Amongst a Portion of the Negroes in the State of South-Carolina, in the Year 1822." [1] Published on October 22, it was designed to explain in greater detail what Governor Bennett and Intendant Hamilton had previously only outlined.*

Thomas Wentworth Higginson—the militant white abolitionist who supported John Brown's Raid and led black troops during the Civil War—based his sketch of the Vesey affair in the Atlantic Monthly *for June, 1861, on this document. Higginson declared the narrative to be "candid and lucid," and by and large historians have not successfully disputed this official story of the insurrectionary events. However, the racist premises, anti-rebel biases, and historical context during which the narrative was written should be taken into account.*

At the head of this conspiracy stood Denmark Vesey, a free negro; with him the idea undoubtedly originated. For several years before he disclosed his intentions to any one, he appears to have been constantly and assiduously engaged in endeavoring to embitter the minds of the colored population against the white. He rendered himself perfectly familiar with all those parts of the Scriptures, which he thought he could pervert to his purpose; and would readily quote them, to prove that slavery was contrary to the laws of God; that slaves were bound to attempt their emancipation, however shocking and bloody might be the consequences, and that such efforts would not only be pleasing to the Almighty, but were absolutely enjoined, and their success predicted in the Scriptures. His favorite texts when

[1] From L. H. Kennedy and T. Parker, *An Official Report of the Trials of Sundry Negroes Charged with an Attempt to Raise an Insurrection in the State of South-Carolina* (Charleston, 1822), pp. 17–60.

he addressed his own color were, "Zechariah, chapter 14th, verses 1, 2 and 3,[2] and Joshua, chapter 4th, verse 21 [3]; and in all his conversations he identified their situation with that of the Israelites. The number of inflammatory pamphlets on slavery brought into Charleston from some of our sister states, within the last four years,[4] (and once from Siera Leone) and distributed amongst the colored population of the city, for which there was a great facility, in consequence of the unrestricted intercourse allowed to persons of color between the different States in the Union; and the speeches in Congress of those opposed to the admission of Missouri into the Union, perhaps garbled and misrepresented, furnished him with ample means for inflaming the minds of the colored population of this state; and by distorting certain parts of those speeches, or selecting from them particular passages, he persuaded but too many that Congress had actually declared them free, and that they were held in bondage contrary to the laws of the land. Even whilst walking through the streets in company with another, he was not idle; for if his companion bowed to a white person he would rebuke him, and observe that all men were born equal, and that he was surprised that any one would degrade himself by such conduct; that he would never cringe to the whites, nor ought any one who had the feelings of a man. When answered, We are slaves, he would sarcastically and indignantly reply, "You deserve to remain slaves"; and if he were further asked, What can we do, he would remark, "Go and buy a spelling book and read the fable of Hercules and the Waggoner"; which he would then repeat, and apply it to their situation. He also sought every opportunity of entering into conversation with white persons when they could be overheard by negroes near by, especially in grog-shops; during which conversation he would artfully introduce some bold remark on slavery; and sometimes, when from the character he was conversing with he

[2] "Behold the day of the Lord cometh, and thy spoil shall be divided in the midst of thee. For I will gather all nations against Jerusalem to battle; and the city shall be taken, and the women ravished; and half of the city shall go forth into captivity; and the residue of the people shall not be cut off from the city. Then shall the Lord go forth, and fight against those nations, as when he fought in the day of battle."

[3] "And they utterly destroyed all that was in the city, both man and woman, young and old, and ox, and sheep, and ass, with the edge of the sword."

[4] As far back as the year 1809, several hundred pamphlets of an insurrectionary character were brought to Charleston, in the ship Minerva, from New-York, by her steward, who was a black man. A citizen of Charleston, a passenger on board, immediately on her arrival informed the Intendant of the circumstance, who promptly repaired, with the City Marshal, to the vessel; but did not arrive there in time to seize them before they were landed. The Steward was, however, committed to prison for trial, and a few of the pamphlets having been procured, he would have been tried for his life had he not entered into an arrangement with the civil authorities of the city to leave the state, never to return therein; and what is a little remarkable, his counsel on that occasion was one of the presiding magistrates of the late court.

found he might be still bolder, he would go so far, that had not his declarations in such situations been clearly proved, they would scarcely have been credited. He continued this course, until sometime after the commencement of the last winter; by which time he had not only obtained incredible influence amongst persons of color, but many feared him more than their owners, and one of them declared, even more than his God.

At this period he sounded Rolla and Ned, two slaves of his Excellency Thomas Bennett, and finding them ready to acquiesce in his schemes, he made the same proposals to Jack, belonging to Mrs. Purcell, and Peter, belonging to Mr. Poyas, who also consented with equal promptness. These men were his first four associates; three of whom, viz: Rolla, Ned and Peter, immediately became his most active agents. Some time after Christmas he was also joined by Gullah Jack, belonging to Mr. Pritchard, and subsequently by Monday, belonging to Mr. Gell; who soon proved themselves to be as fit men for his purpose, and as active as Rolla, Ned and Peter.—These constituted his five principal officers, by whose means, aided by some others whom he employed to go about and travel the country adjacent to Charleston, and amongst the latter of whom the principal agents were Lot Forrester and Frank Ferguson, he engaged great numbers to join in the intended insurrection. He also at his house held nocturnal meetings, for the purpose of interchanging opinions, maturing the plan, collecting and giving information, &c.; at which meetings numbers of the insurgents, both from country and town attended; and where collections were made for the purpose of providing arms, ammunition, &c. and for defraying such expences as might be indispensibly necessary. He also attended meetings at other places appointed by him; at one place in particular on Charleston Neck, about two miles and a half from the city. Besides his five principal officers already mentioned, he had other recruiting agents, though on a smaller scale, amongst whom were William Palmer, Wm. Garner, Charles Drayton and Peirault Strohecker. In order to induce the colored population to join them, every principle which could operate upon the mind of man was artfully employed: Religion, Hope, Fear, Deception, were resorted to as occasion required. All were told, and many believed, that God approved of their designs; those whose fears would have restrained them, were forced to yield by threats of death; those whose prudence and foresight induced them to pause, were cheered with the assurance that assistance from St. Domingo and Africa were at hand; whilst those upon whom none of these principles operated, were excited from despair on being informed, that the whites, perceiving they were becoming too numerous, had resolved to create a false alarm of fire, and as they came out in the dead of the night to kill them, in order to thin their numbers. And strange as it may appear, yet vast numbers of the Africans firmly believed that Gullah Jack was a sorcerer; that he could neither be killed nor taken; and that whilst they retained the charms which he had distributed they would themselves be invulnerable. Add to all this, their belief that Congress had emancipated them, and we may readily credit the declaration of Monday Gell and Perault, that they never spoke to any person of color on the subject, or knew of any one who had been spoken to by the other leaders, who had withheld his assent. Vesey being a free man encountered none of those obstacles which would have been in the way of a slave; his time was at his own disposal, and he could go wherever he pleased, without interruption; qualifications and advantages absolutely necessary for the Chief in a Conspiracy, and which enabled him to travel so much about the country as he did.

On perusing the testimony, the declaration of one or two of the witnesses that this plot had been in agitation for four years will strike the observation of every one; but it must not be supposed therefrom, that recruiting or enlisting had been progressing for that time; or that, for that time there existed any direct proposal from Vesey or any one else for such a measure. Such was not the case. No active measures were taken until near last Christmas. In speaking of this attempt being in agitation for four years, allusion was had to Vesey's conduct and language during that time; and to the dissatisfaction which appeared since, to exist amongst the coloured population. This was about the time that the African congregation, (so called from its being composed wholly of persons of colour and almost entirely of blacks,) was formed, and their Church built in Hampstead [5]; of which Vesey had been a member, and of which his principal associates, Gullah Jack, Monday, Ned and Peter, were also members; and the two last, were class leaders. It was also about this time, that class meetings of the coloured people had become so common as they now are; each class having a coloured preacher or leader as they were termed, named by the Minister of the Church to which he belonged; at which meetings, held usually at night in some retired building, avowedly for religious instruction and worship, no white person attended. That inflamatory and insurrectionary doctrines, without any direct proposal for such an attempt, were inculcated at these meetings or some of them, was positively proved; and further, that they were to be used as places of rendezvous and rallying points, for communicating to all, the exact night and hour, on which the first blow was to be struck. The great impropriety of allowing meetings of any kind to be held solely by slaves, and at such times and places, must forcibly strike every reflecting mind. The African congregation above mentioned was not only composed altogether of coloured persons, but their Ministers were also coloured; and were stated to have been regularly ordained Bishops and Ministers of the Gospel. The influence which such men and class leaders must necessarily acquire

[5] A part of the suburbs of Charleston.

over the minds of the ignorant blacks is evident; and if a disposition exists in them to obtain for their own colour and themselves, the freedom and privileges enjoyed by the whites, by enlisting into their cause perverted religion and fanaticism, that desperation is kindled in their hearers, the consequences of which are but too well known. Is it to be wondered at that, under all the foregoing circumstances, an attempt to create an insurrection should be contemplated!

Vesey perceiving that so far every thing had answered his most sanguine expectations, himself in possession of vast influence over his own colour, and their minds poisoned and embitterred against the white population, began about Christmas 1821, to probe those whom he had selected as leaders; and found as he expected a ready acquiescence in his measures by all of them except Monday Gell, who wavered for some time before he joined. In the selection of his leaders, Vesey shewed great penetration and sound judgment. Rolla was plausible, and possessed uncommon self-possession; bold and ardent, he was not to be deterred from his purpose by danger. Ned's appearance indicated, that he was a man of firm nerves, and desperate courage. Peter was intrepid and resolute, true to his engagements, and cautious in observing secrecy where it was necessary; he was not to be daunted nor impeded by difficulties, and though confident of success, was careful in providing against any obstacles or casualties which might arise, and intent upon discovering every means which might be in their power if thought of before hand. Gullah Jack was regarded as a Sorcerer, and as such feared by the natives of Africa, who believe in witchcraft. He was not only considered invulnerable, but that he could make others so by his charms; and that he could and certainly would provide all his followers with arms. He was artful, cruel, bloody; his disposition in short was diabolical. His influence amongst the Africans was inconceiveable. Monday was firm, resolute, discreet and intelligent.

With these men as his principal officers, amongst whom Peter and Monday was certainly the most active, Vesey began to seduce others at the commencement of the present year. Peter and Monday (and probably the other leaders) kept lists of those who had joined their company or band. As Monday did not join until the business of enlisting had considerably progressed, and proceeded very prudently himself, he had but few on his list, according to his own confession only forty-two; but Peter who had consented as soon as spoken to, and was bold and active in his exertions, had six hundred names on his list; whom he had engaged in Charleston, from that division of the city in which he resided, which was South-Bay. Peter also had in his possession another list of names, or as the witness afterwards explained himself, a memorandum of the whole number engaged, and who amounted as the witness was told to nine thousand, partly from the country and partly from the city. It is true that the witness who made these assertions did not see the lists himself; but he heard it from one who was in daily communication with Peter, and who was then endeavouring, and succeeded in inducing the witness to join; and as Peter wrote a good hand and was active throughout the whole affair, it is impossible to doubt but that he had such lists; but whether the numbers mentioned were really engaged or not, there is no mode of ascertaining; and it is more than probable that they were greatly exaggerated, and perhaps designedly so. That Peter was engaged in enlisting, was positively proved; but so scrupulously and resolutely to the last did he observe his pledge of secrecy to his associates, *that of the whole number arrested and tried, not one of them belonged to Peter's company.* Monday acknowledged that he had kept a list, but had he not become state's evidence, but had died without disclosing as Peter did, as well might we have doubted that *he kept a list.* In the course of the trials it was also stated, that Vesey had a variety of papers and books relating to this transaction, *which he burnt when the discovery of the intended attempt was made.* Monday also burnt his list, *and probably so did Peter at the same time.*

As these leaders only communicated to each other the numbers, and not the names of those whom they had engaged, and who constituted their company; and as with the exception of Monday, none of them betrayed their associates; the companies of Vesey, Peter, Ned, Rolla and Gullah Jack have escaped detection and punishment; with the exception *of a few of Gullah Jack's band,* who were discovered in consequence of one of his men betraying such of his companions as he knew, together with his leader.

In enlisting men the great caution observed by the leaders was remarkable. Few if any domestic servants were spoken to, as *they* were distrusted; and all who were consulted were told, that death would certainly await them if they informed; and Peter whilst he urged one of his agents to speak to others and solicit them to join, at the same time gave him this charge, "but take care and don't mention it to those waiting men who receive presents of old coats, &c. from their masters, or they'll betray us; *I will speak to them.*" The enlistments appear to have been principally confined to Negroes hired or working out, such as Carters, Draymen, Sawyers, Porters, Labourers, Stevidores, Mechanics, those employed in lumber yards, and in short to those who had certain allotted hours at their own disposal, and to the neighbouring country negroes. When the proposal was made to any one to join, such arguments or threats were made use of as would ensure success, and which the leaders had been cautious to prepare before hand, and suit to the different tempers and dispositions they would have to deal with.

As Vesey, from whom all orders emanated, and perhaps to whom only all important information was conveyed, died without confessing any thing, any opinion formed as to the numbers actually engaged in the plot, must be altogether conjectural; but enough has been disclosed to satisfy every reasonable mind, that considerable numbers were concerned. Indeed the plan of attack, which embraced so many points to be assailed at the same instant, affords sufficient evidence of the fact.

The extent of country around Charleston which was embraced in this attempt, has not been so precisely ascertained as to be traced on a map with as much certainty as a division line between two states; but enough has been discovered, to induce a belief, that it extended to the North of Charleston many miles towards Santee, and unquestionably into St. John's Parish; to the South to James' and John's Islands; and to the West beyond Bacon's Bridge over Ashley River. That all who inhabited this extent of country were engaged in the plot, will not be pretended; it was not necessary or perhaps adviseable; for at the season of the year in which the attempt was to be made, all the planters and their families are compelled to be absent from their plantations. If therefore a small number on a plantation or in the neighbourhood were engaged in the plot, and acquainted with the precise night and hour of its execution, it would be an easy matter for them in the course of the preceding day, or, within a few hours of their taking their own departure, to induce many others whose minds were already poisoned to proceed with them. In St. John's Parish four entire plantations of negroes were engaged by Frank Ferguson, as he declared to one of the witnesses; and his statement receives great strength, from the letter of his owner to one of the authors, in reply to one from him requesting certain information in writing. It was principally for the attempt of Jesse, (one of the conspirators) to go to Mr. Ferguson's plantation in St. John's, to inform the negroes of the night and hour they were to be in Charleston, that he was executed; though the declarations made by him independently of this act, shewed that he had heartily embarked in the plot. It was in testimony that the Insurgents *"were trying all round the country, from Georgetown and Santee, round about to Combahee to get people,"* and subsequent to the determination of the trials, it has been distinctly ascertained, that Vesey had been in the country as Far North as South Santee; and Southwardly from Charleston as far as the Euhaws; which is between seventy and eighty miles from the city.

During the period that these enlistments were carrying on, Vesey held frequent meetings of the conspirators at his house; and as arms were necessary to their success, each night, a hat was handed round, and collections made, for the purpose of purchasing them, and also to defray other necessary expenses. A negro, who was a blacksmith, and had been accustomed to make edged tools, was employed to make pike heads and bayonets with sockets, to be fixed at the ends of long poles and used as pikes. Of these pike heads and bayonets, one hundred were said to have been made at an early day, and by the 16th June, as many as two or three hundred, and between three and four hundred daggers.

At one time, Gullah Jack was seen by several witnesses with six of the pike heads, which he said, he had just brought from the blacksmith's; and a bundle containing upwards of twelve well selected poles, neatly trimmed and smoothed off, and about nine or ten feet long, were found concealed on the farm on Charleston Neck, where several of their meetings were held; and which were carried there to have the pike heads and bayonets fixed on them. These were brought before the Court: how many more may have been carried there, and were afterwards removed, destroyed, or effectually concealed; or how many more would have been carried there had the plot not been discovered, is altogether a matter of conjecture; but certain it is, that twelve or twenty poles were more than were requisite for only six pike heads, and as those six pike heads have not been found, there is no reason for disbelieving the testimony of there having been many more made. To presume that the Insurgents had no arms because none were seized, would be drawing an inference in direct opposition to the whole of the evidence. Besides the arms above-mentioned, it was proved that Peter had a sword; that Cha's. Drayton had a gun & sword; that John Horry had a sword; that Pharo Thompson had a sythe converted into a sword; that Adam Yates had a knife, such as are used by Riflemen as dirks, but which from its length was more properly a sword; that Monday had a sword; that Bacchus Hammett gave Peirault a sword and carried another and a pistol to Vesey, together with a keg of powder, that was afterwards made up into fixed ammunition, and which he had stolen from his owner; and that some of the arms of the Revenue Cutter had been stolen, yet none of these arms were found. A dagger rudely made, was found in Rolla's trunk; a quantity of slow match which was supposed to have been stolen out of the Arsenal by Lot was found concealed on one of the wharves, with which the City was to have been fired; and a very considerable number of musket balls were accidently discovered, concealed under water in one of the docks. But the means which the insurgents had in their power of arming themselves were ample. On King-street road, beyond the limits of the city considerably, though within the lines, in a common wooden store, unguarded, were deposited the arms of the Neck Company of Militia, amounting to between two and three hundred muskets and bayonets, and a few swords; the door of which store was to have been opened by Bacchus Hammett immediately as the Insurgents appeared before it, which a party were to have done at the appointed hour. Mr. Duquercron's store on King-street road, also beyond the limits of the City, and but a short distance below the last mentioned store, were deposited for sale about five hundred muskets and bayonets; to which store a body of the same party were to have gone at the appointed hour and secured those arms. To assist in effecting their several purposes, Vesey had made a collection purposely to purchase dark lanthorns. Mr.

Schirer's store in Queen-street, and the other stores with arms, were noted by the chiefs as magazines of arms to which they could resort; especially the stores of those Gun-Smiths, with whom the arms of some of the militia companies are deposited for the purpose of being kept in order. But in addition to these means, the Arsenal in Meeting-street opposite St. Michael's Church, in which the greatest proportion of the arms of the State are deposited, was to have been forced and the arms seized. Let it be remembered that this Arsenal is on the public street, without even a brick wall in front of it, with doors not stronger than those of many dwelling houses, and the difficulty of forcing it will not appear very great. The slaves who were enlisted in Charleston were to endeavour to purloin their owner's arms, and there appeared to be a confidence in the leaders, that a sufficient number in Charleston would from different sources be provided with arms to enable them in the first moments of surprise, and before the whites could possibly assemble, completely to succeed in their first attacks on the Guard House, and the unguarded Arsenals and Stores containing arms; after which they would be at no loss for arms. The negroes from the country were also to bring with them their hoes, hatchets, axes and spades, which might either be used as offensive weapons, or as instruments to break open doors. Had the plot not been discovered, and the Insurrection commenced at the appointed time, they would not have been found unarmed.

Vesey had originally fixed upon the night of the second Monday in July for the attack, as about that time the number of the white inhabitants in the city would be much diminished; those who are either going to the North, or to Sullivan's-Island, or into the upper parts of the State to spend the summer, generally before that time depart; a circumstance which had not escaped the observation of Vesey.—However, in consequence of the discoveries made on the 30th May, and the apprehension of Peter and Mingo Harth the day after, (but who after being examined were discharged) Vesey thought it prudent to fix upon an earlier day for the attack, and changed it some time after to the night of Sunday the 16th of June, which change, though he was able to communicate to his associates in the city, it would appear from his sending messengers into the country for that purpose, as late as the very day preceding the night on which the attempt was to be made, that he had not had sufficient time, or found some difficulty in communicating to his followers in the country; which accounts for their not generally appearing in the city on the night of the 16th of June. Twenty or thirty men however in a canoe did reach the city, and immediately had their arrival reported to Vesey; and with this view may many of those who came into the city on Saturday night and during Sunday have visited Charleston, on which day, great numbers, (certainly above a thousand as will presently be shewn) invariably repair to the city; but the preparations made by the whites, and the number of troops on duty that night, convinced him and his followers that their plot was discovered and the whites on their guard; and as their hope of success was founded on effecting a surprise, Vesey sent them word to depart from the city as soon as possible and wait for further orders; "and the conspirators finding the whole town encompassed at 10 o'clock by the most vigilant patrols, did not dare to shew themselves, whatever might have been their plans. In the progress of the investigation, it was distinctly in proof, that but for those military demonstrations, the effort would unquestionably have been made; and that a meeting took place on Sunday afternoon, the 16th at 4 o'clock, of several of the ringleaders at Denmark Vesey's, for the purpose of making their preliminary arrangements."

The plan of attack as originally formed was still adhered to, with the exception of the change of time before mentioned. It was to commence precisely at 12 o'clock on the night of Sunday the 16th of June; at which hour every one was to move, and the attack at every point to be made at the same moment.—Peter was to lead a party which was to assemble on South-Bay, and to be joined by a force from James' Island; he was then to march up and seize the Arsenal and Guard House opposite St. Michael's Church and secure the arms. From this force, a party was to be detached, whose duty it would be to prevent the Citizens from assembling at their alarm posts, by cutting them off as they arrived. A second body consisting partly of negroes from the country and from the Neck, was to assemble on the Neck, under the command of Ned, and to seize the Arsenal there. A third to assemble at Bennett's Mills, to be headed by Rolla, and, after murdering the Governor and Intendant, to march through the City, or take his station at Cannon's Bridge, and thus prevent the inhabitants of Cannonsborough from entering the City. A fourth, partly from the country, and partly from that portion of the city, was to rendezvous on Gadsden's-wharf, march and attack the upper Guard-House. A fifth, of country and Neck negroes, for whom in particular the pikes which were made had been provided, was to assemble at Bulkley's farm, about two miles and a half from the City, and seize the powder magazine, three miles and a half from town, and then march into the City; and a sixth to assemble at Vesey's, and under his command, to march down to the Guard House. Whilst these attacks were going on, a number of them on horseback were to ride through the streets, and kill every person they might meet, and prevent them from assembling, or extending the alarm. Batteau was to join and march down with Vesey; and Gullah Jack with another body, which was to assemble in Boundary-street at the head of King-street, was to take possession of the arms of the Neck Company, which were deposited in a store as before-mentioned, and also those in Mr. Duquercron's store. Arms being thus from these different sources provided, the City was to have been fired, and an indiscriminate slaughter of the whites to commence, and also of those of their own colour who had not joined them, or did not immediately do so. It was determined that no one should be neuter; "he that is not with me is against me." [6] was their creed. The leaders appeared to have no doubt but that those slaves who had not been particularly spoken to would join them, as soon as the Insurrection had fairly commenced, and the most partial success had been attained. "Let us assemble a sufficient number to commence the work with spirit and we'll not want men, they'll fall in behind us fast enough."

Amongst those unacquainted with the employments, habits and customs of the inhabitants of Charleston and the country and Islands immediately surrounding it, a doubt might arise, how the Insurgents were to provide themselves with horses in the City; and how the negroes from the Islands and the opposite sides of Ashley and Cooper rivers would find a conveyance to town. In neither of these respects, however, was there the least difficulty. There were four sources from which they intended to obtain horses; the three first not only feasible but certain, the last more difficult, but by no means insurmountable. First, numbers of the draymen and carters of the city, who are all persons of colour, and many of whom have their horses both day and night under their controul, (those who are free keeping them in their own yards, and many of the slaves keeping their horses out of their owner's) were to act as horsemen; so were, secondly, some of the butcher's boys, who could with ease provide themselves with horses; thirdly, the slaves at some of the public livery stables were engaged in the plot, and were a short time before the appointed hour to have the horses saddled, and at the hour to open the stable doors, and thus provide their comrades with horses; and fourthly, some of those whose owners were attached to either of the corps of cavalry in the city, were to endeavor to seize and bring of with them their owner's horses. As to the means which those on the Islands &c. would have to reach Charleston, they were abundant. The immense number of canoes of various sizes, (many of which could transport upwards of one hundred men) employed in bringing to the Charleston market, vegetables, stock of every kind and the staple of the country, would have afforded conveyance for thousands. As a matter of information and precaution, the Intendant of Charleston during the trials, and investigations of the plot, when negroes were rather fearful of coming into town, directed the numbers of those who came over in such boats on Sundays from the Islands to be counted, when even at that time, upwards of five hundred entered the city on one Sunday. From this statement some estimate may be formed of the number of negroes who ordinarily come into Charleston on Sunday from different parts of the country; of the facility of trans-

[6] 11th Chapter of St. Luke, 23d verse.

portation afforded by these canoes to those on the islands and rivers, and the foresight of Vesey in fixing on Sunday night for the attack, as on that day the slaves might leave their owner's plantations and come into town without being particularly noticed, which would on any other day be just the reverse.

The attention of the leaders to the most minute particulars is worthy of observation. In order to insure the assemblage of the Insurgents at the exact moment, the negroes who lived near the places of meeting, were requested for that night to conceal in their owner's premises one or more of their comrades; at least Gullah Jack was pursuing this plan, and as it was proved that the order emanated from Vesey, the same orders were no doubt extended to the others. A white man in this city who was a barber and hair dresser, was employed to make a number of wigs and false whiskers of the hair of white persons for some of the Insurgents, with the assistance of which, and by painting their faces, they hoped in the darkness of the night and in the confusion to be mistaken for white men. Such a plan as this would no doubt have assisted Peter in his bold determination to advance singly some distance ahead of his party, and surprise and put to death the sentinel before the Guard House. These wigs and whiskers were the only things by means of which Vesey was thrown off his guard during his imprisonment. The hair dresser who had been employed was carried by the Intendant into Vesey's cell, and Vesey was asked if he knew that man. With the greatest effrontery and composure he denied having ever seen him; at which moment, the Intendant took out of his pocket the very wig made for Vesey himself, which had such an effect upon him, that he exclaimed "good God"—remained silent a moment or two, and then acknowledged that the wig was made for him and that he knew the man.

The principal features in the plan of attack above given were proved by most of the witnesses; but some of them omitted parts, and some stated other particulars, which it would perhaps be tedious and unnecessary to mention. In addition to the foregoing circumstances, it was proved and subsequently acknowledged by Monday, that Vesey had written two letters to St. Domingo on the subject of this plot[7]; but of the character, extent and importance of the correspondence, no satisfactory information has been obtained, and perhaps by no other person but Vesey could this have been given.

What were the views and plans of the Insurgents after they had taken Charleston, had they succeeded in doing so, does not satisfactorily appear; and it is probable they had formed none, but intended to regulate themselves according to circumstances; but they appeared con-

---

[7] Monday never acknowledged *to the Court* that he had written two letters to St. Domingo, but said that Vesey had, and that he in company with Pierault had carried them on board a vessel there bound.

fident, that they would have been joined by such numbers from the country, as to have been able, at that particular season of the year, and with the fortifications on the Neck and around the Harbour, to have retained possession of the city, as long as they might deem it expedient. One or two of the Insurgents said, that Vesey, after robbing the Banks of specie, and plundering the city of all that was most valuable, intended to sail for St. Domingo with his principal adherents; but the informants themselves spoke of it more as a suggestion, than a fixed plan.

The character and condition of most of the Insurgents were such, as rendered them objects the least liable to suspicion. It is a melancholy truth, that the general good conduct of all the leaders, except Gullah Jack, had secured to them not only the unlimited confidence of their owners, but they had been indulged in every comfort, and allowed every priviledge compatible with their situation in the community; and although Gullah Jack was not remarkable for the correctness of his deportment, he by no means sustained a bad character. Vesey himself was free, and had amassed a considerable estate for one of his colour; he was in good business as a carpenter, and enjoyed so much the confidence of the whites, that when he was accused, the charge was not only discredited, but he was not even arrested for several days after, and not until the proof of his guilt had become too strong to be doubted. It is difficult to conceive what motive he had to enter into such a plot (unless it was the one mentioned by one of the witnesses, who said, that Vesey had several children who were slaves, and that he said on one occasion he wished to see them free:) as he himself artfully remarked in his defence on his trial; yet with him it unquestionably originated, and by him was headed. Rolla was the confidential servant of his master; so much so, that when his master's public duties required his absence from his family, they were left under the protection of that slave; and yet that very man, undertook to head a party, whose first act was to be, the murder of that master, who had reposed such confidence in him, and had treated him with great kindness. Ned was also a confidential servant, and his general good conduct was commendable. "Peter was a slave of great value, and for his colour, a first rate ship carpenter. He possessed the confidence of his master, in a remarkable degree, and had been treated with indulgence, liberality and kindness." "Monday enjoyed all the substantial comforts of a free man; (he was) much indulged and trusted by his master; his time and a large proportion of the profits of his labour were at his own disposal. He even kept his master's *arms* and sometimes his money." "He is a most excellent harness-maker, and kept his shop in Meeting-street." "Monday is an *Ebo,* and is now in the prime of life, having been in the country 15 or 20 years." But not only were the leaders of good character and much indulged by their owners, but this was very generally the case with all who were convicted, many of them possessing the highest confidence of their owners, *and not one of bad character.*

Another characteristic of this plot was, that a decided majority of the Insurgents, either did or had belonged to the African Congregation; amongst whom the inlistments were principally and successfully carried on. From the testimony, the presumptions of innocence are in favor of the Bishops and Ministers, (as they styled themselves,) of the Congregation; but two of them have left the state under strong suspicions of having favoured the plot. The class leaders appointed by them, certainly did; two of whom were principals, and Vesey their chief and a fourth leader though not class leaders, yet belonged to the congregation, Rolla being the only exception.

The conduct and behaviour of Vesey and his five leaders during their trial and imprisonment, may be interesting to many. When Vesey was tried, he folded his arms and seemed to pay great attention to the testimony given against him, but with his eyes fixed on the floor. In this situation he remained immoveable, until the witnesses had been examined by the Court and cross-examined by his counsel; when he requested to be allowed to examine the witnesses himself. He at first questioned them in the dictatorial, despotic manner, in which he was probably accustomed to address them; but this not producing the desired effect, he questioned them with affected surprise and concern for hearing false testimony against him; still failing in his purpose, he then examined them strictly as to dates, but could not make them contradict themselves. The evidence being closed, he addressed the Court at considerable length, in which his principal endeavour was to impress them with the idea, that as his situation in life had been such that he could have had no inducement to join in such an attempt, the charge against him must be false; and he attributed it to the great hatred which he alledged the blacks had against him; but his allegations were unsupported by proof. When he received his sentence, the tears trickled down his cheeks; and it is not improbable if he had been placed in a separate cell, he might have made important discoveries; but confined as four of the convicts were in one room, they "mutually supported each other; and died obedient to the stern and emphatic injunction of their comrade, (Peter Poyas.") *"Do not open your lips! Die silent, as you shall see me do."* Rolla when arraigned, affected not to understand the charge against him, and when it was at his request further explained to him, assumed with wonderful adroitness, astonishment and surprise. He was remarkable throughout his trial, for great presence and composure of mind. When he was informed he was convicted and was advised to prepare for death, though he had previously, (but after his trial,) confessed his guilt, he appeared perfectly confounded; but exhibited no signs of fear. In Ned's behaviour there was nothing remarkable; but his countenance was stern and immoveable, even whilst he was receiving the sentence of death: from his looks it was impossible to discover or conjecture what were his feelings. Not so with Peter, for in his countenance were strongly marked disappointed ambition, revenge, indignation, and an anxiety to know how far the discoveries had extended, and the same emotions were exhibited in his conduct. He did not appear to fear personal consequences, for his whole behaviour indicated the reverse; but exhibited an evident anxiety for the success of their plan, in which his whole soul was embarked. His countenance and behaviour were the same when he received his sentence, and his only words were on retiring, "I suppose you'll let me see my wife and family before I die?" and that not in a supplicating tone. When he was asked a day or two after, if it was possible he could wish to see his master and family murdered who had treated him so kindly! he only replied to the question by a smile. Monday's behaviour was not peculiar. When he was before the Court his arms were folded; he heard the testimony given against him, and received his sentence with the utmost firmness and composure. "But no description can accurately convey to others, the impression which the trial, defence and appearance of Gullah Jack made on those who witnessed the workings of his cunning and rude address."—When arrested and brought before the Court in company with another African named Jack, the property of the estate of Pritchard, he assumed so much ignorance, and looked and acted the fool so well, that some of the Court could not believe that this was the Necromancer who was sought after. This conduct he continued when on his trial, until he saw the witnesses and heard the testimony as it progressed against him; when in an instant, his countenance was lighted up as if by lightning, and "his wildness and vehemence of gesture, and the malignant glance with which he eyed the witnesses who appeared against him, all indicated the savage, who indeed had been *caught* but not *tamed*." His courage, however, soon forsook him. When he received sentence of death, he earnestly implored that a fortnight longer might be allowed him, and then that a week longer, which he continued earnestly to solicit until he was taken from the Court Room to his cell; and when he was carried to execution "he gave up his spirit without firmness or composure." He was sentenced on the 9th July to be hung on the 12th.

The whole number arrested were one hundred and thirty-one, of whom sixty-seven were convicted.—From amongst those convicted, thirty-five were executed; the remainder will be sent beyond the limits of the United States, as well as some of those, who though not convicted, are morally guilty; and of those who suffered death, twenty-two were executed at the same time, on the same gallows. The object of punishment being effectually attained by these examples, and the ringleaders being convicted, the arrests stopped here.

One who was not a member of the Court, cannot well conceive the effect produced by the threats used, in preventing a discovery of the plot. The enlistments had been going on and the preparations making actively since Christmas, yet it was not until the 30th May, that the least suspicion was entertained by the whites. Had it not been that one, not authorised by Vesey or the other leaders, and evidently unfit for such a purpose, undertook to enlist, no discovery might have been made; for though the information received on the 14th June, was infinitely more extensive and in detail, and from a very different quarter, yet the first communication and the excitement it occasioned, might have had considerable effect in eliciting the other. The information received on the 30th May, however, so far from leading to a discovery of the plot, was eventually disbelieved; so that the detection was not really made, until two nights preceding the intended exhibition of the dreadful tragedy. The discovery of the plot, however, in sufficient time, in this, as in every other instance, enabled the constituted authorities to crush it in the bud.

The information received on the 30th of May was communicated to the Intendant of Charleston about three o'clock in the afternoon, by a gentleman of great respectability, who that morning had returned from the country. This gentleman stated, "That a favorite and confidential slave of his had communicated to him, on his arrival in town, a conversation which had taken place at the market on the Saturday preceding, between himself and a black man; which afforded strong reasons for believing that a revolt and insurrection were in contemplation among a proportion at least of our black population. The Corporation was forthwith summoned to meet at 5 o'clock, for the purpose of hearing the narrative of the slave who had given this information to his master, to which meeting the attendance of His Excellency the Governor was solicited; with which invitation he promptly complied. Between however, the hours of 3 and 5 o'clock, the gentleman who had conveyed the information to the Intendant, having again examined his slave, was induced to believe, that the negro fellow who had communicated the intelligence of the intended revolt to the slave in question, belonged to Messrs. J. & D. Paul, Broad street, and resided in their premises. Accordingly, with a promptitude worthy of all praise, without waiting for the interposition of the civil authority he applied to the Messrs. Paul, and had the whole of their male servants committed to the Guard-House, until the individual who had accosted the slave of this gentleman, on the occasion previously mentioned, could be identified from among them.

On the assembling of the Corporation at five, the slave of this gentleman was brought before them, having previously identified Mr. Paul's William as the man who had accosted him in the Market. . . .

On this witness being dimissed from the presence of Council, the prisoner (William) was examined. The mode resorted to in his examination was to afford him no intimation of the subject of the information which had been lodged against him, as it was extremely desirable in the first place, to have the testimony of the other witness corroborated as to time and place, that, from the confessions of the prisoner himself, it might appear that he was at the fish-market at the period stated, and that a singular flag, flying on board of a schooner, had formed the subject of his observation. After a vast deal of equivocation, he admitted all these facts, but when the rest of his conversation was put home to him, he flatly denied it, but with so many obvious indications of guilt, that it was deemed unwise to discharge him. He was remanded for the night, to the Guard-House, it having been decided to subject him to solitary confinement in the black hole of the Work-House, where, on the succeeding morning, he was to be conveyed.

On the morning of the 31st he was again examined by the attending Warden at the Guard-House (having during the night, made some disclosures to Capt. Dove) on which occasion he admitted all the conversation which he had held at the fish-market, with the witness before mentioned, and stated that he had received his information from Mingo Harth, who was in possession of the muster-roll of the insurgents.

With the hope of still further disclosures William was conveyed to the Work-House and placed in solitary confinement. The individuals (Mingo Harth and Peter Poyas) against whom he gave information, as those who had communicated to him the intelligence of the plot for raising an insurrection, were forthwith taken up by the Wardens, and their trunks examined. These fellows behaved with so much composure and coolness, and treated the charge, alledged against them with so much levity—(no writings being found in their chests, containing the smallest suspicion, excepting an enigmatical letter; which was then too obscure for explanation, and to which subsequent events only afforded a clue)—that the Wardens (Messrs. Wesner and Condy,) were completely deceived and had these men discharged; but their movements were nevertheless watched, and measures of precaution taken. Things remained in this state for six or seven days, until about the 8th of June, when William, who had been a week in solitary confinement, beginning to fear that he would soon be led forth to the scaffold, for summary execution, confessed, that he had for some time known of the plot, that it was very extensive, embracing an indiscriminate massacre of the whites, and that the blacks were to be headed by an individual, who carried about him a charm which rendered him invulnerable.

Three or four days now elapsed, and notwithstanding all our efforts, we could obtain no confirmation of the disclosures of William, on the contrary, they seemed to have sustained some invalidation, from the circumstance, of one of the individuals (Ned Bennett) whom he named as a person who had information in relation to the insurrection, coming voluntarily to the Intendant, and soliciting an examination, if he was an object of suspicion. In this stage of the business, it was not deemed advisable prematurely to press these examinations, as it might have a tendency to arrest any further developements.

On the night, however, of Friday the 14th, the information of William was amply confirmed, and details infinitely more abundant and interesting afforded. At 8 o'clock on this evening, the Intendant received a visit from a gentleman, who is advantageously known in this community for his worth and respectability.

This gentleman, with an anxiety, which the occasion was well calculated to beget, stated to the Intendant, that, having the most unbounded confidence in a faithful slave belonging to his family, who was distinguished alike for his uncommon intelligence and integrity, he was induced to inform him, that rumours were abroad of an intended insurrection of the blacks, and that it was said, that this movement had been traced to some of the coloured members of Dr. Palmer's church, in which he was known to be a class leader.—On being strongly enjoined to conceal nothing, he, the next day, Friday the 14th, came to his master, and informed him, that the fact was really so, that a public disturbance was contemplated by the blacks, and not a moment should be lost in informing the constituted authorities, as the succeeding Sunday, the 16th, at 12 o'clock, at night, was the period fixed for the rising, which, if not prevented, would inevitably occur at that hour. This slave, it appears, was in no degree connected with the plot, but he had an intimate friend, A—(one of his class) who had been trusted by the conspirators with the secret, and had been solicited by them to join their association; to this A—first appeared to consent, but at no period absolutely sent in his adhesion. According to the statement which he afterwards made himself to the Court, it would seem that it was a subject of great regret and contrition with him, that he had ever appeared to lend his approbation to a scheme so wicked and atrocious, and that he sought occasion to make atonement, by divulging the plot, which on the 14th he did, to the slave of the gentleman in question, his class leader.[8]

As the account given by this slave was remarkably coincident with the one given by William, with whom he had had no communication, and also coincided in its most material points with the plan of attack just given; such measures were taken by his Excellency the Governor, as the occasion required. On the night appointed for the attack, the insurgents found a very strong guard on duty, and by 10 o'clock the whole town was surrounded by the most vigilant patrols; they therefore dared not shew themselves.

[8] Most of the black religious communities in this place, are divided into classes, over which a Leader is placed, having the confidence of the Pastor of the Church.

Notwithstanding the discovery which had been made, and the complete frustration of their plans, yet so true were they in observing their pledge of secrecy to each other, that of all those arrested up to the 22d June, only six of them were convicted. The discovery which had been made and the conviction of those six, amongst whom was their chief and three of his principal leaders, together with Batteau, who though not as principal a leader as the others, was yet an officer, did not however induce them to lay aside their design, for subsequent to these arrests and convictions, it was proposed to make the attempt early on the morning of the 2d July, immediately after the nightly Guards and Patrols had been discharged from duty, and which would be at the beating of the Reville; and some even had the boldness to propose a rescue and general attack, as the convicts were carried forth for execution. Their reason for fixing on so early a day was, their anxiety to save their Chief and Leaders, who were on that day to be executed; but the time between the day on which those six were sentenced, and that on which they were to be executed, was too short, to enable them to concert proper measures; especially as the whites were now on the alert and watchful; and moreover, one of their two remaining Leaders on whom they principally depended, was arrested the very day previous to the execution, a circumstance well calculated to disconcert and deter them. On the 5th July, further information was received from the slave of another gentleman, who voluntarily came forward and offered to reveal all the information he possessed, on condition that his name should never be disclosed. In addition to naming several of his associates, and describing the sorcerer Gullah Jack, who was his leader, so as to lead to his apprehension, he mentioned that the Insurgents had by no means been induced to abandon their original design by the execution which had taken place on the 2d instant; and that their remaining leader Gullah Jack was actively extending the information, that he had resolved to rise and make the attack at day dawn on the morning of the 6th. Want of time to concert measures for this attack also, would probably have prevented its being made; but it was effectually stopped by the arrest of Gullah Jack on the day previous. On the 9th July, sentence of death was passed upon five more, two of whom were Monday and Gullah Jack, and a third, Charles, the slave of the Honorable John Drayton; who though not a leader, had taken so active a part in the business, as to be perhaps as much known in it as the leaders were. It was now thirty-nine days since the civil authorities had received information of this plot, and twenty during which the Court organized for the trial of the Insurgents had been engaged (Sundays excepted); and yet, so true were they to each other, that during all that time only fifteen had been discovered whose connection in the plot was clear, of whom four were used as witnesses. After Monday Gell and Charles

Drayton were convicted there appeared to be a pause in our further discoveries, and some prospect of the investigation closing with their execution and that of John Horry, Harry Haig and Gullah Jack.

On the 9th of July, however, these five men, were called before the Court to receive sentence, and after it had been pronounced, with the most impressive solemnity, they were withdrawn to a common ward in the Work-House, for half an hour, until separate cells could be provided for them. It was at this moment that *Charles Drayton,* overwhelmed with terror and guilt, went up to *Monday* and reproached him with having induced him to join in a scheme which had placed him in such a miserable and perilous situation. To this appeal Monday not only confessed his guilt, but observed to Charles—that their present fate was justly and precisely what they had a right to expect, after their detected and defeated project. On which there immediately ensued between them a conversation on the extent of the guilt of others, in which Monday gave Charles the names of many accomplices whom he had not previously known in the plot; the arrival of the blacksmith to iron the convicts, and the turnkey to convey them to separate cells, interrupted the conversation.

Charles, during the night of the 9th, sent for Mr. Gordon, who has charge of the Work-House, and informed him that he was extremely anxious to see the Intendant, as he had some important disclosures to make. By day-light, on the morning of the 10th, this message was conveyed to the person for whom it was intended, and Charles was visited at sun-rise. He was found, in a state of the most lamentable depression and panic, and he seemed prepared to make the most ample declarations from the fear of death and the consequences of an *hereafter,* if he went out of the world without revealing all that he knew, in relation to the Conspiracy, in which he had been so active an agent. Before his narrative was received, he was most specially put on his guard, that no promises could be made to him of a reversal of his fate, but that he might rest satisfied, his condition could not be worse by his coming out with a full disclosure of all that he knew. He then stated many particulars, that had come to his own knowledge, proving a much wider diffusion of the plot than, at that period, was imagined; and, after giving up the names of several of his comrades, he mentioned the conversation which had been commenced and broken off, in the common ward of the Work-House, between Monday Gell and himself. As Monday, at this period, did not seem disposed to make any confessions to others, whatever he might be inclined to do to his friend Charles, it was considered important, that the conversation between them, should be renewed, and they were brought together in the same cell, and left for twenty-four hours alone; but some little stratagem was employed, to divert the suspicions of Monday, that Charles was confined with him, merely for the purpose of getting information out of him.

On the morning of the 10th, the Court were apprized, generally, of these new disclosures, which Charles had made, but as he was still *closeted* with Monday, he could not be examined on that day, and the Court met and adjourned from day to day until the 13th; on which day Monday Gell's own confession was heard by them. Between the 10th and 13th, *Charles* and *Monday* were separated (having been respited by His Excellency, the Governor, at the request of the Court) and Charles, on his re-examination afforded much important information, which he had derived from Monday. On Monday's having all this brought to his view, he confessed his own guilt, as well as the truth of the statements which he had made to Charles. With the information obtained from Charles, arrests recommenced on the 10th, in the course of which day Peirault belonging to Mr. Strohecker was arrested; whose additional information, with some further details obtained from Harry, belonging to Mr. Haig, in conjunction with the disclosures of Charles and Monday, caused the arrest of upwards of sixty slaves in the course of three or four days. After the trial of these, and a few more subsequently arrested, the civil authorities conceiving that enough had been done to serve as an example, determined to pursue the investigation no further; but should any further information be communicated to them, to bring to trial such only as had taken an active part, and arrange with the owners of the others to send them out of the state.

By the timely discovery of this plot, Carolina has been rescued from the most horrible catastrophe with which it has been threatened, since it has been an independent state; for although success could not possibly have attended the conspirators, yet before their suppression, Charleston would probably have been wrapped in flames—many valuable lives have been sacrificed—and an immense loss of property sustained by the citizens, even though no other distressing occurrences were experienced by them; whilst the plantations in the lower country would have been disorganized, and the agricultural interests have sustained an enormous loss.

9

The Reverend Richard Furman
Writes to Governor
Thomas Bennett

*In a private letter to Governor Thomas Bennett, the
Reverend Richard Furman, president of the South Carolina Baptist State Convention, refuted the claim that the Bible was opposed
to slavery.[1] Instead of prohibiting slaves from practicing religion
as some advocated, Furman argued that blacks should be taught
the Gospel as an "important Security for domestic peace." On December 24, 1822, Furman reiterated these views publicly and at
much greater length in his* Exposition of the Views of the Baptists, Relative to the Coloured Population of the United States
*(Charleston, 1823). The Reverend Frederick Dalcho, minister of
St. Michael's Episcopal Church in Charleston, expressed similar
views in another pamphlet,* Practical Considerations Founded on
the Scriptures Relative to the Slave Population of South-Carolina
(Charleston, 1823).

. . . Before we close this Address, we feel it incumbent on us, to
invite your Attention, Sir, to another Subject; a Subject which though
related to this, is not included in it; and in which we, as Agents of the
Bible Society, are particularly concerned. This is the Apprehension we
have, from Intimations, that in consequence of the late, projected Insurrection, & the Claims laid to a religious Character by several of
those who ranked as Leaders in the nefarious Scheme, Ideas have been
produced in the Minds of many Citizens, unfavorable to the Use of the
Bible among the Negroes; and that Attempts will, probably, be made
to obtain legislative Interference, to prevent their learning to read it,
or to use it freely. —Though we are sensible that the Power of Direction & Control, in this important Concern, does not rest with the Chief
Magistrate of our State; yet we are also sensible, that his Sentiments, &

[1] From the Furman Papers (Columbia, S.C.: University of South Carolina, South
Caroliniana Library). Used with permission of the South Caroliniana Library.

Recommendations have a powerful Influence, in giving Tone to Public Opinion & Feeling; and think that in Cases of Delicacy, where the Cause of Truth, Righteousness, Humanity & Religion are to be advocated, they may be advantageously & laudably employed.

The Sentiment, Sir, that the Doctrines of Holy writ are unfavorable to the holding of Slaves, has, we grant, been a Sentiment which many, & some very worthy Men have advanced; & which some still advocate; but, as we conceive, without just Foundation. Its lawfulness is positively stated in the Old Testament, & is clearly recognized in the New. In the latter a luminus Exhibition is given of Slaves,[2] & their Masters, enjoying Membership together in the Christian Church; while under the immediate Care & Government of the Inspired Apostles; Their respective Duties also are taught, explicitly, and enforced by eternal Sanctions. By these Rules the former are not directed to claim a Right to Liberation, nor encouraged to use Fraud or Force to effect it; but to be faithful, good, & obedient: The latter are required, not to emanciple their Slaves, but to give them the Things which are just and equal; forbearing, Threatening, & remembering, that they also have a Master in Heaven.

The Bible, Sir, as well as all other Things, good & Sacred, which have come into the Hands of Men, may be, & has been abused. But to argue against its Use, from the abuse it has suffered is to adopt a Mode of Reasoning which is not logical, just, nor pious.

The Scriptures are given to Man (without Respect of Persons) to make him wise unto Salvation; and all are required by Divine Authority to read them; because they contain the Words of Eternal Life. To prohibit the Use of them therefore, in respect of any Man or Class of Men, is to contradict & oppose the Divine Authority; & to suppose that the regular Use of them will naturally lead to Conspiracy, Rebellion & Blood, is a Reflection on the Divine Wisdom & Goodness, bordering on Blasphemy. But we have seen that, instead of encouraging Slaves to engage in Schemes of this Nature, they establish Rules of a directly contrary Character, & enforce them by Considerations which far transcend all that Human Munificence can afford as Reward; or that the Punishment of Human Laws can inflict.—Were we only reasoning from the Cause to its Effect, on this Subject, we should naturally arrive at this Conclusion; that whenever the Truths of the Bible are received in an honest Mind, even by Persons in a State of Servitude, they must & will produce happy Effects in favour, not only of Piety & Devotion; but of willing Subordination to lawful Authority, & Conformity to the Principles of Truth, Justice, Good-order, Peace, & Benevolence. But in adverting to Matter of Fact, many can & do testify, that they have seen these Effects produced among the Class of People in Question, really & extensively.

[2] Bond-Servants, or Slaves under the yoke.

Though it is true, that a considerable Number of the Persons who were concerned in the late Conspiracy, professed to be of a religious Character; yet it is also true, that the most leading Characters among them, & the chief of the rest, were Members of an irregular Association, which called itself the African church, & was intimately connected with a similar Body in Philadelphia, from which their Sentiments & Directions in Matters of Religion were chiefly derived: Whose Principles are formed on the Scheme of General Emancipation, for which they are zealous Advocates; & they endeavor to support, by a Misconstruction, or Perversion of the Scriptures. Very few, indeed, of the religious Negroes, in regular Churches among us, were drawn into the Plot; & in some Churches there were not any on whom a Charge of Criminallity has been proved. The Individuals composing the great Body, of well-known, regular, & esteemed Members of Churches, have not been impeached. It would indeed seem that the Conspirators were afraid to trust them: For since the Plot has been discovered, voluntary Information has been given, that Attempts, not then understood, were made to feel the Pulse of some of them, by artful, distant approaches, which not being countenanced were laid aside.

Vesey, the prime Mover in this Plot, was, as we are informed. notorious for his libidinous & petulent Conduct. Glen [Gell?], though co-Preacher among them, &, for one of his Oportunities, of extraordinary Talents, was generally considered as a Sharper, & one commonly chargeable with Falsehoods.

Nothing, that we can discover, has transpired to make it appear, that the Meetings of the religious Negroes, approved by the Churches to which they belong, for reading the Scriptures, learning their Catechisms, & the general Purposes of Devotion & religious Improvement, have been in anywise instrumental in directing or advancing the late horrid Design to which we refer; but on the contrary, we have Reason to believe, they have had a good Influence on the general State of Society, by the Promotion of good Morals, as well as Piety among that Class of People.

This Circumstance corroborates a Sentiment which has been long entertained by some who have been careful in making Observations, as well as in reasoning on this Subject, with the true Interests of Society in view: It is this, that one of the best Securities we have to the domestic Peace & Safety of the State, is found in the Sentiments & correspondent Dispositions of the religious Negroes; which they derive from the Bible.—If this Sentiment is just, it would seem, that instead of taking away the Bible from them, & abridging the truly religious Privileges they have been used to enjoy, to avoid Danger; the better Way would be, to take Measures for bringing them to a more full & just acquaintance with the former; & to secure to them the latter, under Regulations the least liable to abuse. That strict care should be taken to prevent abuses, & the Influence of designing Wicked Men among them is unquestionable, & highly important: And should be seriously regarded by Churches & Ministers, as well as by the Civil Government.

Should Confidence, Respect, & some special Privileges be considered as generally attached, under prudent Regulations, to the Character & State of those who manifest in Religion an Uniform, faithful Regard to just Sentiments, upright Conduct, the due Subordination of Servants, and the general Peace & Good-order of Society, it is believed that such Regard manifested toward them, which is but reasonable, would have a happy Effect; not only on the Mind & Conduct of the Slaves, but on the General Interests of the Community.

But should a Course of Policy, contrary to that which is here advocated, be prefered with respect to the Negroes, either by a Law of the State, or the common Consent of the Citizens, in refferrence to what some Wicked Men among them have done; not only would the Innocent be made to suffer for the Guilty; but the Sufferers, feeling themselves deprived of what they esteem a great Privilege, connected with their spiritual and eternal Interests, would, of course, feel unhappy, & be brought under the Influence of a strong Temptation to become indifferent to the Interests of their Masters, if not to hearken to the Voice of Seduction; the State, it is feared, would lose an important Security for its domestic Peace; & the Gospel would suffer Obstruction in its Operations & benign Influence, by that Arrest which Benevolence & Piety would experience, while employed in desseminating the Word of Life among the Poor, & promoting the Use of those Means of Grace which are designed by Heaven for the Conversion and Salvation of Sinners.

We submit these Considerations to your Excellency, & remain with high Respect,

Sir,
Your obedient
Humble Servant.
[Richard Furman]

His Excellency
Governor Bennett

10

The Proslavery Argument Restated

The Vesey Plot provoked considerable discussion about the propriety of the institution of slavery itself. Yet while some may have had doubts, most Carolinians merely repeated their long-standing arguments in favor of bondage. These apologetics for slaveholding were summarized by "A Columbian," a pseudonym for the leading jurist Henry William Desaussure of the Chancery Court. Desaussure's articles first appeared in the Columbia South Carolina State Gazette *in September and October, 1822, and were soon reprinted in pamphlet form.*[1]

We state . . . that the importation and slavery of the blacks was imposed upon us by the British Government, which refused to listen to the petitions of the Colonies against such importations.

That slavery, when the blacks were reduced to that state in this country, was universally considered lawful; and the scriptures no where prohibit slavery. Every power which now denounces it, encouraged and practised it, and particularly Great Britain, France, Spain, and Portugal. Northern capital and shipping were also employed in the trade. . . .

That the slaves cost an enormous sum of money, and are as much the property of their holders, as any other property, of any other owners—and that they cannot be justly or lawfully deprived of this property, but by their own consent, and at a fair and full price. . . .

There is too another view of the subject which ought not to be overlooked.

It is well known that the southern and western states are chiefly or in a great degree cultivated by the slaves. The climate of the sea coast is insalubrious in the summer and autumn to white settlers, but healthy to blacks; arising apparently from a difference of constitution founded in nature or in the effect of climate acting on one race for many centuries.

[1] From "A Columbian," [Chancellor Henry William Desaussure,] *A Series of Numbers Addressed to the Public, on the Subject of the Slaves and Free People of Colour. . . .* (Columbia, S.C.: State Gazette Office, 1822).

Of the 1,500,000 slaves, it is computed that at least 500,000 are employed in agriculture, the product of whose labor, besides feeding themselves and the country, furnishes an immence mass of products in Tobacco, in Flour, in Rice, Cotton, Lumber and Naval Stores.— These form the basis of an immense coasting and foreign trade, which enriches the citizens, fills the coffers of the government, employs the shipping and the seamen of the middle and eastern states, and produces a constant and beneficial intercourse between the remote parts of the Union.

Drive out these cultivators of the earth, and the southern, and part of the western states, would for many years, perhaps centuries, be a dreary waste, and a howling wilderness. The immense gap made in the population could not be replaced in two hundred years; and a great part of the sea coast must forever remain as pestilential, as desolate, and as depopulated as the Maremmes of Italy, or the deserts of Africa.

The sudden expulsion of such a great body of laborers, has proved ruinous to some, and very injurious to all the nations who have ever ventured on the perilous and cruel experiment. . . .

We are next led to inquire into the practicability and effect of emancipation.

It must be obvious that this measure can never be adopted and carried into execution, but with the consent of the southern and western states, and by compensation to the slave holders, for the privation of their property. The government of the United States has no authority to touch the subject; and are even bound by the constitution to ensure domestic tranquillity, and to protect the several states from domestic insurrection: It is bound also to protect the citizens in the secure enjoyment of that species of property, as well as every other, and it has heretofore done so faithfully. . . .

It will not then be denied that if the interests or policy of the United States should require the emancipation of the blacks, the government which asks that concession of the states, (for it cannot enforce it of right,) will be bound to make compensation to their owners. The enormous amount which that would cost, for the whole mass, has been shewn to exceed the financial powers of this country in so overwhelming a degree, as to render that scheme impracticable.

If a different plan should be adopted, and those only should be purchased for emancipation, who might be born after this period, this also is full of difficulties. The number of births must be very great, from 1,550,000 persons, who never suffer from famine, who have the best medical attendance, without cost to themselves, and who have no apprehensions of marrying very early, and having children in abundance, because they know they will be taken care of, and cloathed and fed at all events. . . .

The whole of this detail has been given to shew how impossible it would be for the pecuniary means of this country to pay the owners of this property either the gross sum of 450,000,000 of dollars for the whole mass of slaves, if emancipated at once, or the sum of 15,000,000 annually, for all those born after the contract between the government and the people. . . .

If it were possible for the government to purchase and pay for the slaves, they could not be transferred to Africa, but at an enormous and overwhelming expense: and experience shows that such a body of people could not be transported across the ocean without great sufferings, miseries and destruction on the passage, and probably utter annihilation on their arrival in Africa. And that locating them on any part of the North American continent, would not remove the difficulty in any degree. . . .

Emancipation then cannot take place, by purchase.

Let us then put the impossible case—that it should be carried into execution by main force, against the wishes of the proprietors and to the destruction of their interests, and let us examine what would be the effects of such a measure, and how it would work upon the United States. I put out of the way all the difficulties which would occur in such an undertaking, the resistance of the proprietors, the discords, the civil wars, the exterminating domestic broils, the dissolution of the Union, and the interference of foreign powers—and we will suppose the thing accomplished in peace. The emancipation of these people, must be either on condition of the full enjoyment of equal rights and privileges, or they must be placed on a footing of inferiority. If the latter should be pursued as the safer course, the inequality would of course be in the privation of political rights; the blacks would be permitted to pursue their occupation to acquire property, to enlarge it, and to enjoy every privilege of free men, except the right of voting at elections, the right of eligibility to office, the right of sitting on juries, and some other political rights.

Would this content these people? those have profited little by the lessons drawn from history, and from an intercourse with mankind, who suppose that they would remain long contented with this state of exclusion from political rights. It is a principle deeply rooted in the human mind, always to look forward with the hope of acquiring a better state than we now enjoy. To-morrow is to be the day of happiness sketched by our fancy in our day-dreams. . . .

It cannot be doubted that if the blacks should be emancipated and put on a footing with the whites, as to civil rights, but excluded from political rights, their course would be precisely that of all who have preceded them in that situation and career.—They would never cease to contend for a participation of all political privileges. Denmark Vesey, the head and animating spirit of the late plot in Charleston, was free, at ease in his circumstances, protected in his rights of person and property, and unoppressed: But he was excluded from political rights, and was disconted: he sought them through appalling difficulties, and in the pursuit of his object, disregarded the dangers which confronted him, and defied the death which he encountered.—The emancipated blacks of the southern and western states, would bear a portion of one to two, or about 1,500,000 blacks to 3,000,000 whites. They would acquire property, obtain education, become ambitious, and aspire to share in the government. This would lead to fierce contentions, and ultimately to civil wars, inhuman, desolating to individuals, and ruinous to the country within, and weakening it against foreign powers without. If their claims were successfully repelled, we should have a discontented population, always ready for a change, always eager for an opportunity to rebel, and to acquire the long coveted right of participating in the government.

Should they succeed by force, or by solicitation acting on the fear, or on the policy of the whites, in acquiring the object of their desires, they would then be put on a footing of perfect equality with the whites. . . .

That state of equality would include the right of exercising their industry and talents in every department and walk of public and private life. They might not only be cultivators of the earth, day-labourers, artizans, and manufactures; but merchants and professional men. They might according to law, glide into our families as physicians in the perfect confidence of that delicate relation; they might vindicate or violate our rights as advocates; sit in judgment upon our lives and property as jurors and judges; and instruct and guide our consciences as pastors. They might vote and control the popular elections; be themselves elected to the state legislatures, and to congress; command our armies and navies; preside over our councils, as Presidents and Ministers of state; and represent the dignity and the interests of the nation as ambassadors in foreign countries. We might hear a white member of congress from Massachusetts, or Connecticut allude to the argument or compliment the speech, of his honorable black friend from Pennsylvania[2] or Virginia; of his yellow friend from Maryland or South Carolina; of the tawney gentleman from Georgia or Tennessee; or of the spotted or brindled gentleman from Louisiana or Arkansaw.

This would be the legitimate fruit of equal rights between the whites and blacks. If it be said that this could not take place because our prejudices would counteract the exercise of the right, let it be answered how those prejudices could produce that counteraction in the sea coast districts of Virginia, North Carolina, South-Carolina,

[2] There are upwards of 30,000 free blacks, entitled to equal privileges with the whites in Pennsylvania; 30,000 in the state of New-York; and 12,000, in New Jersey.

Georgia, and Louisiana, where the blacks greatly exceed the whites in number? Many of the blacks would acquire wealth by industry, or other means; and wealth would bring education and ambition. They would sometimes be elected in the districts spoken of, and the heterogeneous mixture would take place, which has been described. Nor would this be all—wealth and power produce a certain degree of respect, however unworthy the possessors, or abhorrent the circumstances. The wealthy and the powerful among the blacks would find multitudes among the poorest and most ignorant whites, and perhaps even among some in moderate circumstances, who would bow down and worship these Idols. They would find no difficulty in procuring friends, supporters, wives and connections of every kind among them. The plea of these degraded whites would be, "our poverty and not our will consented." . . .

Thus some of the blacks, who inherit the cunning, as well as the punic faith of the ancient Carthagenians, their predecessors, and countrymen, would find ways and means to advance themselves, to mingle with many of the whites, to create a new race, in violation of nature, of vile complexion and odious character, who would tarnish the national reputation, as well as colour, and humble it in the dust. . . .

Such would be the unfortunate fate of this country, should this detestable scheme for blending ever be adopted. But it is impossible that it could ever be carried into full execution. There is a moral impossibility, that a high spirited free people, nourished with liberty from earliest infancy, as their best inheritance, can consent to degrade themselves, by generally mingling on equal terms with the slaves, whom they have been accustomed to despise for their vices, and their brutality. They cannot bear with patience the dishonor of their blood and their name.

The two races never can assimilate perfectly. The mixture will be partial, and incomplete—sufficient perhaps to do much evil, and no good. The whites can never forget that they had been masters; and could never lay aside the tone of superiority. The blacks could never forget that they had been slaves; and they would retain either the base and crouching spirit of slaves, or would attempt to throw the cloak of oblivion over their origin, by assuming a pert and braggadocio air of defiance and insult, as a substitute for that calm self respect which they could never feel.

Are the blacks now prepared, or could their descendants be prepared for the enjoyment of liberty or political rights? The answer founded on experience must be in the negative. . . .

Are the slaves, it is again asked, possessed of the qualities necessary to convert them with safety at once into freemen, with all political privileges? Are they trained and brought to that state of mind, which feels a proud obedience to the laws, though it would disdain submission to any other power? The answer must be in the negative. The body of them would either be the blind and violent instruments of some of their own cunning and base leaders, or of profligate white demagogues, who would condescend to use so coarse an instrument, to gain power; or they would be a dead, inert mass, mere hewers of wood and drawers of water. They would either be mischievously active, or uselessly inactive.

Could the northern states be satisfied to become the confidential friends, the brothers, the equal members of the same political body, with these dark, and savage barbarians? Could they serve in the same councils, eat at the same tables, and marry their sons and daughters to them? Could they rely on their public patriotism, or their private virtues, in those critical emergencies which try men's souls? They could not—they would not do any of these things: they have had experience of free blacks [whose] . . . conduct is at times servile and contemptible; at other times, insolent and arrogant. . . .

But different would be our case; with us it is a struggle for life, for character, for colour, for dignity, for government and mastery—in short for every thing dear to men, and most especially to free white men.

It is a vain hope to expect that these two races of people can blend and assimilate, and live in harmony together. It would be a perpetual struggle for power, and then for existence itself. When the French Convention in its madness emancipated the slaves of St. Domingo, and its orators pronounced the dreadful dogma, let the earth and its inhabitants perish, rather than a principle, (the principle of universal freedom,) it little imagined that this decree would produce the extermination of the whites, the utter destruction of that fine colony, and the ruin of the best commerce which France enjoyed;—yet such were the fruits—and such would be the case in the southern states, in the struggle and civil wars which would inevitably follow, if the blacks were emancipated; unless the whites, feeling that their existence depended on it, put forth their strength vigorously, and subdued them promptly. There could, indeed, be no doubt of the issue, if they did justice to their own strength and talents, unless the interposition of foreign powers, the active energy of the Haytians in aid of their black brethren, (to whom these last have already turned their eyes, and addressed their letters as their natural allies,) and the apathy of the northern states, should overwhelm the southern whites.

Let our northern friends take a view of either event, and look to the consequences. Should the whites subdue the blacks, the situation of the latter would be brought back to that which it is now—with their numbers, thinned by slaughter and misery, and their minds embittered and discontented by their sufferings. They would be slaves without that confidence and good will which now subsists pretty generally between the masters & slaves, founded on mutual services and kindness. Their condition would then be much worse than it is at present. A stern despotism would add to the weight of their chains.

Should the blacks subdue the whites, it would be a war of extermination. Men accustomed to freedom and to superiority, could not submit to the domination of their former slaves. They would fight to the last extremity; and when hope was gone, the few who survived would abandon the country, and take refuge among their brethren in the nothern states.

What sort of neighbors, what kind of friends the black empires of the south and west would be to the north, is left to the calm and deliberate consideration of the northern statesmen. It will be for them to decide whether they would prefer the present race, who are masters, and who are united to them by every tie which binds men together—a common origin and colour, a common religion and language, similar habits and feelings, laws, governments and institutions of all kinds—to be their friends and associates in peace and in war; or to have the blacks, descendants of the barbarian Africans, who have never in any age or under any circumstances been distinguished by virtues or talents—to be their neighbors and their allies or their enemies.

It cannot be doubted for one moment, which they would choose. It would be a gross injustice to their well known judgment, to entertain the smallest doubt. But, the argument is put to them in this shape, in order to bring them to reflection. Without intending to do a real injury, or to produce any lasting ill consequences, many of the northern citizens, indulge even in the public prints in reflections and reasonings which, if followed out into their consequences, must produce all the ill effects of discontent and rebellion in the minds of these slaves. They are thus sporting with inflammable substances. Let them reflect seriously where that would end, and then pause. The wise and the good should then interpose and prevent fools from casting about firebrands, which may light up a conflagration, that could not be extinguished without torrents of blood.

If, as we have attempted to show, the slaves can neither be purchased, and transported to other countries, nor emancipated with advantage to themselves, or safety to the whites, there remains no other course, than to retain them in their present condition. Some alterations and improvements can and ought to be made in the plan of treating and managing them.

The present code contains many harsh enactments which are never enforced, and have no other effect than to excite prejudices against us among those who can judge of us only by the provisions of the statute book. It should be revised and adapted to the feelings and habits of the present times; that is, it should be a humane code. The slaves should be put more effectually under the protection of the laws, against abuse and cruelty; and secured absolutely in the enjoyment of an abundant supply of food and cloathing adapted to their condition, with moderate labour, not above their strength. The system, having secured these essential points, should be one of strictness, and of steady superintendance. It is in vain to expect to maintain subordination, without the strong hand of power; and that should be exhibited steadily and uniformly. It must be left to the wisdom of the Legislative body, combining the experience and the judgment of many minds, to prepare, digest, and complete a code adequate to all these objects. But it may be permitted to a private citizen to suggest a few hints for the consideration of others. The great fundamental principle, it is believed, should be, that the slaves should be kept as much confined as possible to agricultural labours. These, so employed, are found to be the most orderly and obedient of the slaves. And now that the foreign admixture of native Africans is absolutely and permanently prohibited by law, and almost wholly so in practice, and that leaven of barbarism which was heretofore continually infused into the mass is thus withheld, there may be a reasonable hope that the descendants, born and bred in the country, may gradually become a docile, and in some degree a civilized people.

There should be no black mechanics or artizans, at least in the cities. These are placed by the nature of their employments, much more from under the eye and inspection of their masters, and they acquire vicious habits injurious to themselves, as well as their owners, and of evil example to other slaves. In the sea-coast towns, often filled with many worthless and idle strangers, from the West-India Islands, the black mechanics, artists, draymen, and wharfingers, are thrown into bad company who infuse false notions and delusive hopes into their minds, which render them dissatisfied with their condition, and prepare them for plots and other mischief.

It is as true as it is trite, that knowledge is power. Education therefore should on no account be permitted. I am aware that this may be considered a hard measure, to close the book of knowledge on the human mind, and shut it out from the delights of learning: Nor would I insist upon it, if it were possible ever to incorporate the black race with the white race, and make one people of them. But as that is impossible, it is a favour to them to keep them in ignorance, and contentment, with their lot. . . .

The slaves also should have no separate place of worship; a station should be appropriated for them in every place of worship used by the whites, where they should be able to see and to hear, and they as well as their masters should be taught the mild doctrines of the gospel, which, whilst they instruct the slave to be obedient, and to serve industriously, for conscience sake, and not as eye servants, teach the master also that he is bound to treat his slaves with gentleness and kindness, and to provide for their comfort, in sickness as well as in health, in infancy, and old age, as well as in the vigor of useful life. Many other regulations will doubtless be framed by the wisdom of the legislature for the double purpose of ensuring kind treatment and complete protection, on the one hand, and for maintaining on the other hand the proper subordination of the slaves. And when our northern brethren are fully satisfied that all has been done which can be done, to ameliorate the condition of these people, consistent with their station, and that no other system can be devised, which is practicable and safe, then they will cease to throw out those reproachful remarks which can do no good, and may do much harm. For we are quite sure that even enthusiasts, who are led away by a morbid feeling of false humanity, would not do evil for its own sake; nor even venture to act on the vile maxim ascribed to the Jesuits, that evil may be lawfully done, that good may come of it—a maxim which Paschal triumphantly refuted, and which the good feeling and common sense of mankind has banished from society. . . .

A COLUMBIAN

11

A Charleston Editor Refutes the "Calumnies" Against the South and Proposes to Eliminate the Free Black Population

Originally published as a diatribe against antislavery Congressmen during the Missouri Debates of 1819–21, Edwin C. Holland—a leading Charleston literary figure and editor of the Times—revised this pamphlet in reaction to the Vesey Conspiracy.[1] Critical of religious "missionaries" and the meddling attitudes of Northerners, Holland was tolerant of the free mulatto group because they informed against revolts. He also expressed his sexual fears openly, and proposed measures that would remove free blacks from the state and police all Negroes—the "Jacobins of the country," in Holland's phrase—more rigorously.

. . . The people of the North and East . . . take the liberty of interfering in the designing of some of our most important local regulations and of directing the steps of our constituted authorities. We are not only dictated to, but we are slandered in their public prints, denounced in their pulpits, and calumniated in pamphlets and orations. We are exposed to still greater perils, by the swarm of Missionaries, white and *black,* that are perpetually visiting us, who, with the Sacred Volume of God in one hand, breathing peace to the whole family of man, scatter, at the same time, with the other, the fire-brands of discord and destruction, and *secretly* disperse among our Negro Population, the seeds of discontent and sedition. It is an acknowledged fact, that some of these religious itinerants, these apostolic vagabonds, after receiving the charities which the philanthropy and open-hearted generosity of our people have bestowed, have, by the means of *Tracts* and other modes of instruction, all professedly *religious* in their character, excited among our Negroes such a spirit of dissatisfaction and revolt, as has, in the end, brought down upon

[1] From E. C. Holland, *A Refutation of the Calumnies Circulated Against the Southern and Western States.* . . . (Charleston, S.C.: A.E. Miller, October 29, 1822).

them the vengeance of offended humanity, and given to the gallows and to exile, the deluded instigators of a most diabolical and unholy Insurrection. Those who are intimately acquainted with the efficient causes of the late intended Insurrection in Charleston and the districts adjoining, which, from the testimony as well of many of those who have been executed, as from that of the hundreds who either knew of or were engaged in the plot, was to have been conducted with a ferocious barbarity, at which humanity shudders and turns pale; those, we repeat, who are acquainted with the rise and progress of that nefarious plot, know how blasphemously the word of God was tortured, in order to sanction the unholy butchery that was contemplated, and what a powerful agency was put into operation by the dispersion among our Negroes, of *religious magazines, news paper paragraphs* and *insulated texts of scripture;* all throwing such a delusive light upon their condition as was calculated to bewilder and deceive, and finally, to precipitate them into ruin. Religion was stripped of her pure and spotless robe, and, panoplied like a fury, was made to fight under the banners of the most frightful Conspiracy that imagination can conceive, and her voice was heard instigating the midnight ruffian and coward, to creep silently to the pillow of his unsuspecting master, and at one "fell swoop" to murder *him* in the unconscious hour of sleep, prostitute the partner of his bosom, violate the child of his affections, and dash out the brains of his innocent and unoffending infant. The measure of desolation was not even yet full; after robbing our banks, and seizing on our shipping, killing all but the *captains,* who were to be reserved as *pilots,* their atrocious footsteps were to have been lighted from our shores by a *general conflagration,* and our city, that proudly swells with life and with wealth, was to have been left an awful monument of the most ferocious guilt. Such are a few of the barbarities to which we would have been exposed had the late intended Insurrection been crowned with success. But the activity and intelligence of a wise and efficient police, strengthened and enlightened as they were by the protecting interposition of a benificent Providence, have frustrated the wicked designs of our barbarous and inhuman enemies, and consigned to a bloody and ignominious fate the *master spirits* of the Revolt. Notwithstanding all these projected atrocities, however, and with a full knowledge of the facts upon the subject, we have, nevertheless, been vilified and abused for having visited upon the heads of their stupid and flagitious instigators, the penalty which the Laws of our Country award, and which the vengeance of violated humanity required. . . .

We repeat, the people of the North and East are, or affect to be, totally ignorant of the actual state and character of our Negro Population; they represent the condition of their bondage as a perpetual revolution of labor and severity, rendered still more deplorable by an utter destitution of all the comforts of life. Our Negroes according to these candid and accurate observers, are in every respect illy provided, badly fed and badly clothed; worked beyond their physical capacity while in health; neglected while in sickness; going always to their labor with the most dogged reluctance, confined to it by the severity of the cart-whip, and denied, in fine, all the ordinary enjoyments of existence. Now, the very reverse of this is the truth; and it is within the province of those who are continually defaming us, to ascertain it; yet, notwithstanding that the most abundant testimony is at hand to satisfy the most curious inquirer upon the subject, and every candid and enlightened observer finds himself at every step furnished with the most ample refutation of these charges, the calumny has nevertheless been industriously propagated and upheld with a malignity of design, and an utter contempt of truth, at war with every thing like fair argument, or the most ordinary regard for OUR feelings. . . .

Although the utter impracticability of effecting any permanent change in their condition, by an insurrection among our Slaves, has been, we think, fully demonstrated, it is nevertheless indispensible to our safety to watch all their motions with a careful and scrutinising eye—and to pursue such a system of policy, in relation to them, as will effectually prevent all secret combinations among them, hostile to our peace. Every possible precaution should be adopted, that is calculated, in the remotest degree, to save us from a catastrophe which at all times threatens us, and of the horrors of which, the imagination can form no definite idea. The Crisis through which we have so recently and providentially passed, had long been anticipated by those who were minute observers of the passing events of the times. A general spirit of insubordination among our slaves and free negroes— springing from the relaxation of discipline on the part of the whites— had been long discernable—nor are the other auxilliary causes so occult that they cannot be easily pointed out.

We regard our negroes as the "*Jacobins*" of the country, against whom we should always be upon our guard, and who, although we fear no permanent effects from any insurrectionary movements on their part, should be watched with an eye of steady and unremitted observation.

We look upon the existence of our Free Blacks among us, as the greatest and most deplorable evil with which we are unhappily afflicted. They are, generally speaking, an idle, lazy, insolent set of vagabonds, who live by theft or gambling, or other means equally vicious and demoralising. And who, from their general carriage and insolent behaviour in the community, are a perpetual source of irritation to ourselves, and a fruitful cause of dissatisfaction to our slaves. Our slaves, when they look around them and see persons of their *own color* enjoying a *comparative* degree of *freedom*, and assuming privileges beyond their own condition, naturally become dissatisfied with their lot, until the feverish restlessness of this disposition foments itself into insurrection, and the "black flood of long-retained spleen" breaks down every principle of duty and obedience. We would respectfully recommend to the Legislature, therefore, *the expediency of removing this evil, and of rooting it out of the land.* A law, banishing them, male and female, from the State, under the penalty of death, or of perpetual servitude, upon their return—or placing such a tax upon them, as, from its severity, would render it impracticable for them to remain among us—is desirable. Either of these modes presents a feasible and easy method of clearing the country of this detestable *caste*. The example of a sister State[2] in this latter particular, gives us a wholesome lesson of instruction. Our philanthrophic brethren at the North and East, will, no doubt, afford them an asylum, and *we* have every disposition to get rid of them—Under such a dispensation, therefore, all parties might be satisfied. Should the necessity of such an expedient appear obvious to the Legislature, we ought, in common humanity, to see that their departure from our shores should be attended with every necessary comfort and convenience.—An appropriation of funds, therefore, to meet the exigencies of such an event, and to provide for those who might be incapable of providing for themselves, would be necessary. If we are compelled, from our situation, to pass over some of the more rigid and fundamental principles of *abstract* justice, let the encroachment be made with as little individual distress as possible.

There are many enlightened and intelligent men who are of opinion, that the same measures should be adopted in relation to our Free Mulattoes—and that they are as serious an affliction, both to the morals and security of the State, as the Free Blacks themselves. We are, however, of an opinion, directly the reverse, and are decidedly opposed to any system of legislation that would end in banishing *them*. They are, in our estimation, (but perhaps we have viewed the subject in an improper light) a *barrier* between our own color and that of the black—and, in cases of *insurrection*, are more likely to enlist themselves under the banners of the whites. Most of them are industrious, sober, hard-working mechanics, who have large families and considerable property: and as far as we are acquainted with their temper, and disposition of their feelings, abhor the idea of an association with the *blacks* in any enterprise that may have for its object the revolution of their condition. It must be recollected also, that the greater part of them own slaves themselves, and are, therefore, so far interested in this species of property, as to keep them on the watch, and induce them to disclose any plans that may be in-

[2] Georgia.

jurious to our peace.—Experience justifies this conclusion. The important discoveries, in most instances of insurrection, particularly in the last, have been made through the immediate instrumentality and advice of this class. Would it be generous then to drive them from the comforts of their present situation, and exile them from our shores, when we at the same time acknowledge the value of the services they have performed? We think not. . . .

[But] let it never be forgotten, that "our Negroes are truely the *Jacobins* of the country; that they are the *anarchists* and the *domestic enemy; the common enemy of civilized society,* and the barbarians who would, if they could, become the destroyers *of our race.*"

12

Thomas Pinckney Favors Excluding Black Workers from Charleston

As the legislative session of November-December, 1822, approached, leading South Carolinians began to suggest certain measures which might alleviate the danger of future conspiracies. In a widely acclaimed pamphlet "Achates," (a pseudonym for Thomas Pinckney, the famous soldier, diplomat, and governor from the revolutionary generation), urged that the ratio of blacks to whites in Charleston be reduced by employing white workers instead of blacks.[1] This would also increase the effective military force of the city.

The following Reflections are from the pen of a Soldier and a Patriot of the Revolution; whose name (did we feel ourselves at liberty to use it) would stamp a peculiar weight and value on his opinions.

They were written after the public disturbances in this place, during an excursion into the interior, and have been transmitted to a few friends for their perusal, who have deemed them worthy of a more comprehensive dissemination than a single manuscript copy could possibly have afforded.— It will be sufficiently obvious that these Reflections are the result of much patient thinking on a subject well calculated to arouse the anxieties of patriotism, and to invoke all that the maturity of experience is capable of yielding. . . .

Previous to the proposal of any plan for preventing the recurrence of similar danger, it may be useful to advert to the causes which produced the late conspiracy. The following may be assigned as some of the most obvious:—1st, The example of St. Domingo, and (probably) the encouragement received from thence.—2dly, The indiscreet zeal in favor of universal liberty, expressed by many of our fellow-citizens in the States north and east of Maryland; aided by the Black population of those States.—3dly, The idleness, dissipation, and improper indulgencies permitted among all classes of the Negroes in Charleston, and particularly among the domestics: and, as the most dangerous of

---

[1] From *Reflections, Occasioned by the late Disturbances in Charleston. By Achates* (Charleston, S.C.: A. E. Miller, November 4, 1822).

those indulgencies, their being taught to read and write: the first bringing the powerful operation of the Press to act on their uninformed and easily deluded minds; and the latter furnishing them with an instrument to carry into execution the mischievous suggestions of the former.—4th, The facility of obtaining money afforded by the nature of their occupations to those employed as mechanics, draymen, fishermen, butchers, porters, hucksters, &c.—5th, The disparity of numbers between the white and black inhabitants of the City. No effort of ours can remove some of these causes, but over others we may exercise control. . . .

If we examine the last census, and refer to that taken twenty years previous, we shall find that this evil is rapidly increasing; for at the former period the white population of Charleston exceeded the other, while in the last census the black population was to the white nearly as 22 to 14.—Now, as it must be admitted that this excess of physical force does diminish the great superiority which their means and qualifications give to our citizens, a reliance on this circumstance must have formed the prinicipal encouragement to the late attempt; for without it, mad and wild as they appear to have been, they would not have dared to venture on a contest of force. How imperative is then the policy of removing this rapidly increasing evil—this *sine qua non* of insurrection!

The next questions then, which naturally occur, are, to what degree will it be necessary to extend the reduction? And what substitute can be obtained to occupy the employments now filled by the Negroes?

. . . The benefits which will be derived from the change, will be, in the first place, security: not merely that we and our families shall be safe from these horrors, but, that we and they shall feel, and be perfectly assured that we are so; that we may retire to our repose at night, with the certain knowledge of our immunity from the dagger of the treacherous internal assassin, and all the horrors which were so fatally exhibited at St. Domingo, and were distinctly threatened here. Another advantage is, that all the labor and domestic business of the City, will be better performed, and all articles committed to the charge of subordinate agents more carefully preserved.

But, it is not merely exemption from the disadvantages attending the employment of slaves, that will result from the change of system, but great positive benefits will attend the introduction and employment of so many white inhabitants. The most obvious, is the effective force which will thereby be added to the militia of the City. If, in the place of 22,432 coloured persons now maintained there, only half the number of white inhabitants were introduced; as all the mechanics, the draymen, the fishermen, and the porters, would of course be males, more than five thousand effective men would be added to our muster-roll; whereby, not only Charleston would be perfectly secure, but all thoughts of servile insurrection in the country, would be forever banished; for with a militia force of seven or eight thousand men, well armed and accoutred, which would then compose the militia of Charleston, on one side, and the numerous white population of the upper country, on the other; it would be more than madness for any portion of the country slaves to meditate an insurrection, destitute as they are of most of the advantages and facilities for such an enter-prize, of which those in Charleston might have availed themselves. . . .

The appeal is made to the sober reason and judgment of those who have so valuable a stake in the decision. An attempt has been made to show that the measure recommended is not only highly beneficial, but, that it is also practicable; and the whole is, with due deference, submitted to the consideration of those to whom are confided the safety and the welfare of the public.

ACHATES.

13

Charleston Citizens Petition the State Legislature

The hostility toward free blacks and slave artisans, the fear of white involvement in slave revolts, and proposals to strengthen the military force of the state—all of which surfaced during and after the trials—were manifested in the following petition to the South Carolina legislature by a group of Charlestonians in the fall of 1822. Under the heading "Slave Conspiracies and Crime," the southern historian U. B. Phillips included this selection in his Plantation and Frontier Documents *(Cleveland, Ohio: A. H. Clark Co., 1909), Vol. II, pp. 103–116.*

MEMORIAL OF THE CITIZENS OF CHARLESTON TO THE SENATE AND HOUSE OF REPRESENTATIVES OF THE STATE OF SOUTH CAROLINA (CHARLESTON, 1822)

At a moment of anxiety and in a season of deep solicitude, resulting from the recent discovery of a projected insurrection among our colored population, your Memorialists submit to you the following considerations:

Under the influence of mild and generous feelings, the owners of slaves in our state were rearing up a system, which extended many privileges to our negroes; afforded them greater protection; relieved them from numerous restraints; enabled them to assemble without the presence of a white person for the purpose of social intercourse or religious worship; yielding to them the facilities of acquiring most of the comforts and many of the luxuries of improved society; and what is of more importance, affording them means of enlarging their minds and extending their information; a system, whose establishment many persons could not reflect on without concern, and whose rapid extension, the experienced among us could not observe but "with fear and trembling," nevertheless, a system which met the approbation of by far the greater number of our citizens, who exulted in what they termed the progress of liberal ideas upon the subject of slavery, whilst many good and pious persons fondly cherished the expectation that our negroes would be influenced in their conduct towards their owners by sentiments of affection and gratitude.

The tranquility and good order manifested for a time among the slaves, induced your memorialists to regard the extension of their privileges, in a favourable light, and to entertain the hope that as they were more indulged, they would become more satisfied with their condition and more attached to the whites.

But in the midst of these promising appearances, whilst the citizens were reposing the utmost confidence in the fidelity of the negroes, the latter were plotting the destruction of the former. A plan was perfected—a corps was organized—arms were collected, and every thing arranged to overwhelm us with calamity—a calamity from which we were preserved by the fidelity of a single slave, who disclosed to us a plot, which in its origin, extent and design, may well bear comparison with the most atrocious of the West Indian insurrectionary schemes. No regard was to be paid to age or sex—no discrimination to be made between the benevolent master and the severe slave-holder, without even respecting the sacred character of our Clergy, who had been assiduous in instructing them in the duties of life, and encouraging them in the pursuit of Heaven; the slaves had resolved to seize on the arsenals, destroy the guard, murder the citizens, and envelope the town in one extended conflagration. The discovery of the plot, but a few days before the period resolved on for its execution, fortunately preserved us from these horrors, and brought many of the conspirators to justice. But although the immediate danger has passed away, yet the causes from which it originated your memorialists conceive to exist in full vigor and activity, and will, as they conscientiously believe, produce, before many years, a series of the most appalling distresses, unless speedily removed by the most resolute and most determined laws. To the enacting of such laws, the attention of the Legislature is solicited by your memorialists, who, after the most attentive investigation into the origin, design and extent of the late projected insurrection—after a careful inquiry into the existing evils of our slave system, and after mature reflection on the remedies to be adopted, humbly recommend that laws be passed to the following effects:—

1st. To send out of our State, never again to return, all the free persons of color.

In considering this subject, it naturally resolves itself into two parts: 1st. the evils to be expected from the movements of the free people of color from themselves, and 2nd. those which arise from the influence which the existence of such a class of persons must produce upon our slave system.

In considering, first, the evils to be apprehended more immediately from the free people of color themselves, we must consider the relation in which they stand both to the whites and the slaves. They form a third class in our society, enjoying more privileges than the slaves, and yet possessing few of the rights of the master; a class of persons having and exercising the power of moving unrestrained over every part of the State; of acquiring property, of amassing wealth to an unlimited extent, of procuring information on every subject, and of uniting themselves in associations or societies—yet still a class, deprived of all political rights, subjected equally with slaves to the police regulations for persons of color, and sensible that by no peaceable and legal methods can they render themselves other than a degraded class in your society. Thus it appears that they have sufficient of liberty to appreciate the blessings of freedom; and are sufficiently shackled to be sensible they enjoy comparatively few of those blessings. But it is the very constitution of the human mind, that its desires progress in a ratio proportioned to the increase of its acquisitions; and in no respect is this more observable than in its efforts after freedom. Restraints are always irksome, but restraints on one portion of the community, from which the other are exempt, become doubly so from comparison; it therefore follows from the very nature of things, that the free people of color must be discontented with their situation, and will embrace the first favorable opportunity of attaining all the privileges enjoyed by the whites, and from which, with deep regret, they see themselves cut off. The efforts of men to obtain any given object are always proportioned to the animation of their hopes or the energy of their despair. The hopes of the free negroes will increase with their numbers, and when they shall have equalled the whites, which it can easily be shown will happen before many years are passed, they will expect and claim all the privileges, rights and immunities of citizens, which if denied them, as they must be, they will be driven by despair to obtain by force what cannot be effected in any other way; and then, indeed, will the evil have become of such magnitude as will render it almost impossible to remove it. . . .

If we judge from the evidence afforded by the last ten years, the ratio of increase among the whites is diminishing, whilst that of the free persons of color is increasing.

But there are other causes which must operate upon these relative numbers, and must render the free persons of color in a few years more numerous than the whites—at the same time evincing how dangerous this class must prove, if suffered to remain among us.

The Free people will never emigrate; they have so little to hope for, and so much to dread, from any change of place, that they will adhere to the spot of their nativity, under the pressure of any inconvenience, rather than seek to improve their condition in distant countries. As they multiply, they are bred up to the mechanical arts, or perform such labor as is usually performed by the poorer class of whites; of course they must come in competition with this class, and before the lapse of many years, the quantity of labor will greatly exceed the demand, and employment must be sought where the demand is greater—one class must therefore emigrate; but the free people of color will not emigrate; consequently the whites must; so that as the free people of color are extending their lines, the whites are contracting theirs. This is not mere speculation, but a fact sufficiently exemplified already. Every winter, considerable number of Germans, Swiss and Scotch arrive in Charleston, with the avowed intention of settling among us, but are soon induced to emigrate towards the west, by perceiving most of the mechanical arts performed by free persons of color. Thus we learn, that the existence of this class among us, is in the highest degree detrimental to our safety.

But in another point of view, the residence of free negroes among us, is pregnant with evils, evils arising from the influence which the existence of such a class of persons must have upon our slave system.

The superior condition of the free persons of color, excites discontent among our slaves, who continually have before their eyes, persons of the same color, many of whom they have known in slavery, and with all of whom they associate on terms of equality—freed from the control of masters, working where they please, going whither they please, and expending their money how they please—the slave seeing this, finds his labor irksome; he becomes dissatisfied with his state, he pants after liberty! A liberty he can never hope to acquire by purchase or faithful services, for the Legislature has deemed it expedient to close the door against emancipation, his only chance for freedom is to combine with others and endeavor to incite an insurrection; an insurrection which offers to the free colored man as many temptations as to the slave—for as the slave is desirous of being on equality with him, so he likewise is desirous of being placed on the same footing with the whites. It is therefore the interest of the free persons of color, to cherish a spirit of discontent among the slaves, as they hope to avail themselves of their assistance to promote their own schemes of ambition. There is identity of interest between the slave and the free person of color, whilst there is none between the latter class and the whites; but there is not only an identity of interest but also an identity of feeling among the colored people of both descriptions—they are associated by color, connected by marriages, and by friendships. Many of the free negroes have parents, brothers, sisters and children, who are slaves; should an insurrection occur, they would have every inducement to join it; they would be distrustful of the whites, and the whites would be naturally distrustful of them; they would therefore carry over to slaves their intelligence and numbers, and would serve as channels for communication between slaves of the different portions of the state. But it may be remarked, that in the late projected insurrection, very few of the free people of color were engaged—let it however, not be forgotten, that Denmark Vesey was a free person; he who projected and planned the insurrection; who was the leader of the conspirators, and the most active in collecting the materials.—Had he not been free, it would have been impossible for him to communicate so extensively with the slaves in the country, without whose co-operation, the slaves in the city would not have dared to make the attempt to emancipate themselves.

But it is said, great inconvenience will result to the free persons of color, and we ought not to inflict so much distress on an innocent race of persons. Your memorialists are aware of the inconvenience to which the free persons of color will be subjected if compelled to emigrate. But they are sensible that a partial evil must frequently be tolerated for the promotion of the general welfare, and the only inquiry to be made is, whether the good to be received by the state, exceeds any evil which can possibly arise to the free people of color. Now your memorialists conceive there is no comparison between them; the evils which the free people of color will experience, must in its very nature, be temporary. In a few years they will have acquired new habits, found out new channels of industry, and formed new connections—whilst those remaining amongst us, will be a source of continual apprehension to the whites; of continual discontent to the slaves, and sooner or later, the inevitable cause of a disastrous and bloody commotion in our state.

It becomes us, however painful it may prove, to sacrifice feeling to reason, and mistaken compassion to a stern policy, and expel from our territory every free person of color, that we may extinguish at once every gleam of hope which the slaves may indulge of ever being free—and that we may proceed to govern them on the only principle that can maintain slavery, the "principle of fear."

2nd, your Memorialists are decidedly of opinion, that the number of negroes to be hired out, should be limited by law, and that no negro should be allowed to work as a mechanic unless under the immediate control and inspection of his master. By far the greater portion of negroes who work out, are released in a considerable degree from the controul of their masters—laboring or forbearing to labour, as their interest or inclination prompts, rendering unto their owners, only a monthly account; and provided they but settle the wages with punctuality are permitted to regulate their own conduct; the consequence is, they assemble together whenever they wish, and having their time at their own disposal, can be convened at any given and fixed period, and having regular and stated meetings, can originate, prepare and mature their own plans for insurrection. Whereas, the slaves who are kept in the yards of their masters, are immediately under their eyes, and cannot fix upon a period for assembling—they

know not at what hour they may be called for by their owners, or
for how long a period they may obtain leave of absence—they cannot,
therefore, act in concert and "concert is the very life of a conspiracy."

But there is another consideration. The facility of obtaining work
is not always the same. At one period the demand for labor is considerable; at another the demand is comparatively small; the consequence is, the labor of the slaves hired out is very irregular, and a
quantity of time is consumed in idleness. Irregularity of habits is thus
acquired; this irregularity produces restlessness of disposition, which
delights in mischief and detests quiet. The same remarks will apply
to the negro mechanics, who having a stated portion of labor to
perform, are masters of the remainder of the day, when the work is
ended. The time in the evenings, and on the Sabbath is so entirely
at their disposal, that the most ample opportunity is afforded of
forming combinations and devising schemes. Should a law be passed
limiting the number of slaves to be hired out and confining the exercise of the mechanical arts to white persons (except in the cases above
specified,) the result will be that a large portion of the black population now in the city, will be removed into the country, and their places
be supplied by white laborers from Europe and the Northern States.
In this manner we will exchange a dangerous portion of our population for a sound and healthy class of persons "whose feelings will be
our feelings, and whose interests our interests."

The late intended Insurrection forcibly proves the truth of the
above remarks; for with a very few exceptions, the negroes engaged in
that conspiracy were mechanics or persons working out. Great inconvenience, perhaps even considerable misery, may be experienced
by many worthy citizens, who at present are maintained by the hire
of their slaves. But to obtain important objects by effecting considerable change or reform, great sacrifices must be made, and great difficulties encountered. This is an affair in which temporizing expedients
will avail nothing. We must meet the difficulties with resolution, and
overcome them by the most vigorous and determined course of action.
They are difficulties which, if eluded now, will meet us again in their
progress, multiply and crowd upon us until we are involved in confusion and disorder.

3rd. Your memorialists also recommend to the Legislature to pre-
scribe the mode in which our persons of color shall dress.—Their apparel has become so expensive as to tempt the slaves to dishonesty;
to give them ideas not consistent with their conditions; to render
them insolent to the whites, and so fond of parade and show as to
cause it extremely difficult to keep them at home. Your memorialists
therefore recommend that they be permitted to dress only in coarse
stuffs, such as coarse woolens or worsted stuffs for winter—and coarse
cotton stuffs for summer—felt hats, and coarse cotton handkerchiefs.

Every distinction should be created between the whites and the negroes, calculated to make the latter feel the superiority of the former. It is not the intention of your memorialists to embrace in these sumptuary regulations "livery servants," as liveries however costly, are still badges of servitude. The object is to prevent the slaves from wearing silks, satins, crapes, lace, muslins, and such costly stuffs, as are looked upon and considered the luxury of dress.

4th. The next topic to which your memorialists would invite the attention of the Legislature, is the organization of a regular, efficient military force, in lieu of the City Guard, as at present constituted. The City Guard, as now organized, are of little benefit to the city. Most of them are shop-keepers or retailers of spirituous liquors to the negroes. It is therefore their interest and it is notorious that this interest induces them to permit such of the negroes as are their customers, to pass unmolested through our streets after the bell has rung, and the watch has set. Independently of this circumstance, the members of the Guard are employed in some occupation throughout the day, and when night comes are totally incapacitated from serving as sentinels. In such a city as ours, where there is a large slave population, we should be extremely vigilant; a regular well disciplined force, well officered, and distinct from the body of the citizens, generally, should be kept on duty night and day. It is of equal importance to the city and country that such a body be organized, for insurrections, though they may break out on the plantations, must necessarily have their origin in the city. We should always act as if we had an enemy in the very bosom of the State, prepared to rise upon and surprise the whites, whenever an opportunity be afforded.

5th. It is further recommended by your memorialists that a law be passed, preventing persons of color from holding real property. Many of them are becoming rich, and some of them are already owners of plantations. It is impossible to calculate the evil which may arise from any number of these people possessing extensive plantations. Living in the country, they must, in a great measure, be removed from the vigilance of the whites. They can harbour any number of runaway negroes; their plantations may become the rendezvous of the desperate and discontented among the slaves, and having within themselves the means of support, they may carry on their schemes of destruction, without any likelihood of detection. Neither should they possess real estate in the city, as it will enable them to become landlords to many white persons, who lease from them lands and houses. *Now* the laws respecting landlords and tenants are such, that unless the tenant be punctual in the payment of his rents, it places great power in the hands of the landlord,—a power which should never be permitted to those who, by the laws and policy of our State, are considered a degraded and inferior class.

6th. Your memorialists have viewed with deep regret the influx into Carolina of slaves from the middle states. These slaves are of the most worthless and abandoned characters, taken out of the jails and houses of correction; the greater portion are criminals, whose punishments are commuted into banishment. Yet this degraded and villainous body of negroes are continually pouring in upon us—mingling with our colored population, and contaminating the minds of our most valuable domestics. Your memorialists therefore most earnestly entreat the Legislature to make the bringing of slaves into our state highly penal.

7th. It is deemed requisite to prevent negroes from residing upon premises where no white persons reside. It is our policy to place the slaves under the inspection of their masters as much as possible, and every care should be taken to prevent their associating and leagueing together.

8th. Your memorialists consider the laws now in force, so far as they relate to white persons concerned in insurrections of the slaves, extremely defective, as those laws only extend to white persons assisting the negroes in a state of actual insurrection—whereas it is equally criminal to incite the slaves to insurrection. Your memorialists therefore recommend that the laws now in force be so far amended as to subject to the punishment of death all white persons who shall be principals, advisers or abettors in any actual or projected insurrection of the slaves.

And we recommend that a law be passed, prohibiting under severe penalties, all persons from teaching negroes to read and write.

With these observations and recommendations, it remains only to add the hopes of your memorialists, that on a subject of such deep and extensive concern, such measures may be adopted as are calculated to afford protection to our property and security for our lives.

14

The South Carolina Legislature Further Represses the Black Population

The suppression of the Vesey Conspiracy led directly to more stringent enforcement of the South Carolina slave codes and to greater repression of the black population throughout the South. One piece of concrete legislation passed by the state's assembly on December 1, 1822 (and amended the following year) was a new act "for the better regulation and government" of blacks.[1] The third section providing for the detention of Negro seamen who landed at South Carolina ports created considerable controversy with northern states and with England.

AN ACT FOR THE BETTER REGULATION AND GOVERNMENT OF FREE NEGROES AND PERSONS OF COLOR, AND FOR OTHER PURPOSES

Section 1. *Be it enacted by the honorable the Senate and House of Representatives now met and sitting in General Assembly, and by the authority of the same,* That, from and after the passing of this act, no free negro or person of color, who shall leave this State, shall be suffered to return; and every person who shall offend herein shall be liable to the penalties of the act passed on the twentieth day of December, in the year one thousand eight hundred and twenty, entitled "An act to restrain the emancipation of slaves, and to prevent free persons of color from entering the State, and for other purposes."

Sec. 2. *And be it further enacted,* That every free male negro or person of color, between the ages of fifteen and fifty years, within this State, who may not be a native of said State, or shall not have resided therein five years next preceding the passing of this act, shall pay a tax of fifty dollars per annum; and in case said tax shall not be paid, the said free male person of color shall be subject to the penalties of the act against free persons of color coming into this State, passed on

[1] From "Free Colored Seamen, ..." *House Reports,* No. 80, 27th Cong., 3rd sess., January 20, 1843, pp. 21–23.

149

the twentieth day of December, one thousand eight hunderd and twenty.

Sec. 3. *And be it further enacted by the authority aforesaid,* That if any vessel shall come into any port or harbor of this State, from any other State or foreign port, having on board any free negroes or persons of color, as cooks, stewards, mariners, or in any other employment on board of said vessel, such free negroes or persons of color shall be liable to be seized and confined in jail, until said vessel shall clear out and depart from this State; and that, when said vessel is ready to sail, the captain of said vessel shall be bound to carry away the said free negro or free person of color, and to pay the expenses of his detention; and, in case of his neglect or refusal so to do, he shall be liable to be indicted, and, on conviction thereof, shall be fined in a sum not less than one thousand dollars and imprisoned not less than two months; and such free negroes or persons of color shall be deemed and taken as absolute slaves, and sold in conformity to the provisions of the act passed on the twentieth day of December, one thousand eight hundred and twenty, aforesaid.

Sec. 4. *And be it further enacted by the authority aforesaid,* That the sheriff of Charleston district, and each and every other sheriff of this State, shall be empowered and specially enjoined to carry the provisions of this act into effect, each of whom shall be entitled to one moiety of the proceeds of the sale of all free negroes and free persons of color that may happen to be sold under the provisions of the foregoing clause: *Provided* the prosecution be had at his information.

Sec. 5. *And be it further enacted,* That it shall be the duty of the harbor master of the port of Charleston to report to the sheriff of Charleston district the arrival of all free negroes or free persons of color who may arrive on board any vessel coming into the harbor of Charleston from any other Sate or foreign port.

Sec. 6. *And be it further enacted,* That, from and after the passing of this act, it shall be altogether unlawful for any person or persons to hire to any male slave or slaves his or their time; and in case any male slave or slaves be so permitted by their owner or owners to hire out their own time, labor, or service, the said slave or slaves shall be liable to seizure and forfeiture, in the same manner as has been heretofore enacted in the act in the case of slaves coming into this State contrary to the provisions of the same.

Sec. 7. *And be it further enacted,* That, from and after the first day of June next, every free male negro, mulatto, or mestizo, in this State, above the age of fifteen years, shall be compelled to have a guardian, who shall be a respectable freeholder of the district in which said free negro, mulatto, or mestizo, shall reside; and it shall be the duty of the said guardian to go before the clerk of the court of the said district, and before him signify his acceptance of the trust, in writing; and at the same time he shall give to the clerk aforesaid his certificate, that the said negro, mulatto, or mestizo, for whom he is guardian, is of good character and correct habits; which acceptance and certificate shall be recorded in said office by the clerk, who shall receive for the same fifty cents; and if any free male negro, mulatto, or mestizo, shall be unable to conform to the requisitions of this act, then and in that case such person or persons shall be dealt with as this act directs for persons of color coming into this State contrary to law; and the amount of sales shall be divided, one-half to the informer, and the other half for the use of the State.

Sec. 8. *And be it further enacted by the authority aforesaid,* That if any person or persons shall counsel, aid, or hire, any slave or slaves, free negroes, or persons of color, to raise a rebellion or insurrection within this State, whether any rebellion or insurrection do actually take place or not, every such person or persons, on conviction thereof, shall be adjudged felons, and suffer death without benefit of clergy.

Sec. 9. *And be it further enacted by the authority aforesaid,* That the commissioners of the cross roads for Charleston neck be, and they are hereby declared to be, justices of the peace, ex-officio, in that part of the parish of St. Phillip's without the corporate limits of Charleston, for all purposes except for the trial of causes small and mean.

In the Senate house, the first day of December, in the year of our Lord one thousand eight hundred and twenty-two, and in the forty-seventh year of the independence of the United States of America.

THE REBELLION IN HISTORY

15

"A Colored American":
Brave Patriots

In 1850, an anonymous "Colored American" published a brief pamphlet which included a personal reminiscence of the circumstances of the Vesey Conspiracy.[1] The author has been variously identified as the fugitive slave Henry Bibb or the black editor Thomas Hamilton, but his true identity remains a mystery. The account is significant, however, for its discussion of the impact of the new laws on the aspirations of South Carolina slaves, the methods used to extract confessions, the "solemn farce" of the trials, the opportunism of white politicians, and the black community's desire to wear black dress and crepe to mourn its dead heroes.

. . . A Governor was elected to preside over the State for two years, who, in his Message to the Legislative Assembly in Columbia, recommended, among other things, "some provisional law be enacted for the protection of the free native born colored inhabitants of the State, and punishment for free colored foreigners who might visit that State under any circumstances, except as cooks and stewards aboard of some vessel sailing into the port of Charleston, or servants to gentlemen travelling in the State."

Here was the beginning and ground work for modern persecution against the free colored American people. Many of the circumstances connected with this matter I distinctly recollect, which is extremely fierce and savage in its nature. It began in the latter part of 1819, and

[1] From "A Colored American," *The Late Contemplated Insurrection in Charleston, S.C. . . .* (New York: Printed for the Author, 1850), pp. 4–9.

153

has continued to operate with demoniac ferocity upon defenceless, innocent free colored Americans, up to the present day. Perhaps it was about three years after this period that the philanthropic and patriotic Denmark Vesey, well known for his industrious habits as a carpenter, and moral pursuits in life as a Christian, in full communion in one of the Established churches in Charleston, with his coadjutor, Peter Poyas, a ship carpenter of some eminence, a holy and devout man, and four other equally worthy patriots, suffered martyrdom, merely for an oral review of their grievances, in their outraged rights and privileges, perpetrated on them and their enslaved brethren by the enactment of new and cruel laws for that express purpose, without any justifiable cause, and, as it had been alleged, for a contemplated insurrection of the slaves in Charleston in the month of June, 1822.

As I have already stated, the recommendation of the Governor, with reference to ameliorating the condition of the free colored people, appeared to be just the thing that was wanted as an excuse for those of the new school party to foist themselves into public favor, on a substantial platform; that is, to commence a fresh and unprovoked public persecution against the orderly, well-behaved, free colored people in Charleston, who at that time appeared to be growing into affluence and respectability. The subject of the recommendation of the Governor was referred to the Judicial Committee, of which Mr. Prioleau, a gentlemen of great influence and respectability, and deservedly popular with all parties of citizens, was, I think, chairman—a new party man, a quid, who reported recommendations of laws adverse, not only towards free colored foreigners, but against native born South Carolinians—denying to that useful and industrious class of citizens many privileges and rights they had heretofore enjoyed. Besides this gross innovation on liberty and the rights of man, the Committee reported the propriety of the Legislature to enact laws forbidding slaves in future, no matter how enterprizing, industrious, or meritorious their moral character might be, from being manumitted, except by special law of the Legislature when in session in Columbia; and then the manumitted slave be expelled immediately beyond the limits of the State, never to return within its precincts under severe penalties: which Report was accepted and adopted as a part of the fundamental laws of the State of South Carolina.

Hence the prospects of the slaves for freedom were blasted; many of whom had toiled anxiously at night to earn sufficient means to purchase freedom for themselves; all of whom aspired to the manly boon of freedom, the declaration of their masters to the contrary notwithstanding. Freedom many of the slaves resolved to have at all hazards. Many of them, in confidence reposed in their masters, in addition to their wages, paid large sums of money to their masters—

hard earnings at night work, for the express purpose of purchasing their freedom; all of which, by the enactment of erroneous and cruel laws, was lost to the poor slaves forever.

Several years after the enactment of laws to cut off entirely all hopes, and to prevent the slaves from acquiring their liberty by purchase, as the sequel of this sad narrative will tell, it is probable that a party of these disappointed slaves, justly incensed with the cruel passage of such uncivilized laws, which were a great and intolerable hinderance to their peace and happiness, had conspired to free themselves from the yoke of the most unholy bondage ever invented by man in that liberty-loving country—to become owners of their own sacred persons, over the bodies of their masters. In this matter, however, they failed owing to one of the party who was found to be a traitor to their supposed righteous cause, who communed with a free colored man on the subject of their intention to make an attempt to liberate themselves, who in turn communicated the whole subject matter to the constituted authorities of the city of Charleston; which timely information saved the city from a bloody servile contest. But it resulted in the capture of the entire band of patriots, and in their subsequent execution—the most barbarous on record in that day—notwithstanding the sanctity of their cause, made holy by the American Revolution.

The mock and summary trial of those brave men, after the alleged plot was discovered and the party taken prisoners, exceeds credence, and will ever blight the escutcheon of the Palmetto State. A Court was summoned for the express purpose of trying the contemplated conspirators, composed of gentlemen slaveholders, upon the plan of Judge Lynch, for which the South is peculiarly celebrated. The proceedings were, as usual when slave interests are supposed to be interfered with, a solemn farce; and in this form the business was conducted. Freeholders were readily selected, pre-disposed to condemn and hang every prisoner brought before them on the charge of insurrection ("as a terror to the slaves, to keep them in awe for a quarter of a century," as one of the prosecutors said, and that there was "nothing too bad for the slaves to contemplate doing, but the masters had the ability to punish them for it,") without sufficient lawful evidence that was necessary to convict anybody except in the Slave States. The prisoners were arraigned in the most despotic form of the darkest gone-by age, where they were truly forlorn. No lawyer dared to defend them fairly or professionally. I think the Governor and one of the Judges of the Supreme Court were threatened with violence for expressing an opinion adverse to the ruling party of the city at that time.

Under such charges as were brought against the accused, one of the prisoners, whose name was Pharo, acted as States-evidence on the promise of rewards, with security for his life; which promise the honorable Court failed to keep, and Pharo was condemned and hung with twenty-one others of the so-called conspirators, at the lines of Charleston, after every information was extracted from him, and, as it was alleged, he proved himself to be a false witness. All the arrangements having been prepared and ready for the accommodation and sitting of the Court, the prisoner was brought out of his dungeon and securely fixed in the hall of the prison house, without a friend to support him in this dreadful emergency, where accusation against him was pronounced by the Court, charging the individual prisoner with a criminal meeting with one or more other slaves who contemplated to raise an insurrection, with an intent to overthrow the present form of Government in Charleston—to establish a rule of their own. The accused, after his arrest, was cut off from all communication whatever with his acquaintances, and was not allowed to see, nor to have an interview, nor to consult with a friend on any occasion; neither was he allowed to see or confront his accuser face to face. O how cruelly this part of the arrangement was carried out with unchristian ferocity! Indeed all the condemnation of culprits that did occur on that awful and melancholy occasion, in sending thirty-six brave men to a premature, but honorable, grave, (Colonel Isaac Hayne, of Revolutionary memory, died on the scaffold,) was cowardly and shamefully done in secret, and upon very slight circumstantial and secret evidence alone. The accused was tried, not by a jury, oh, no! He was condemned to die, and none but slaveholders, who would taunt him, were permitted to speak with the prisoner on any consideration.

In this horrible situation he was led out of prison to be executed, without friend or relative to assuage or console the culprit in his overwhelming calamity. Nay, the endearing ties of nature were ruthlessly sundered by the demon "office-hunter"; neither wife nor children, ah, no! no colored persons whatever were allowed to manifest the slightest grief for affliction in their family. Even the affliction of death, which comes of the power of God, in his Divine Providence, was treated with disregard; nor were the free colored people allowed to wear a bit of crape to mourn the loss of father, mother, brother, sister, daughter or son, but the act was construed into sympathy for the contemplated conspirators, (such was the rage of leading young men, who were looking forward to political advancement, and who knew that oppressing the colored people was the sure road in which to obtain that end,) and punished accordingly.

The matter of hanging the contemplated conspirators, and whipping and stripping the peaceable colored people of their black dress, crape, &c., continued for several weeks, and would perhaps have continued much longer. There was a very large number of persons already imprisoned, waiting their turn for the scaffold; but some of the citizens who had already suffered great loss in having their slaves hung without full remuneration for their value, and the fears of others who were surfeited in seeing, and having their property in human flesh sacrificed in order to gratify and pave the way of a few young men to office, without sufficient pay for their loss of property in the condemned slaves (Governor Ben—tt, the then executive of the State, perhaps would have hesitated to take $10,000 for two of his slaves that were executed for being declared leaders of the contemplated conspiracy. They were men above the ordinary standing of first-rate slaves, of deep piety and experience—ingenious engineers and millwrights; indeed, it was said of them they were above mediocrity); when one of the freeholders, as I have been informed, devised the following plan to rid themselves of the odious measures:—

A rash youth had, by his advice and zealous counsel, put the city under. He sent into the interior of the country, beyond the residence of any of the reported contemplated conspirators, and had two of his slaves brought before the august assembled Court, to discover what effect their appearance would have on the secret evidence, dressed as they were in their country rags. The secret witnesses, after reviewing carefully the persons brought before them for inspection, declared that there was no accusation against them, and they were discharged free from blame into the hands of their owners: the identical slaves were washed and dressed fashionably, and again presented before the Court for examination, on charges pretended to be preferred against them, when the same disinterested, pure witness, who had previously declared these men innocent of any criminal charge against the State, without hesitation, on their second and improved appearance before the Court, pronounced these very men participants in the scheme of the contemplated conspiracy.

The success of this method on the part of the Court to detect false witness was complete, for they had become surfeited of their own abominable work; and stayed the execution of more than a hundred valiant victims prepared by their order for the scaffold, as the Court themselves declared in a publication issued by authority from one of the public presses in Charleston, the contents of which has escaped my memory. I recollect this much of their statement, however, viz., "that many others, including a blind man formerly from St. Domingo, were fit subjects for the gallows; but motives of humanity prevented their execution." The motives of humanity alleged by the Court, I apprehend were not praiseworthy motives to discover false witness or arrest the execution of the patrician band; ah, no! but after a gluttonous destruction of the lives of thirty-six honorable and brave men, for their own self-protection against prospective loss. Some of the honorable members of the Court owned slaves who were implicated in the affair of the contemplated insurrection. That circumstance, perhaps was one of the chief motives of humanity that influenced the Court to stay their hand and authority.

This disgraceful, wholesale murder of thirty-six remarkably upright and worthy men, principally to make sure a popular platform for office-hunters to be elevated upon, is without parallel, even in Charleston. The day on which twenty-two of the patriots were hung, or rather sacrificed to the wicked principles of slavery, at one time, owing to some bad arrangement in preparing the ropes—some of which were too long, others not properly adjusted so as to choke effectually the sufferers to death, but so as to give them the power of utterance, whilst their feet could touch the ground—they, in their agony of strangulation, begged earnestly to be despatched; which was done with pistol-shot by the Captain of the City Guard, who was always prepared for such an emergency; i.e. shooting slaves.

I recollect seeing him shoot down dead a colored man, who did not give him the slightest offence, in Bull street, Charleston, opposite the residence of Major Hamilton, sen. The man whom he shot was in some difficulty with his wife, and the Captain passing by at the time, ordered him to surrender; but the man declining to obey his order, was shot, and fell into the arms of death for his temerity. I never heard of his being called to account for his noble deed, except it be his re-election to the captaincy, a snug sinecure of the City Guard, for many years after in succession. Perhaps he paid for the man, or was let off the responsibility, in virtue of his office. Oh! when we reflect that God is no respecter of persons, and meditate upon the high-handed tyranny and outrage practised upon colored Americans by their lighter skinned brothers, without fear of a general and manly outbreak for liberty, we are forcibly brought to this conclusion, that it is surpassing fortunate for these States that the slaves generally have not the endowment of those eminent men, whose patriotism led on the sons of 1776 to deeds of renown. Denmark Vesey, according to the printed report, by the authority of the city of Charleston, if my memory is correct, was a native of Africa, from whence he was taken (as millions of his benighted countrymen are kidnapped) in his youth, and carried to St. Domingo, one of the French islands in the West Indies, prior to that gallant people declaring themselves independent of the French nation. It is there, in that country, perhaps, the seed of patriotism was sown in the heart of Vesey, the head and front of the alleged contemplated conspiracy, which might have had an influence on him, nobly to hazard his valuable life against such odds, the army of the Northern States, in arranging and developing a plan upon the most extensive scale for the attempted emancipation of his enslaved brethren. It was said, also, of the blind man, whom the Court of Freeholders had seen fit to excuse from sharing the fate of thirty-six of his less fortunate brethren on the scaffold, owing to his blindness—his name I do not recollect—but of whom it was said, that he was a West India Frenchman, of the Haytian Republic; it was also said that he gave considerable aid with his judicious council and advice to that patrician band of worthies, in the movements of the alleged contemplated conspiracy, the matter of which plan was nearly or quite consummated, only waiting the proper period for concentrate action. The arrangements, it was said, were more extensive for a general attack upon the city, with prospects of successful execution than any heretofore contemplated insurrection meditated by the slaves, the entire body of whom were men of great respectability and intelligence in their respective spheres of life, many of whom were head men, entrusted with the entire control and management of their owners' business. They were well aware of the importance and magnitude of the hazardous contemplated enterprize. Indeed, had the affair riped into execution, nothing short of Uncle Sam's long and ponderous arm, and that from the Northern States, would have availed the South much good in a contest for Liberty brought about by a determined revolutionary spirit of her slaves, led on by such patriotic bravery as Denmark Vesey, Peter Poyas, and other martyrs in the art of Freedom, eminently possessed. . . .

A COLORED AMERICAN.

PHILADELPHIA, January, 1850.

16

Joseph C. Carroll: The National Crisis of the 1820s

Writing in the 1930s, the black scholar Joseph C. Carroll in the first full-scale study of nineteenth-century American slave revolts placed the Vesey Plot in the context of the sectional crisis of the 1820s and the emergence of the antislavery movement in the North.[1] Though Carroll's discussion of the politics of the 1820s should be supplemented with more recent studies, such as William W. Freehling's Prelude to Civil War *(New York, 1966), his information on the reaction to the plot and its impact on later black protests is quite suggestive.*

It was thought by all those who were opposed to slavery that the law of 1808, which prohibited the slave trade, had at last severed the vital artery of that infamous institution and that it would die out in the South just as it had in the North. But never were they so badly mistaken, for the rise of the Cotton Kingdom had made slavery fasten itself upon the South with a firmer grasp than ever, and men like John C. Calhoun were not only denying that slavery was an evil, but defending it as a positive good. The churches of the South, through their pulpits, were proving that slavery had always had divine sanction, and the one famous text which the white clergy preached to the slaves was "Servants obey your masters." On the other hand, the conviction was slowly taking possession of the people of the North that the whole system was wrong and should be checked. On both ethical and economic grounds the North came to oppose the extension of slavery. The South at the same time was wide awake to the issues of the moment. She was quick to see that the only way to prevent further legislation unfriendly to slavery, was to increase the number of slave states, and thus increase its representation in the Senate of the United States. In this lay her only hope of keeping pace with the free states in the Senate. For the North had outgrown the South in population, and had the representation in the Senate been

---

[1] From Joseph C. Carroll, *Slave Insurrections in the United States, 1800–1865* (Boston: Chapman and Grimes, 1938), pp. 83–84, 102–13.

based on population as it was in the House, the free states would have been able to dominate both branches of the National Congress.

The Missouri Compromise of 1820

The admission of Missouri brought the slavery question to the focus of the national consciousness. When the Sixteenth Congress opened in December, 1819, a great debate ensued by reason of this question. The debate assumed and involved a deep constitutional principle as well as an ethical and economic question. In this debate the nation's best forensic talent was displayed. Senator Rufus King of New York, who seems to have made the greatest impression on Denmark Vesey, made the fullest, most thorough, and exhaustive presentation of all. It was said that he unravelled with ingenious and subtle analysis many sophistical issues of the slaveholders, and laid down the position of the natural liberty of man, and its incompatibility with slavery; and that the great slaveholders gnawed their lips, and clinched their fists as they heard him. The outcome of the nation-wide discussion was the Missouri Compromise of 1820, which the aged Thomas Jefferson afterward said alarmed him like a fire bell in the night. The Compromise attempted to localize slavery by providing that it should be prohibited in all the remainder of the Louisiana Territory above thirty-six degrees and thirty minutes north latitude, the southern boundary of Missouri.

No doubt the nation-wide discussion that centered about the Missouri Compromise had its influence upon the slaves. Their interest vacillated back and forth as they caught bits of the eloquent anti-slavery utterances of Northern statesmen. In Jones County, North Carolina, in 1821, the Insurrectionary spirit manifested itself and the militia had to be called out to check it. All during this period of agitation and excitement, there was one man at least who was using it to good advantage in leading the slaves of South Carolina to believe that Congress had actually already emancipated them, and that they were being held contrary to the laws of God and the supreme law of the land.

The "Vis A Tergo" of Denmark Vesey

The whites in this as in the case of the whole insurrectionary movement, were always mystified whenever they ventured to seek the cause of the outbreak. It seems that all the confederates of Vesey's organization were well treated by their masters. It was the opinion of one editor that the whole plan originated in the ambitions of free Negroes, and was to have been carried out by those, who in most respects, were treated more like gentlemen than slaves. As for Vesey himself, it would seem that he had less cause for complaint than any of them. He was a free man, well established in business as a carpenter, and flourishing to the extent that for several years he had employed a number of men working for him in order that he might fulfill his contracts. Concerning Vesey, one journalist said that he was a *free black man*, as free as he should have been, and owned property worth about eight thousand dollars. "Therefore it was not resistance to 'tyranny,' but the Prince of Darkness that prompted his devilish plan." When the judge of the Court passed sentence upon him he dwelt upon the favorable situation of Vesey, which he had enjoyed among them for many years. . . .

Some of the Southern whites claimed that the Negroes revolted because they were excited over a church squabble; or because they had been too much indulged, especially in being allowed to learn to read and write. The Southern Baptist Convention thought it was because the Negroes were not Baptists. . . .

It was the candid opinion of the Baptist Convention of South Carolina that the deliverance of the city and state from the conspirators was due to nothing less than a special intervention of Divine Goodness. They, therefore, urged the governor to appoint a day of Thanksgiving. They went further, and assured the governor that the Baptists of the State regarded slavery as sanctioned by the Bible and proved to be a divine institution by the history of ancient and modern nations. . . . It was also the opinion of [one] writer that to prevent the recurrence of the evil the Negro artisans and mechanics should be displaced by white workers; that the free people of color should be sent out of the State; and that legal restrictions should be placed on the education of Negroes. One Charleston paper declared that the agitation of the Missouri question had made the slaves discontented with their situation, and had assisted in producing the diabolical plot.

While the trials and executions were going on, a New York journalist remarked that Charleston was getting rid of its black population without the aid of the Colonization Society. "There are about fifty more in confinement . . . who will probably be strung up with as little ceremony as they string up weak fish in the Fulton Market."

It is strange that it never occurred to many of the whites of the South, that the best motive for insurrections was the fact that Negroes were slaves and wanted to be free. Moreover, the South made the mistake of thinking that it could prevent insurrections by means of harsh repressive measures, which made the status of the slaves harder, and gave them additional motives for rebellion. Denmark Vesey could have gone to Liberia, where there would have been no bounds to his political aspirations. For it is certain that a man of his talent and ambition might have been governor of a state or even president of the republic. But when approached by a representative of the American

Colonization Society, he replied: "No, I shall stay here and see what can be done for my people." Herein lay his *"Vis A Tergo,"* the desire to help his people.

The Sequel of Denmark Vesey

It is said that Denmark Vesey predicted just before his death that the insurrectionary movement would still go on. One free Negro having created such an alarm, the state felt that something had to be done to prevent further trouble which might arise from the presence of other free Negroes within its borders. An act had been passed two years before, [in 1820,] which forbade free Negroes to enter the state, and those already in the state were not allowed to return in case they should have occasion to leave. . . .

The act of 1820 which up to the time of the Denmark Vesey Insurrection seems to have been forgotten was now strictly enforced. In December, 1822, the legislature of South Carolina passed the Negro-Seaman's Act, which provided for the arrest and imprisonment of free Negroes coming into Charleston harbor from other states and from abroad. . . . The Act also provided that captains of ships should be fined one thousand dollars if they failed to take said Negroes with them when they left the port. The Act remained on the statute book of South Carolina, though it greatly interfered with interstate commerce and involved the United States in serious controversies with foreign nations. . . .

South Carolina restricted the movements of the slaves by prohibiting them from hiring out their time, labor, or service, on penalty of being seized and sold from their owners. All free Negroes above fifteen years of age were required to have some respectable white person as guardian. This guardian was requested to give to the authorities a statement in writing that the free person of color was of good and correct habits. Whenever any such free person of color failed to live up to the reputation given by his guardian, he was to be sold into slavery; one half of the price from such sales was to be given to the informer, and the other half to the state. It was also enacted that any persons who might be guilty of rebellion or insurrection within the State, whether the rebellion took place as planned or not, should be adjudged felons and suffer death without benefit of clergy. In order to keep the Negroes in check in the country around Charleston, the Commissioners of the Cross Road at Charleston Neck were declared to be Justices of the peace, in that part of the Parish of Saint Phillips without the city limits. Complaints were made to the Legislature concerning the number of schools which were kept within the city of Charleston, by persons of color. Accordingly it was made a State prison offense to be guilty of teaching a black man how to read and write. Idleness and the congregating of slaves in large numbers on Sundays was another source of infection. These were prohibited except under strict surveillance of white men. The gathering of slaves in Charleston from the plantations was prohibited. Police regulations on the plantations became more rigid. In short there was a tightening up all around. Masters mistrusted their slaves however genuine in affection and loyalty they might appear. The bondsmen's privileges were curtailed, and the least signs of insubordination were punished.

Before the winter of 1822–23 was over it was reported that the city of Charleston was raising a little standing army of one hundred and fifty men, for its own defense. This it was estimated would cost the city six thousand dollars a year. "Thus slavery was both a political and a moral pestilence."

Another sequel to Vesey's Insurrection was the battle of pens which usually raged on such occasions between the North and the South. Out of the many communications which passed back and forth between editors of the two sections of the country I have selected only a few, for they are too numerous to attempt to include all of them. After so many executions had been performed under the influence of popular excitement, the city of Charleston found it necessary to make some kind of apology for her actions. Because misery likes company, one of the Charleston papers made the following comparison: In 1741 New York executed 35, Charleston in 1822 executed 35, New York transported 85, making a total of 120; Charleston transported 37, making a total of 72, which shows that the Southern city was more merciful than that one of the North. *The New York Daily Advertiser* denounced the proceedings at Charleston as, "A Bloody Sacrifice." . . .

The *Boston Recorder* denounced the proceedings at Charleston as "unlawful, unjust, and cruel." To this a Charleston paper replied: "It arises from a limited knowledge of facts, and is unjust and unchristian; the people of Charleston have acted just as any other enlightened and humane people would have acted under similar circumstances, and it is unjust for those unacquainted with those circumstances to suspect their motives, or condemn their proceedings." . . .

The outbreak in Charleston in 1822 seems not to have given much impetus to the insurrectionary movement among the Negroes as a whole, so far as the records show. On September 20, 1822, a Charleston editor said: "A letter from Beaufort dated 16th inst., states that, on the night previous, ten Negroes belonging to as many respectable families in that place, had been apprehended as concerned in attempting to raise an insurrection of the Blacks in this state." When the letter was written the town Council were in secret session examining the Negroes. The mail from Beaufort, due in Charleston on the following Sunday, probably furnished the editor with more definite information. He said that he trusted that it was only a branch of the Denmark Vesey Insurrection and not the sowing of new seed of mischief, "which must and shall be exterminated."

As a result of the Insurrection in Charleston one would expect to find that there were outbursts in the neighboring State of North Carolina. But . . . much to the relief of the masters of that Commonwealth, there were no visible signs of its effect there. Not until 1826 was there manifested any outward signs of discontent among the slaves. In that year at Newbern, North Carolina, there was an attempted insurrection, led by forty slaves who took up a position finally in a swamp, where they were surrounded and all killed. After that there was nothing to disturb slavery's peaceful course until Nat Turner's Insurrection in Virginia in 1831.

17
Richard Wade: Reconsiderations and Revisions

> *In 1964, Richard Wade, a professor at the University
> of Chicago, reexamined the evidence left by the Vesey Affair and
> reached the conclusion that "no conspiracy in fact existed."* [1]
> *To support his case, Wade cited the hysteria of white Charles-
> tonians, the skepticism of some top officials, discrepancies in the
> trial record and manuscript confessions, the comparative free-
> dom from discontent of urban slaves, and the growing racial
> tensions in South Carolina. "Charleston stumbled into tragedy,"
> concluded Wade, and the plot "was probably never more than
> loose talk by aggrieved and embittered men." However, Wade's
> skeptical conclusions have been criticized in part by Sterling
> Stuckey's "Remembering Denmark Vesey,"* Negro Digest, *XV
> (Feb. 1966), 28–41, and by William W. Freehling's* Prelude to
> Civil War *(New York, 1966), 53–61.*

. . . The standard source [on the Vesey Affair] is a long pamphlet
containing the court's record of the trial, published by the city in
1822 under the title of *An Official Report of the Trials of Sundry
Negroes* and edited by two members of the court. This document
conveyed special authenticity because the testimony and confessions
purported to be as "originally taken, without even changing the phraseology, which was generally in the very words and by the witnesses." Indeed, the court had instructed the editors *"not to suppress any part of
it."* [24] Scholars had few other sources to turn to. Charleston newspapers
imposed a nearly perfect blackout on the details of the episode
throughout the summer, confining themselves to a simple recording
of sentences and executions. And contemporaries left only a few scattered items to help fill out the slight skeleton provided by the council's
publication.

[1] From Richard Wade, "The Vesey Plot: A Reconsideration," *Journal of Southern
History,* XXX (May, 1964), 148–61. Copyright © 1964 by the Southern Historical
Association. Reprinted by permission of the managing editor and the author.
Original numbering of footnotes has been retained.
[24] *Official Report,* iii.

Hence, historians accepted the only facts available and drew their accounts from the official record. They did not question the court's findings but rather dwelt on certain aspects of the episode. Some, like Carter G. Woodson and Ulrich B. Phillips, emphasized the extent and precision of the planning.[25] Others centered on the extraordinary quality of the rebels, especially their leader. Dwight Dumond found Denmark Vesey a "brilliant man," familiar with the Bible, and acquainted with the debates in Congress over the admission of Missouri to the Union. He concluded that "few men were better informed . . . in the history of race relations." John Hope Franklin characterized Vesey as "a sensitive, liberty-loving person" who "believed in equality for everyone and resolved to do something for his slave brothers." Still others were impressed with the unity of the Negroes which made the plot possible. Herbert Aptheker, for example, quoted the report of two Negroes who said they "never spoke to any person of color on the subject, or knew of any who had been spoken to by the other leaders, who had withheld his assent." [26]

More important was the broader meaning of the conspiracy. Most authors viewed it in the context of the resistance of Negroes to the institution of slavery. Along with Nat Turner, they placed Denmark Vesey at the head of the list of colored rebels. For some his plot demonstrated the latent urge for freedom that lay beneath the regime of bondage; for others it revealed an ugly layer of hatred and revenge contained only by stringent laws and alert policemen.

But all accepted the official version: that a widespread conspiracy existed and only a last-minute betrayal rescued the city from insurrection and civil war. Whether the author was Negro or white, Northerner or Southerner, opponent of or apologist for slavery, there was no quarrel on this point. Historians who otherwise disagreed on many issues did not question the conventional story. Hence there was little incentive for reappraisal.[27]

Yet, in spite of the apparent agreement of most contemporaries and

[25] Carter G. Woodson, *The Negro in Our History* (Washington, 1927), 180; Ulrich B. Phillips, "The Slave Labor Problem in the Charleston District," *Political Science Quarterly*, XXII (September 1907), 429–30.

[26] Dwight Lowell Dumond, *Antislavery: The Crusade for Freedom in America* (Ann Arbor, Mich., 1961), 114; John Hope Franklin, *From Slavery to Freedom: A History of American Negroes* (New York, 1956), 210; Herbert Aptheker, *American Negro Slave Revolts* (New York, 1943), 270.

[27] In a paper delivered to the Southern Historical Association meeting in 1957 Thomas T. Hamilton of the University of Wichita evidently developed some doubts about the case from "irregularities in the trials and testimony." Presumably this skepticism stemmed from a close reading of the text. *Journal of Southern History*, XXIV (February 1958), 71. Standard accounts of the Vesey plot include Anne King Gregorie, "Denmark Vesey," *Dictionary of American Biography*, XIX, 258–59; John Lofton, "Negro Insurrectionist," *Antioch Review*, XVIII (Summer 1958), 183–96; and John M. Lofton, Jr., "Denmark Vesey's Call to Arms," *Journal of Negro History*, XXXIII (October 1948), 395–417.

the consensus of subsequent historians, there is persuasive evidence that no conspiracy in fact existed, or at most that it was a vague and unformulated plan in the minds or on the tongues of a few colored townsmen. No elaborate network had been established in the countryside; no cache of arms lay hidden about the city; no date for an uprising had been set; no underground apparatus, carefully organized and secretly maintained, awaited a signal to fire Charleston and murder the whites. What did exist were strong grievances on one side and deep fears on the other. Combined with a number of somewhat unrelated circumstances, they made it possible for many people, both white and Negro, to believe in the existence of a widespread scheme to overturn the institution of slavery.

The first note of skepticism came from a respected judge, a longtime resident of Charleston. Watching the mounting excitement in June, and privy to the proceedings of the court, he warned in a newspaper letter against the "Melancholy Effect of Popular Excitement." In an oblique parable he recounted an episode "within the recollection of thousands" when a freeholders' court had hastily hanged a slave, Billy, for sounding a false alarm to the patrols by blowing a horn. Although "no evidence was given whatever as to a motive for sounding the horn, and the horn was actually found covered and even filled with cobwebs, they condemned that man to die the next day!" The only testimony had been provided by another slave who "was first whipped severely to extort a confession, and then, with his eyes bound, commanded to prepare for instant death from a sabre" if he would not divulge the needed information. Many of the worthiest men in the area protested and asked for "a more deliberate hearing." It did no good, however. "Billy was hung amidst crowds of execrating spectators," the "popular demand for a victim" being so great that it was doubtful whether even a Governor's pardon could have saved him.[28]

The letter was unsigned, but everyone knew its author was of "commanding authority." Moreover, published at the time of the newspaper blackout, it obviously came from someone close to those involved in the trial. In fact, its author was William Johnson, a judge and brother-in-law of the Governor. His daughter observed that when the article appeared, the freeholders "took up the cudgels, supposing it was a slur at them—guilty conscience you know" and "threatened their anathemas at him." Johnson responded with a pamphlet, which his daughter characterized as asserting the "entire innocence of the slaves" and in which he pointed out that the charge against Billy had been "an attempt to raise an insurrection." [29] The moral could hardly

[28] Charleston *Courier,* June 21, 1822.

[29] Anna Hayes Johnson to Elizabeth E. W. Haywood, Charleston, July 24, 1822, in Ernest Haywood Papers. For the court's reply see Charleston *Courier,* June 29, 1822.

be clearer: he feared the court would bend to the popular hysteria and find guilt where there was none.[30]

His daughter, too, soon took this view. Her letters spanning the two months of the crisis moved from frenzy to skepticism. At the beginning of the trouble she wrote that the conspirators spoke of "rapine and murder" with "the coolness of demons" and that "the plot is computed to be about 30,000—the children were to have been spiked and murdered &c." [31] A few weeks later the tone became more measured, the numbers involved much fewer, and she could "thank God none of our slaves have been found in the plot, though there are twenty of them in the yard." [32]

Still later some deeper doubts crept in. "You know," Miss Johnson wrote, "that the leading characteristic of our state is our impetuosity and ardency of feeling which unavoidably lays them [the people] open to deception and consequently leads them on to error in action." Not much, however, could be done about it: "you might as well attempt to 'fetter tides with silken bands' as to make them listen to reason when under this excitement." Yet she concluded that in a few days "the unfortunate creatures are to be hung—it is most horrible—it makes my blood curdle when I think of it, but they are guilty most certainly." [33] Her final letter mentions no plot at all and is obsessed with "the most awful tragedy in this . . . city that comes within the recollection of man"—the mass executions. "Certainly," she added, the whole affair "will throw our city back at least ten years." [34] By the end, Miss Johnson, if she believed a conspiracy existed at all, thought it surely had not extended far enough to justify the massive retaliation of the courts.

The criticism by Governor Thomas Bennett was much more precise. The court should not have "closed its doors upon the community" in its secret proceedings and "shut out those accidental rays which occasionally illuminate the obscurity." Moreover, he found the testimony gathered by the judges "equivocal, the offspring of treachery or

[30] "If it was intended as it would seem to be to make this moral, and the story which accompanies applicable to a supposed existing state of things in our community, . . . " wrote the Mayor [Intendant], "I have only to remark that the *discretion* of the writer is altogether equal to the unjust libel he has insinuated against his Fellow Citizens." The Mayor contended that the measures adopted were taken "in a spirit of the most perfect justice and moderation." *Southern Patriot and Commercial Advertiser,* June 22, 1822.

[31] Anna Hayes Johnson to Elizabeth E. W. Haywood, Charleston, June 23, 1822, in Ernest Haywood Papers.

[32] Anna Hayes Johnson to Elizabeth E. W. Haywood, Charleston, July 18, 1822, *ibid.*

[33] Anna Hayes Johnson to Elizabeth E. W. Haywood, Charleston, July 24, 1822, *ibid.*

[34] Anna Hayes Johnson to Elizabeth E. W. Haywood, Charleston, July 27, 1822, *ibid.*

revenge, and the hope of immunity." "Nor should it be less a source of embarassment and concern," he continued, contesting the official version of the city, "that the testimony should be received under pledges of inviolable secrecy" and "that the accused should be convicted, and sentenced to death, without seeing the persons, or hearing the voices of those who testified to their guilt." [35]

The Governor noted particularly that the decisive information came from three witnesses "while they were under the impression that they would have their life spared." Their testimony not only facilitated "the detection of the general plan of conspiracy, but enabled the court to convict a number of the principal offenders." While questioned "two of them were sometimes closeted together," achieving a uniformity of evidence. In one case William, "the slave of Mr. Palmer," was convicted "exclusively on the testimony of two of the persons under sentence of death." He protested his innocence, claimed he had attended no meetings and had never talked about a plot, and demonstrated his high reputation in many ways. Worse still, Charles Drayton "predicated his claim of escape [from the gallows] on the number of convictions he could make" with his story. "Nothing," Governor Bennett asserted, "could exceed the chilling depravity of this man."

Though the Governor probably believed in a plot of some kind, he could not take the one described by the city very seriously. "It is scarcely possible to imagine one, more crude or imperfect," he said. "They were unprovided with arms," and except for a few pennies that had been subscribed, "no effort was used to procure them." The leaders showed "no confidence in each other"; in fact, they were "in many instances unknown to each other." They had "no definite plans of attack concerted; nor place of rendezvous fixed." Yet the city represented the danger as "mature and within a few hours of consummation."

He went on to say that the idea of an insurrection itself seemed unlikely, although some of the reasons he gave are less convincing. "The liberal and enlightened humanity of our Fellow Citizens, produce many attachments, that operate as checks on the spirit of insubordination." Indeed, there were "unsurmountable obstacles"—the "habitual respect" of the slaves "for an obedience to the authority of their owners; their natural indolence, and want of means and opportunities to form combinations; their characteristic cowardice and treachery, excited by a knowledge of the positive ability of the state to crush in an instant their boldest enterprise." The Governor's view of the episode was plain. "The public mind had been raised to a pitch of

---

[35] Message of Governor Thomas Bennett to the Senate and House of Representatives of the State of South Carolina, November 28, 1822 (South Carolina Archives Division). The Charleston delegation thought the Governor's message too harsh on the city's handling of the episode. Charleston *Mercury,* December 18, 1822.

excitement" over the rumor of a slave revolt and "sought relief in an exhibition of truth." [36] Instead, the action of the city created further panic and confusion.

A close examination of the published record of the trial tends to confirm the Governor's doubts. Though the testimony seems at first reading to suggest a ripe plan, the important evidence is missing at the critical points. For example, the transcript stated that "the whole numbers engaged" were 9,000, "partly from the country and partly from the city." But, it added, "it is true that the witness who had made these assertions did not see the lists [of accomplices] himself; but he heard from one who was in daily communication with Peter, . . . and as Peter wrote a good hand and was active throughout the whole affair, it is impossible to doubt that he had such lists." To be sure, the judges then contended that the larger figure was "greatly exaggerated, and perhaps designedly so." [37] Yet not a single roster of names ever turned up.

If the numbers were conjectural, the extent of the conspiracy was even more so. The report estimated the infected area covered not only the regions around the city but neighboring parishes as well. All through the crisis, however, no one detected any activity in the rural sections.[38] The charge that some of the central figures had acquaintances in the surrounding area was not accompanied by any evidence of complicity. Indeed, one black testified that Pierre Lewis told him "something serious would happen" but that "I was country born, and he was afraid to trust me." [39]

On the matter of weapons the official record reveals the same ambivalence. A blacksmith was supposed to have made some long pikes, six of which a few witnesses claimed existed. But the pikes were never located, thereby forcing the court into a curious logic: "as those six pike heads have not been found, there is no reason for disbelieving the testimony of there hav[ing] been many more made." Later the transcript mentions that "one hundred (pike heads and bayonets) were said to have been made at an early day, and by the 16th June, as many as two or three hundred, and between three and four hundred daggers." And there was still more. "Besides the above mentioned, it was proved that Peter had a sword; that Charles Drayton had a gun & sword; that John Henry had a sword; that Pharo Thompson had a

[36] Message of Governor Thomas Bennett.

[37] *Official Report*, 25–26.

[38] Nonetheless, a prominent planter explained "the orderly conduct of the negroes in any district within 40 miles of Charleston, is no evidence that they were ignorant of the intended attempt. A more orderly gang than my own is not to be found in this state—and one of Denmark Vesey's directives was, that they should assume the most implicit obedience." *Official Report*, 28n–31n. The plot presumably stretched as far as 70 or 80 miles from the city. *Ibid.*, 31.

[39] *Ibid.*, 159.

scythe converted into a sword; that Adam Yates had a knife . . . that Monday had a sword"; and that Bacchus Hammett gave a sword and a gun to others. Yet, except for these few individual weapons, no arms cache was uncovered. "To presume that the Insurgents had no arms because none were seized," the judges concluded, "would be drawing an inference in direct opposition to the whole of the evidence." [40] Since the city published the full text of the trial to allay suspicions both in Charleston and in the North that some injustice had been done, the inconclusiveness of the case at the crucial points is significant.[41]

Equally important is the fact that the printed transcript is at odds in both wording and substance with manuscript records of the witnesses. For example, the confessions of Bacchus Hammett and John Enslow, among the few surviving original documents, have been carefully edited in the authorized version. Some passages were omitted; facts not mentioned in the original interrogation were added; even the tone of the narrative was changed with the alterations.[42]

For example, while Bacchus Hammett is reported to have testified: "At Vesey's they wanted to make a collection to make pikes for the country people, but the men had no money," [43] the manuscript suggests something different: "Denmark told me in March, he was getting arms fast, about 150 to 200 pikes made, and there was a great deal of money placed in his hands for the purpose." [44] Again the *Official Report* lists names of accomplices. "Bellisle Yates I have seen at meetings, and Adam Yates and Napham Yates and Dean Mitchell, and Caesar Smith, and George a Stevidore [sic]." It also includes Jack McNeil, Prince Righton, Jerry Cohen. None appear in the original confession.[45]

At some points the manuscript included material not found at all in the printed version. To use but a single instance, the confession of Bacchus [actually John's confession—ED.] is quite explicit on a rebellion in Georgetown which would precede the Charleston uprising. "I also heard them say that they were well informed in Georgetown. That they would let the principal Men know the time of the attack,

[40] *Ibid.,* 32.

[41] The Washington *Daily National Intelligencer* of August 3, 1822, noted that the Charleston *City Gazette* promised that "a succinct account of the whole transaction shall be given to the world. It will bring to view a scheme of wildness and of wickedness, enough to make us smile at the folly, did we not shudder at the indiscriminate mischief of the plan and its objects. Those (they were but few) who at first thought we had no cause for alarm, must be overwhelmed with conviction to the contrary."

[42] Bacchus, the Slave of Benjamin Hammett, Confession, and The Confession of Mr. Enslow's Boy John, 1822, in William and Benjamin Hammett Papers.

[43] *Official Report,* 146.

[44] Bacchus, the Slave of Benjamin Hammett, Confession, and The Confession of Mr. Enslow's Boy John (Duke University Library).

[45] *Official Report,* 146, 7.

being a short distance from Charleston, would commence a day or two before." The plan was simple. "Kill all the whites between there and Charleston, make their way through the woods and be in time to assist these people in town. It is also said by them that the Population in Georgetown could be killed in one half hour." Yet the city's account contains no mention of this extraordinary dimension of the plot.

The discrepancies seem deliberate since the preface of the pamphlet went to great pains to say that "the whole evidence has been given in each particular case, in the order of its trial, and wherever any additional, or incidental testimony has been disclosed against any criminal subsequently to his conviction, sentence or execution, it has been noticed." "In most cases," the judges contended, "it was as originally taken, without even changing the phraseology" and using "the very words" of the witnesses.[46] Yet these two depositions indicate that little confidence can be placed in the authenticity of the official account.[47]

Strangely, historians have received it less skeptically than some contemporaries. While many newspapers outside the state approved the silence of the Charleston press during the trial, some also looked forward to "a succinct account of the whole transaction" that had been promised by the court. When it arrived, however, there was disappointment. "We doubt the policy of the present publication," wrote a reader of the Boston *Daily Advertiser*. "If intended to awe the blacks, it would seem the executions and banishments *silently* made, would be more terrible, but if really designed as an appeal, and a justification to the American people and to the world, as to the justice of the sentences, it appears either too much or too little." The "historical part," he concluded, "is too loose." [48]

In fact, the explanation of the whole episode lay in the "historical part." If a genuine conspiracy was lacking, tension between the races was not. In the years before the "plot," several developments had worsened relations that always were uneasy. The census figures conveniently summed up white fears. Officially Negroes outnumbered whites 14,127 to 10,653.[49] During the summer when many families left the city to escape the heat, the colored majority was even larger. Thomas Pinckney, in an extended post-mortem on the grim event, expressed the consequent anxiety. He called the imbalance "the principal encouragement to the late attempt, for without it, mad and wild as they

---

[46] *Ibid.*, iii.

[47] Indeed, a close reading of the report suggests that the object of the trials was not to discover the extent of the plot but rather to awe the Negroes by a show of force. "The object of punishment being effectually attained by these examples, and the ring leaders being convicted," the court explained, "the arrests stopped here." *Ibid.*, 48, 59.

[48] Boston *Daily Advertiser*, October 8, 1822.

[49] *Census for 1820, Published by Authority of an Act of Congress, Under the Direction of the Secretary of State* (Washington, 1821), 26.

appear to have been, they would not have dared to venture on a contest of force." In a word, numerical superiority was the "*sine qua non* of insurrection." [50]

Numbers alone, however, would not have produced panic. Some rural areas had a higher percentage of slaves than the city without the same alarm. It was the kind of colored population, not its mere predominance, that frightened white leaders. Charleston's Negroes, like urban blacks elsewhere, were a far different lot than their country brothers. They were more advanced, engaged in higher tasks, more literate, more independent, and less servile than those on plantations. Not confined to the field or the big house, many found employment as draymen, porters, fishermen, hucksters, butchers, barbers, carpenters, and even as clerks and bookkeepers. Their work took these slaves away from the constant surveillance of their masters and generated a measure of self-reliance not usually found in the "peculiar institution." Added to this was an urban environment that provided churches, livery stables, cook houses, and grog shops as centers of informal community life.

Even the domestics who comprised the bulk of urban bondsmen in Charleston afforded slight comfort, though they were popularly believed to be loyally attached to the families of their owners.[51] In fact, Pinckney thought them "certainly the most dangerous" because they had an "intimate acquaintance with all circumstances relating to the interior of the dwellings," because of "the confidence reposed in them," and because of "information they unavoidably obtain, from hearing the conversation, and observing the habitual transactions of their owners." Having "the amplest means for treacherous bloodshed and devastation," this group would comprise the core of a conspiracy. Yet these slaves, he complained, had been "so pampered" by "indulgencies," even "being taught to read and write," that the "considerable control" embodied in ordinances and state laws had been frustrated by the "weakness of many proprietors." [52]

Nearly all those believed to be ringleaders by the court came from one or another of these areas of colored life. Denmark Vesey, who "stood at the head of this conspiracy" according to the court's report, was a successful carpenter who had bought his freedom with money won in a lottery in 1801 [actually 1800—Ed.] Since he was the only free Negro executed (six others were questioned and dismissed), offi-

---

[50] Achates [Thomas Pinckney], *Reflections Occasioned by the Late Disturbances in Charleston* (Charleston, 1822), 10.

[51] The *Official Report* contained the conventional view. "Few if any domestic servants were spoken to [by the leaders], as *they* were distrusted." *Ibid.*, 26. Pinckney's appraisal of the domestics suggests that he did not wholly trust the analysis of the court even though he believed in the existence of the plot.

[52] Pinckney, *Reflections*, 6–9.

cials assumed "the idea undoubtedly originated with him" and that he concocted the plot. His house and shop became the rendezvous of the rebels and he the moving genius. For several years before he "disclosed his intentions to anyone," the court declared, "he appears to have been constantly and assiduously engaged in endeavoring to embitter the minds of the coloured population against the white." He "rendered himself perfectly familiar" with the Bible and used whatever parts "he could pervert to his purpose; and would readily quote them, to prove that slavery was contrary to the laws of God." Moreover, he distributed "inflammatory pamphlets" among the bondsmen. He even "sought every opportunity" to "introduce some bold remark on slavery" into conversations with whites while in the presence of other Negroes.[53]

His associates were no less impressive. Monday Gell not only hired his own time but kept a shop on Meeting Street where he made harness; his owner entrusted arms as well as money to him. Governor Bennett once called him "the projector of the plot" and its "most active partisan." [54] Peter Poyas was a "first rate ship carpenter" who had an excellent reputation and the implicit confidence of his master. Two others belonged to the Governor of the state, and one of them tended the family's business when his owner was at the capital. Only Gullah Jack, who claimed to be a sorcerer with mysterious powers, seemed irregular.

White fears fixed on this colored urban elite, on those who managed to "succeed" a little in bondage. To the whites of Charleston, the character of the city's Negro population made an uprising seem possible, indeed, reasonable. The Negroes were, as a group of residents put it, the "most condensed and most intelligent." [55] Moreover, the extent of literacy brought the "powerful operation of the Press" on "their uninformed and easily deluded minds" and, more precisely, made them privy to events outside the city and the South. The example of Santo Domingo, where the blacks had risen successfully against the whites, and the debate over the Missouri Compromise were thought to have "directly or indirectly" heightened the unrest and encouraged insurrectionary activity.[56] In sum, both the quality and the quantity of Charleston slaves rendered the whites uneasy.

The Negroes, too, were edgy, for things had not gone well for them

---

[53] *Official Report*, 17–19. Later in the testimony, however, the court contended that Vesey "enjoyed so much the confidence of the whites, that when he was accused, the charge was not only discredited, but he was not even arrested for several days after, and not until proof of his guilt had become too strong to be doubted." This does not square well with the previous description of years of agitation and bold confrontation with whites.

[54] Message of Governor Thomas Bennett.

[55] *Southern Patriot and Commercial Advertiser*, August 21, 1822.

[56] Pinckney, *Reflections*, 9.

in the preceding months. New state legislation had made manumission more difficult, nearly closing the door on those who hoped to get their freedom either by purchase or the generosity of their masters.[57] Such "uncivilized laws," "A Colored American" recalled, were "a great and intolerable hindrance" to the slaves' "peace and happiness," since some had already made arrangements to buy their liberty.[58]

Another cause of controversy was the closing of an independent Methodist church established for colored people. In this sanctuary many blacks had found both spiritual consolation and brief relief from servitude. When it was closed down in 1821, the Negro community became embittered. Bible-class leaders especially felt aggrieved because it deprived them of one of the few positions of modest status open to bondsmen. The resentment of this articulate group was scarcely a secret. In fact, the city later charged that almost all the ringleaders were connected with this church.[59]

The atmosphere, then, was charged with fears and grievances. No doubt conversations among whites turned often, if hesitantly, to the topic; and certainly in the grog shops, in Negro quarters, and on the job, the slaves talked about their difficulties. The gap between the races was great, calculatedly so, and was quickly filled by gossip and rumor. Blacks heard the whites were going to "thin out" the colored population, that a false alarm would bring out the militia and volunteers to butcher the slaves on the spot, that new restraints were under consideration in city hall and the state legislature. Circulating among the whites were equally hair-raising notions: a servile uprising, the seizure of the city, the carrying off of women after all males had been exterminated.

Under these circumstances anything specific—names, places, target dates—seemed to give substance to the rumor, suggesting that a plot not only existed but was ripe. Prudence dictated preventive action and a withering show of force by the city. Not only the ringleaders but even those remotely connected had to be swiftly seized, tried, and punished. Hence, the chance encounter of Devany Prioleau with William Paul on the wharf on May 25, 1822, with its garbled but ominous portent, set off a chain of events that did not end until thirty-five had been executed, still more deported, and a town frozen in terror for almost a summer.

Thus Charleston stumbled into tragedy. The "plot" was probably never more than loose talk by aggrieved and embittered men. Curi-

---

[57] *Acts and Resolutions of the General Assembly of the State of South-Carolina Passed in December, 1820* (Columbia, 1821), 22–24.

[58] A Colored American, *Late Contemplated Insurrection*, 5.

[59] The church included both slaves and free blacks. Though some accounts emphasize the petition of free Negroes to the legislature for the privilege of conducting their own worship, the report of the trial asserts that nearly all the bondsmen involved also belonged to the African church and that many were class leaders.

ously, its reputation as a full-scale revolt has endured, in part, because both sides in the slavery controversy believed insurrections to be essential to their broader argument. Apologists for the "peculiar institution" contended that the stringent laws against Negroes in the South were needed to protect whites from violence; opponents of slavery asserted that the urge for freedom was so embedded in human nature that none would passively remain enchained. In either event the Denmark Vesey uprising became a convenient illustration of a larger view of bondage. No closer examination seemed necessary. What *both* Aptheker and Phillips could accept as fact, it was assumed, must necessarily be true.

But the very agreement tended to obscure the important reality. For a concerted revolt against slavery was actually less likely in a city than in the countryside. The chances for success anywhere, of course, were never very good, but ordinary circumstances favored a Nat Turner over a Denmark Vesey. The reasons for this are clear. Nowhere, not even in Charleston, did the blacks have the great numerical superiority that was present on many plantations. Moreover, police forces in the towns, large and well organized, constituted a more powerful deterrent than the vigilante patrol system characteristic of places with scattered populations. And ironically, the urban environment proved inhospitable to conspiracies because it provided a wider latitude to the slave, a measure of independence within bondage, and some relief from the constant surveillance of the master. This comparative freedom deflected the discontent, leading Negroes to try to exploit their modest advantages rather than to organize for desperate measures.

The white community, however, could see only the dangers. The Negroes in Charleston were not only numerous but quite different from the imbruted field hands of the cane and cotton country. Many mastered skills, learned to read and write, joined churches and in every way tried to comport themselves as free men. This was the source of the fear. They seemed capable both of resenting their bondage and organizing an insurrection against it. It was not difficult to translate a few rumors into a widespread conspiracy. Indeed, it was so easy that historians, too, have done so for nearly a century and a half.

Afterword: The Judgment of History

Whether the Vesey conspiracy was a genuine slave plot or merely a white panic is, in a limited sense, irrelevant, since the tradition of insurrection and the memory of Vesey still survive in the black ghettos of twentieth-century America. However, Richard Wade's analysis of the Vesey affair, his use of evidence, and his major conclusion that "no conspiracy in fact existed" deserve to be subjected to serious criticism.

Wade's findings—that the rebels had "at most . . . a vague and unformulated plan," but no "elaborate network" in the countryside or the city, and that "no cache of arms lay hidden" and "no date for an uprising had been set"—can be easily refuted if we follow the lead of scholars like William W. Freehling and Sterling Stuckey (see Bibliographical Note). Given the caliber of the leaders and their discipline of silence over the recruits, there is no reason why they should have disclosed their full plan of action to the court, even under coercion. Since the magistrates admitted that only a minority of the participants had been detected, why should those arrested have revealed the whole scheme when there was still a possibility of those at large beginning the revolt? Besides, the complete plans were probably known to only a few top leaders, most of whom died without disclosing any information, and even the "vague" plans uncovered were sufficient to seize the city had the revolt actually occurred.

Though Vesey may have been unable to create an "elaborate" rural following, where communications were difficult, he probably had mustered enough plantation support to carry out the plans. Regarding the urban underground, where communications were easier, the fact that several score of blacks were convicted points to a city organization adequate to begin a rebellion, not counting those recruits who remained undetected by the authorities and those blacks who might have joined in once the uprising began.

The absence of a cache of arms may be explained by the refusal of defendants to divulge such information or by the fact that Peter Poyas and Mingo Harth had enough time to secrete the arms after their temporary release. Also, Vesey and Gullah Jack were at large long after the discovery of the plot. There must have been places to conceal arms in the black community where whites would never find them, and, in any event, the rebels intended to capture the arms needed by surprise attacks on homes, stores, and arsenals. The lack of rosters of names can be explained on similar grounds, as well as by the fact that each leader was supposed to keep track of his own recruits—a point further verified when many of the accused denied knowing each other. Such group-organization suggests, moreover, the extensiveness of the plot rather than its non-existence.

Since several blacks testified that Vesey had set July 14 for the commencement of the insurrection and then advanced it to June 16 after the initial arrests, the argument that no date had been set seems to be a misreading of the evidence. Indeed, what is most striking about the trial testimony as a whole is the great correspondence of names, places, times, numbers, dates, and other *specific* information—all of which points more to the reality of a conspiracy than to an unfounded panic among whites.

The fears of uncontrolled white hysteria and unwarranted persecution of blacks expressed publicly and privately by Justice Johnson, Anna Johnson, and Governor Bennett prove exactly the opposite of Wade's contentions. Such evidence demonstrates that the Johnsons and Bennett emphatically believed that a conspiracy existed, even though they questioned its extent and the court's means of uncovering it. In other words, no white Charlestonian at the time, including those with a vested interest in skepticism, thought that the conspiracy was just "loose talk." Even Wade concedes that Bennett "probably believed in a plot of some kind," and, according to Freehling, who carefully examined all of the sources, "Bennett believed that a serious conspiracy was afoot, but he doubted that it involved more than eighty Negroes and questioned whether it ever came close to being consummated. . . . In my judgment," concludes Freehling, "Bennett's position, but not Wade's, is consistent with all the evidence. While the terrorized community exaggerated the extent of the danger, there was, in fact, a conspiracy worth getting excited about."

Concerning the discrepancies between the printed and manuscript versions of the court record, a line-by-line comparison of the two documents reveals that some reorganization of evidence occurred, but there was no *change* in the testimony, except for the deleted sentences about poisoning water wells. Moreover, the manuscript confessions of Bacchus Hammet and John Enslow need not be identical to the printed record (or to the manuscript version for that matter) since these confessions were probably taken in jail before they were reiterated in court for the record.

Wade's final claims—that "a concerted revolt against slavery was actually less likely in a city than in the country," because urban blacks enjoyed (relative to plantation slaves) better treatment, higher living standards, "modest advantages," "a measure of independence within bondage," and "comparative freedom," while they lacked "great numerical superiority," all of which "deflected their discontent"—can be criticized on several grounds. First, many urban rebellions or conspiracies occurred before Vesey's attempt; the New York City insurrection of 1712 and the Gabriel Plot near Richmond, Virginia, in 1800, for example, suggest that urban uprisings were at least as "likely" as rural ones. Second, though blacks only slightly outnumbered whites in the city of Charleston, in the surrounding plantation districts the black-white ratio favored slaves overpowering their masters. White urban guards may have been a better deterrent than rural patrols, but for black rebels communication and organization were less difficult in cities than between outlying plantations. Third, the living conditions and treatment of urban house servants and slave artisans may have been superior than those for rural field hands; but the bulk of urban day-laborers and factory slaves were, according to my own research on "industrial slavery" (see Bibliographical Note) no more comfortable in terms of food, clothing, shelter, and working conditions than plantation bondsmen. Since urban slaves attempted to escape as frequently (proportional to their numbers) as rural slaves, city slaves seemed to feel as oppressed as their rural counterparts. Even if some urban slaves received comparatively greater privileges, they did not necessarily feel less oppressed, for as the fugitive slave Peter Randolph recalled, urban slavery "as seen here by the casual observer might be supposed not to be so hard as one would imagine. . . . But Slavery is *Slavery*, wherever it is found." Thus, when all of the arguments and documents are assessed, the judgment of Sterling Stuckey appears sound: "Denmark Vesey did lead a conspiracy [which] must be regarded as one of the most courageous ever to threaten the racist foundation of America. . . . He stands today, as he stood yesterday, as an awesome projection of the possibilities for militant action on the part of a people who have for centuries been made to bow down in fear."

Robert Starobin
Ithaca, New York
December, 1969

Bibliographical Note

The most important sources for a study of the Denmark Vesey Conspiracy and the trials which ensued are the explanations of the affair by the Governor of South Carolina, the Intendant of Charleston, and the Magistrates' Court. These documents are the public letter by Governor Thomas Bennett, Charleston, S.C., August 10, 1822, printed in the Washington, D.C., *Daily National Intelligencer,* August 24, 1822 and in *Niles' Weekly Register,* XXXIII (September 7, 1822), 9–12; James Hamilton, Jr., *An Account of the Late Intended Insurrection Among A Portion of the Blacks of This City. Published By the Authority of the Corporation of Charleston* (Charleston, S.C.: A. E. Miller, August 16, 1822)—which went through several editions and was reprinted in Boston; and Lionel H. Kennedy and Thomas Parker, *An Official Report of the Trials of Sundry Negroes, Charged with an Attempt to Raise an Insurrection in the State of South-Carolina . . .* (Charleston, S.C.: James R. Schenck, October 22, 1822), which follows in most respects a manuscript version in the South Carolina Department of Archives and History.

Collections of private papers in manuscript form which contain valuable material concerning the slave conspiracy and the reaction to it include the following: the Hammett Papers (Duke University Library); Cheves Papers (South Carolina Historical Society); the Haywood and the Arnold-Screven Papers (University of North Carolina Library); the Furman and the Williams-Chestnut-Manning Papers (University of South Carolina Library); the Jefferson and the Monroe Papers (Library of Congress); Poinsett Papers (Historical Society of Pennsylvania); Secretary of War Papers (National Archives) and Governors' Papers containing Bennett's Message No. 2 to the state legislature (South Carolina Department of Archives and History). In addition, the memorial of Charleston citizens to the South Carolina legislature for the fall of 1822 is reprinted in U. B. Phillips, ed., *Plantation and Frontier Documents,* Vol. II (Cleveland, Ohio: A. H. Clark Co., 1909), while letters and documents concerning the Negro Seamen Acts can be found in *House Reports,* No. 80, 27th Congress, 3rd session, January 20, 1843. (Philip M. Hamer, "Great Britain, the United States, and the Negro Seamen Acts, 1822–1848," *Journal of Southern History,* I (1935), 3–28, discusses the legal and diplomatic results of this legislation.)

Although the daily newspapers (especially southern ones) tended to suppress the news of the Vesey Conspiracy, still the bare outlines of the plot and the controversy it produced can be followed most conveniently in the following newspapers for 1822: the Charleston *City Gazette;* Charleston *Courier;* Charleston *Mercury;* Columbia *South-Carolina State Gazette;* Washington, D.C., *Daily National Intelligencer;* and the New York *Daily Advertiser. Niles' Weekly Register,* Baltimore, Md., carried only a few items.

The Vesey Conspiracy did, however, precipitate the publishing of several pamphlets, the most interesting of which are: William Johnson, *To the*

Public of Charleston (Charleston, S.C.: C. C. Sebring, July 4, 1822); "A Columbian" (Chancellor Henry William Desaussure), *A Series of Numbers Addressed to the Public, on the Subject of the Slave and Free People of Colour* (Columbia, S.C.: State Gazette Office, October, 1822); Edwin C. Holland, *A Refutation of the Calumnies Circulated Against the Southern and Western States, Respecting the Institution and Existence of Slavery Among Them* (Charleston, S.C.: A. E. Miller, October 29, 1822); (Thomas Pinckney), *Reflections, Occasioned By the Late Disturbances in Charleston. By Achates* (Charleston, S.C.: A. E. Miller, November 4, 1822); *Rev. Dr. Richard Furman's Exposition of the Views of the Baptists, Relative to the Coloured Population of the United States* (Charleston, S.C.: A. E. Miller, January, 1823); and the Reverend Frederick Dalcho, *Practical Considerations Founded on the Scriptures Relative to the Slave Population of South Carolina, By a South Carolinian* (Charleston, S.C.: A. E. Miller, 1823).

Historians who have dealt with the Vesey Conspiracy include: "A Colored American," *The Late Contemplated Insurrection in Charleston, S.C.* (New York: Printed for the Author, 1850); William C. Nell, *The Colored Patriots of the American Revolution . . .* (Boston: Robert F. Wallcut, 1855); (Thomas Wentworth Higginson), "Denmark Vesey," *Atlantic Monthly*, VII (June, 1861), 728–44, reprinted as *Black Rebellion* (New York: Arno Press, 1969); William Wells Brown, *The Negro in the American Rebellion* (Boston: Lee and Shepard, 1867); Archibald H. Grimke, "Right on the Scaffold," American Negro Academy *Occasional Papers*, No. 7 (Washington, D.C.: The Academy, 1901); U. B. Phillips, "The Slave Labor Problem in the Charleston District," *Political Science Quarterly*, XXII (September, 1907), 416–39; U. B. Phillips, *American Negro Slavery* (New York: D. Appleton, 1918); Theodore D. Jervey, *Robert Y. Hayne and His Times* (New York: The Macmillan Company, 1909); H. M. Henry, *The Police Control of the Slave in South Carolina* (Emory, Va.: n.p., 1914); Joseph C. Carroll, *Slave Insurrections in the United States, 1800–1865* (Boston: Chapman and Grimes, 1938); Herbert Aptheker, *American Negro Slave Revolts* (New York: Columbia University Press, 1943); Donald G. Morgan, *Justice William Johnson* (Columbia, S.C.: University of South Carolina Press, 1954); John M. Lofton, "Denmark Vesey's Call to Arms," *Journal of Negro History*, XXXIII (October, 1948), 395–417; John M. Lofton, *Insurrection in South Carolina: The Turbulent World of Denmark Vesey* (Yellow Springs, Ohio: The Antioch Press, 1964); Richard C. Wade, "The Vesey Plot: A Reconsideration," *Journal of Southern History*, XXX (May, 1964), 143–61; Richard C. Wade, *Slavery in the Cities* (New York: Oxford University Press, 1964); William W. Freehling, *Prelude to Civil War* (New York: Harper and Row, Publishers, 1966); and Sterling Stuckey, "Remembering Denmark Vesey—Agitator or Insurrectionist?" *Negro Digest*, XV (February, 1966), 28–41. Winthrop Jordan's *White Over Black: American Attitudes toward the Negro, 1550–1812* (Baltimore: Penguin Books, Inc., 1969) dicusses white racial attitudes in early American history and the reaction to colonial slave revolts. Robert Starobin's *Industrial Slavery in the Old South* (New York: Oxford University Press, 1970) analyzes the working and living conditions and the resistance to slavery by those bondsmen used in manufacturing, milling, mining, lumbering, and transportation enterprises between the 1790s and 1861.

Index